DATE DUE

MAY 11 '78	MY 4		
AUG 31 78	JL 2 6		
OCT 14 '80	AP 2 8		
GAYLORD			PRINTED IN U.S.A.

The Nouveau Roman:

A Study in the Practice of Writing

In the same series

Stendhal Michael Wood
Thomas Hardy: The Poetic Structure Jean R. Brooks
Aldous Huxley Keith May

In preparation

Kafka Franz Kuna
Flaubert Jonathan Culler
Henry James and the French Literary Mind Philip Grover

Novelists and Their World

General Editor: Graham Hough
Professor of English at the University of Cambridge

The Nouveau Roman:

A Study in the Practice of Writing

Stephen Heath

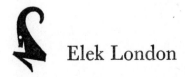

Elek London

ISBN 0 236 15414 1

Published in Great Britain by
ELEK BOOKS LIMITED
54–58 Caledonian Road, London N1 9RN

Printed in Great Britain by
Clarke, Doble & Brendon Limited,
Plymouth

16 ⨍
EB

For Dominique

Contents

Ts'ui Pên diría una vez : *Me retiro a escribir un libro.* Y otra : *Me retiro a construir un laberinto.* Todos imaginaron dos obras; nadie pensó que libro y laberinto eran un solo objeto

J. L. Borges, 'El jardín de senderos que se bifurcan'

Preface

To write a book on the *nouveau roman* is already a paradox. How, after all, is one to write about a project the whole impetus of which is centred in its aim for foundation as *experience of reading*? It is as well, then, to recognize from the outset the limits of this book, fragmentary and repetitive as it is, which offers no more than, literally, a *pre-text* to the nouveau roman. Written in French, it might well have been called *Lire le nouveau roman,* for if it functions properly as an introduction, it is precisely in so far as it emphasizes and prepares for the problem of reading posed by modern French writing in the novel. Thus the reader will find here neither a detailed descriptive history of the nouveau roman nor an exhaustive analysis, work by work, of all the novelists who have been associated with the nouveau roman, a procedure that could only be —for reasons that I hope will become clear—essentially reductive. No apologies need be offered for the number of novels and novelists not directly discussed in the short course of this book.

What *is* in question here is an attempt to present the context of ideas and research directed towards the investigation of the nature and possibilities of the novel form as represented in the work of some of the key French novelists writing today, from Nathalie Sarraute to Philippe Sollers. The latter, strictly speaking, comes *after* the nouveau roman but in the kind of account I am attempting this is not a reason for excluding him from consideration. The extension of my argument to take stock of the work accomplished by Sollers and the *Tel Quel* group with which he is associated seemed necessary in order to obtain some sort of perspective on the practitioners of the nouveau roman as generally understood and to re-emphasize certain premises central to my discussion of the nouveau roman and to the situation of it which I am here concerned to propose. My aim is not to define narrow boundaries for something called the nouveau roman, including this and excluding that novel or novelist, but to present a certain contemporary work situated in the context of a shift in literary consciousness that I shall call *the practice of writing*.

The term 'work' should be stressed, for it is essentially a work that is carried out by these writers, a work in and on the novel form which runs into and stems from a constant process of reflection on the whole nature of the novel. It is a question for these novelists, that is, of a *practice* of *writing*. There is thus nothing of the habitual rigid distinction between novel and theoretical writing (so that I am uneasy about the term 'novelist' in this context), though the degree of connection and interaction may vary from writer to writer, and this fact is reflected in the present essay, the purpose of which has involved giving major attention to the theoretical reflections of the novelists discussed and to the writings of those thinkers whose work has been of seminal importance in this fundamental questioning of the novel form. The differences in length and organization between the various chapters devoted to particular authors again followed necessarily from the nature and purpose of my account. There could have been no question of treating every writer in the same way nor, as has been indicated, of treating each writer 'exhaustively'. Each novelist to whom particular reference is made is presented in the terms he or she seems to demand, but also in the terms of the general aim of this book, the presentation of an exploration of the novel form. In however modest a fashion, this book does ask to be read straight through as a discussion of that particular literary form, and does, in fact, represent an offshoot from a larger work in progress devoted to a study of that form in relation to the implications of the term 'realism'. But this last point is a personal note, of interest perhaps only to myself.

It is pleasing to be able to record here my gratitude to those who have afforded me the benefit of their help and encouragement. The teaching of Raymond Williams and Terry Eagleton gave meaning to three years spent as an undergraduate at Jesus College, Cambridge. A research fellowship at Downing College has made possible, among other things, the writing of this book and the advice I received from two of my colleagues there, Brian Vickers and Christopher Prendergast, both of whom struggled with versions of the manuscript, made it so much easier. Professor Graham Hough has offered me help of every kind, as have M. and Mme Pierre Maillard: to them, as to my parents for their unfailing support, I am deeply grateful. My greatest debt, however, is to the work and teaching of Roland Barthes. The pages of this book, for all their inadequacy, would not have been written without the help of his example.

Stephen Heath, Paris, May 1969

Various circumstances have delayed the publication of this book. In the meantime a good deal of new work has appeared from the various writers with whom it deals and I have tried to revise my text to take account of this. Nothing of the argument has changed, however, and the book is substantially that completed in 1969. Parts of Chapter 2 appeared in the Winter 1970 issue of *Novel* and I am grateful to the Editors for permission to reprint that material here. I should like to thank Les Editions de Minuit, Editions Gallimard and Editions du Seuil, and the authors of the books published by them, for their kind permission to quote from copyright material. Full details of first publication are given in the Bibliography.

S.H., Paris, November 1971

I

The Practice of Writing

'Idéal littéraire, finir par savoir ne plus mettre sur sa page que du "lecteur".'

PAUL VALÉRY

'ce système de significations, qui est à l'intérieur du livre, va être une image du système de significations à l'intérieur duquel le lecteur est pris, dans toute sa vie quotidienne, et à l'intérieur duquel il est perdu.'

MICHEL BUTOR

'La Société française allait être l'historien, je ne devais être que le secrétaire.'[1] Balzac's famous project in the *Comédie Humaine* poses a problem of writing, but the writing itself does not in any way represent a problem. The problem is the task—its extent, its magnitude, its performance—not the means by which the task is to be performed. Witness in this respect the relationship posited between the novelist and the reality to be described : the novelist is, as it were, a scribe *taking down* his contemporary and immediately pre-contemporary society from a kind of visual dictation. The chronology of the task is clear for Balzac in his role as secretary to Society : observation, *then* expression : 'l'auteur pense être d'accord avec toute intelligence, haute ou basse, en composant l'art littéraire de deux parties bien distinctes : *l'observation—l'expression*.'[2] Cuvier, *poet* of the nineteenth century ('n'est-il pas le plus grand poète de notre siècle?'[3]), who finds a place in Balzac's pantheon of the four great lives of the age ('Quatre hommes auront eu une vie immense :

[1] *La Comédie Humaine* (Pléiade edition) I, p. 7.
[2] Ibid. XI, p. 174.
[3] Ibid. IX, p. 29.

15

Napoléon, Cuvier, O'Connell, et je veux être le quatrième'[4]), expressed the relationship of the natural sciences to the world they study as that of 'deux vastes tableaux, dont l'un devrait être la copie de l'autre',[5] a formulation that captures equally the intended relationship between the science of social observation of Balzac (that 'docteur ès sciences sociales'[6]) and the French society observed. The 'tableau de la Société'[7] is to be copied in a 'reproduction rigoureuse',[8] and the *Comédie Humaine* will be the vast tableau of the 'natural history' of Society, standing in relation to its object as the natural sciences stand to theirs for Cuvier.

The problem posed by the writing of the *Comédie Humaine* is then precisely that of the natural sciences of the period, one of classification and the establishment of a valid scientific typology, and the importance of the place held in Balzac's thinking by Cuvier and Saint-Hilaire causes no surprise. The act of reproduction that is the *Comédie Humaine* involves an order, 'cette multitude d'existences exigeaient des *cadres*, et, qu'on me pardonne cette expression, des *galeries*. De là, les divisions si *naturelles* de mon ouvrage . . .':[9] it involves, that is, a construction, but the construction is natural, realistic in the nineteenth-century sense of the term, faithful to the object it copies or describes. This is the point of the concern to establish a scientific typology as opposed to the Romantic typology of a Walter Scott, a concern and a contrast explicitly developed and worked out in the introductions written by Félix Davin, at Balzac's prompting, for the *Etudes philosophiques* and the *Etudes de moeurs au XIXe siècle*.[10] The copy is more than a copy, the novelist must 'surprendre le sens caché dans cet immense assemblage de figures, de passions et d'événements',[11] must, in an act of understanding, seize the significance of the outward circulation of the social reality ('Chez moi . . . l'observation était déjà devenue intuitive . . . elle saisissait si bien les détails extérieurs qu'elle allait sur le champ au-delà'[12]), and arrest its movement in a final moment of comprehension. This comprehension for Balzac is a mode of evaluation; writing 'à la lueur de deux Vérités éternelles: la Religion, la Monarchie',[13] Balzac will demonstrate to the reader the malaise of contemporary society,

4 *Lettres à Madame Hanska*, ed. R. Pierrot (Paris, 1968), II, p. 374.
5 G. Cuvier, *Rapport historique sur les progrès des sciences naturelles depuis 1789* (Paris, 1810), p. 4.   6 *Comédie Humaine* VI, p. 183.
7 Ibid. I, p. 8.   8 Ibid. I, p. 7.
9 Ibid. I, p. 13 (my italics)   10 Ibid. XI, pp. 203–51.
11 Ibid. I, p. 7.   12 Ibid. VI, p. 66.
13 Ibid. I, p. 9.

reveal, for instance, 'le sentiment d'insubordination sociale caché sous le mot *égalité*'.[14] This final stage, as its description as 'final' suggests, succeeds, in Balzac's chronology of literary production, the reproduction of the reality, of, in Davin's words, 'la vie telle qu'elle est'.[15] It *attends* (and that attention is, of course, its guarantee) the reproduction to demonstrate and confirm its typicality as commentary, whether that of the author ('Quand à Paris une femme a résolu de faire métier et marchandise de sa beauté, ce n'est pas une raison pour qu'elle fasse fortune . . . *Voici pourquoi* . . .[16]), that of an observer figure, type of the novelist in the analytical comprehension of his probing observation (as, for example, Bianchon the surgeon : 'entre la nécessité de faire fortune et la dépravation des combinaisons, il n'y a pas d'obstacle, car le sentiment religieux manque en France . . . Voilà ce que se disent tous ceux qui contemplent, comme moi, la société dans ses entrailles.'[17]), or, as generally is the case, that of the two together.

Thus a chronology of the writing of the *Comédie Humaine* might be proposed as something like : observation—expression or reproduction—commentary. All the inadequacy and naïvety of such a schema can be recognized at once : what is in question here is simply the fact that it is in terms of such a schema that the writing of the *Comédie Humaine* is proposed and, drawing out the implications of this proposition, that that which is, after all, the centre of the *Comédie Humaine* is absent, or rather, non-problematically present : namely, the activity of writing. 'Le monde écrit';[18] Davin's description of the *Comédie Humaine* is exact, but the writing is understood merely as mirroring imitation. The *Comédie Humaine* is not a process of composition but of representation, and it is this latter emphasis that provides all the images for the activity of scription which are largely drawn from painting—'tableau', 'cadres', 'galeries', and so on. Balzac 'takes down' the 'real' 'realistically' and the word 'realistically' here poses a problem not at the level of the writing, but at that of the observation the writing records. Hence language and writing can be regarded, as a passage in *Illusions perdues* suggests, as perfected instruments, having, like the printing press, an 'evolutionary' development, progressing from early crudity to the

14 Ibid. IV, p. 978.   15 Ibid. XI, p. 244.
16 Ibid. VI, p. 264 (my italics).
17 Ibid. VI, p. 501.
18 Ibid. XI, p. 213.

achievement of their present perfection.[19] Language, in fact, is taken-for-granted in Balzac's project, which therefore defines itself firmly in what might be called, after Husserl, the *natural attitude* towards reality. Balzac's language, the instrument of the *Comédie Humaine*, is conceived in terms of what Michel Foucault has characterized as the positivist dream : 'un langage qui serait maintenu au ras de ce qu'on sait : un *langage-tableau*.'[20] Language is thought of as self-effacing in the process of the presentation of things, in the reproduction of society, not grasped in its specificity as the milieu of the articulation of the reality known by a given linguistic community. Balzac's writing is thus a writing that knows no limits, or, if there are limits, they are not at the level of the writing itself, but 'outside', referred to as History or Society or even God. (This *exteriority* can be seen as a fundamental assumption of traditional conceptions of literary realism : 'ce qui définit le réalisme, ce n'est pas l'origine du modèle, c'est son extériorité à la parole qui l'accomplit.'[21]) It is here that the fact of the 'perfection' of Balzac's writing may be understood; not source of the real, but instrument of its representation, its limits are the limits of the real itself (and not vice versa) : it is the quicksilver of a mirror that directly reflects in image the tableau of Society. Certainly Balzac can acknowledge limits in the reflection : 'Paris est un véritable océan. Jetez-y la sonde, vous n'en connaîtrez jamais la profondeur. Parcourez-le, décrivez-le? quelque soin que vous mettiez à le parcourir, à le décrire; quelque nombreux et intéressés que soient les explorateurs de cette mer, il s'y rencontrera toujours un lieu vierge . . . quelque chose d'inouï, oublié par les plongeurs littéraires.'[22] Limits such as these, however, in no way call into question the perfection of the writing; they are but the limits imposed by the magnitude of the task Balzac sets himself in the project of the *Comédie Humaine*, that task the accomplishment of which was to allow him, rightfully, to take his place alongside Cuvier in the gallery of the great men of the age.

[19] Ibid. IV, p. 588: 'pour arriver à leur perfection, l'écriture, le langage peut-être . . . ont eu les mêmes tâtonnements que la typographie et la papeterie.' Modern linguistics rejects this kind of speculation: 'The truth is that every language so far studied, no matter how "backward" or "uncivilized" the people speaking it, has proved on investigation to be a complex and highly developed system of communication. Moreover, there is absolutely no correlation between the different stages of cultural development through which societies have "evolved" and the "type" of language spoken in these stages of cultural development.' John Lyons, *Introduction to Theoretical Linguistics* (Cambridge, 1969), p. 44.
[20] *Les Mots et les Choses* (Paris, 1966), p. 309 (my italics).
[21] Roland Barthes, *Essais critiques* (Paris, 1964), p. 199.
[22] *Comédie Humaine* II, p. 856.

This attitude to writing is basic to realist literature, understanding by that not simply what is historically known as Realism, but equally Naturalism (which questions Realism at the level of its social comprehension not at that of its writing : 'Le réaliste', comments Maupassant in discussing the progress from Realism to Naturalism, 'ne se préoccupe que du fait brutal sans en comprendre l'importance relative et sans en noter les répercussions.'[23]) and also the vast majority of novels published today. With reference to work done by Roman Jakobson and Mikhail Bakhtin, one can describe this realist writing as *metonymic* and *monologistic*.[24] Jakobson distinguishes two fundamental modes of arrangement in verbal behaviour; selection and combination :

'The selection is produced on the base of equivalence, similarity and dissimilarity, synonymity and antonymity, while the combination, the build-up of the sequence, is based on contiguity.'[25]

These two modes Jakobson characterizes as the metaphoric and the metonymic respectively, since they find their most condensed expression in those two rhetorical tropes. As Jakobson points out,[26] it is the latter mode, the metonymic, that typifies realist writing, a writing that traces the real in, on its terms, a potentially endless notation ('il s'y rencontrera toujours un lieu vierge'), an endless passage from detail to detail in a monologue of re-presentation. Here is the basic sense of Bakhtin's idea of monologistic writing : realist writing is face to face with the real in a direct relation of instrumentality, it covers the real exactly in its progression, leaving no trace, absent in that which, outside it, founds and guarantees its realism.[27]

Realism then, as it has come to be understood in connection with the novel, is always grasped finally in terms of some notion of the representation of 'Reality', which is reflected in the literary work as

---

[23] Préface, *Lettres de Gustave Flaubert à Georges Sand* (Paris, 1884), p. xv.

[24] Cf. R. Jakobson, 'Linguistics and Poetics', in *Style and Language*, ed. T. Sebeok (Cambridge, Mass., 1966); *Fundamentals of Language* (with M. Halle) (The Hague, 1956); M. Bakhtin, *Rabelais and his World* (Cambridge, Mass., 1969); *La Poétique de Dostoevski* (Paris, 1970).

[25] 'Linguistics and Poetics', p. 358.

[26] *Fundamentals of Language*, pp. 53–4.

[27] It has been necessary to sketch here the attitude to writing proposed in Balzac's project. This does not mean, however, that that proposition is to be accepted without question. On the contrary, to *read* the Balzac text it would be crucial to bring out the conventions of its structuration as a text which found its very *readability* as 'realistic'. Cf. Roland Barthes, *S/Z* (Paris, 1970; discussed below, pp. 210 ff.).

in a mirror. It is in the development of the novel in the nineteenth century, under the impetus of the desire to achieve a 'social realism', that the relation of realism in the novel and image of the mirror is definitively forged. Thus George Eliot, for example, can offer her novels naturally as an attempt to 'give a faithful account of men and things as they have mirrored themselves in my mind'.[28] This is the same kind of 'innocence' that was encountered in Balzac's description of the *Comédie Humaine* as a 'visual dictation' : the idea of an *account* introduces a notion of selection but without in any way revealing a problem, without challenging the assumptions of the natural attitude; no problem is posed by saying that the account is to be a *realistic* account and, indeed, it is precisely this that prevents the recognition of any problem. Yet if the term 'realistic' is examined and the question formulated as to what is 'realistic' (and the work I shall be concerned with in this book is one element in our ability to formulate this question), it will be seen that the answer cannot lie in any absolute conception of 'Reality' (of '*the* Reality'), but, on the contrary, in the recognition of the representation of reality which a particular society proposes and assumes as 'Reality'. 'Reality', that is, needs to be understood not as an absolute and immutable given but as a production within which representation will depend on (and, dialectically, contribute to) what the French Marxist theoretician Louis Althusser has described as 'practical ideology', a complex formation of montages of notions, representations, images and of modes of action, gestures, attitudes, the whole ensemble functioning as practical norms which govern the concrete stance of men in relation to the objects and problems of their social and individual existence; in short, the lived relation of men to their world.[29] In this sense, the 'realistic' is not substantial but formal (a process of significant 'fictions'), and, in connection with the novel, it may be described in the notion of the *vraisemblable* of a particular society, the generally received picture of what may be regarded as 'realistic'; such a *vraisemblable* being founded in our own culture by, amongst other things, the novel itself. Evidently, this *vraisemblable* is not recognized as such, but rather as, precisely, 'Reality'; its function is the naturalization of that reality articulated by a society as *the* 'Reality' and its success is the degree to which it remains unknown as a form, to which it is received as mirror of 'Reality', ever confirmed by a fixed source exterior to its discourse.

[28] *Adam Bede*, Ch. XVII.
[29] See below p. 190.

20

It is within the space of this discourse that the realism of a literary work for a society is defined. For a particular society, in fact, the work that is realistic is that which repeats the received forms of 'Reality'. It is a question of reiterating the society's system of intelligibility. There is a moment in *A la recherche du temps perdu* when the narrator, arrived at a restaurant just outside Paris and awaiting Saint-Loup, studies the owner of the restaurant and comments : 'il avait l'habitude de comparer toujours ce qu'il entendait ou lisait à un certain texte déjà connu et sentait s'éveiller son admiration s'il ne voyait pas de différences.'[30] The mode of realism that has been described here is exactly that : the repetition of a certain text which is, in its very familiarity (its 'naturalness'), diffuse, unknown as text. *Nombres* by Philippe Sollers speaks of the 'theatre' of representation 'où nous allons et venons encore, récitant sans y penser le texte ancien, embrouillé, menteur . . .'[31] What founds this text in part, and to an extent that has grown steadily since the beginning of the nineteenth century, is the novel and what assures this foundation is its readability ('unreadable' being a term with which we trace the horizon of our sense, of our desire not to read our limits). This readability is relayed by a series of codes and conventions, by the text of the already known and written : that work is readable, therefore, which is cast within their horizon, which repeats them in their naturalized transparence. In these terms, the novel, through the development of realist writing (and most of the novels written today are 'Balzacian' in the sense of their commitment to the premisses of that writing), has become the form of a certain social seeing; a form, like other social forms (and this is the guarantee of its stability), to be learned, repeated and consumed. It is thus, as Sartre tried to say in *La Nausée*, that we conceive and live our lives as novels, within the conventions (though they are not felt as such) which the novel provides. There is a passage in his *Logiques* in which Philippe Sollers gives a very powerful description of this condition :

'LE ROMAN EST LA MANIÈRE DONT CETTE SOCIÉTÉ SE PARLE, la manière dont l'individu DOIT SE VIVRE pour y être accepté. Il est donc essentiel que le point de vue "romanesque" soit omniprésent, évident, intouchable; qu'il ait ses chefs-d'oeuvre indéfiniment cités, commentés, rappelés; ses tentatives difficiles; ses demi-réussites; ses échecs. Il est essentiel qu'il dispose de tous les registres : naturaliste, réaliste, fan-

[30] Pléiade edition, II, p. 406.
[31] *Nombres* (Paris, 1968), p. 37.

21

tastique, imaginaire, moral, psychologique et infra-psychologique, poétique, pornographique, politique, expérimental. Tout se passe d'ailleurs comme si ces livres étaient désormais écrits par avance; comme s'ils faisaient partie de cette parole et de cette pensée anonymes, toutes-puissantes, qui à l'intérieur et à l'extérieur, de l'information publique jusqu'à l'intimité la plus silencieuse, règnent, exagérément visibles et par conséquent invisibles. Notre *identité* en dépend, ce qu'on pense de nous, ce que nous pensons de nous-mêmes, la façon dont notre vie est insensiblement amenée à composition. Qui reconnaît-on en nous sinon un personnage de roman? (Qui reconnaissez-vous en moi qui vous parle sinon un personnage de roman?) Quelle parole échapperait à cette parole insidieuse, incessante, et qui semble toujours être là avant que nous y pensions?"[32]

The limits of the novel are confounded with the limits of the natural attitude, hence its naturalness, its triumphant mirroring, and Sollers can define it precisely as an area of man's captivity, the area in which he is held captive then indeed being termed 'the readable'.

The basis of this repetition, as was seen earlier, is an absence of writing; language is lost in a monologue of re-presentation. The purpose of this book is to present one moment in the development of a radical shift of emphasis in the novel from this monologistic realism to what I shall call *the practice of writing*. This shift is not to be understood in the traditional terms of a change from 'social realism' to 'psychological realism' or whatever, but in terms of the deconstruction of the very 'innocence' of realism. Its foundation is a profound experience of language and form and the demonstration of that experience in the writing of the novel which, transgressed, is no longer repetition and self-effacement but work and self-presentation as *text*. Its 'realism' is not the mirroring of some 'Reality' but an attention to the forms of the intelligibility in which the real is produced, a dramatization of possibilities of language, forms of articulation, limitations, of its own horizon.

This attention may be defined as an activity of *hesitation*. The term is explicit enough in *Finnegans Wake*, signed as an 'HeCit-Ency', the text as 'scribenery', 'epiepistle to which . . . we must ceaselessly return', activating a perpetual circulation of signs only within which is to be read any subject ('author', 'history', etc.); as it is too in *A la recherche du temps perdu* where the painful ex-

[32] *Logiques* (Paris, 1968), p. 228.

perience of the child, in the moment of awakening, of a hesitation of the conventional forms, through the habitual stability of which the subject realizes his presence, becomes the work of Proust's text which can find an 'essence' only in the activity of reading these forms, the text thus taking the status of 'la seule vie par conséquent réellement vécue'; as it is again in Thomas Mann's *Zauberberg*, where Hans, plaything of dialectical rivalries, is the figure of the dramatization of a shifting series of forms, of a whole space of discourse that moves on the scene of the text in that incompletion of interpretation which gives the irony of the book and defines it within a Nietzschean perspective. These texts of the practice of writing variously propose themselves in terms of an activity of *reactivation* : it is a question not of the repetition of the *vraisemblable* of a society but of the reading of the forms of that *vraisemblable*; not a monologue, the repetition of a discourse as absence of discourse, but a dialogue, a mise-en-scène of forms. The series of forms of realist writing, naturalized as writing 'without thickness', as non-formal, miming 'Reality' as its direct expression, is now deconstructed, grasped as production. In the space of the text in the practice of writing there is no longer a movement forward to the fixing of some final Sense or Truth, but on the contrary, an attention to a plurality, to a dialogue of texts, founding and founded in an intertextuality to be read in, precisely, a *practice* of writing. As Sollers has emphasized : 'La "réalité" n'est plus, ainsi, l'éternel morceau préexistant à découper dans tel ou tel sens, mais LE PROCÈS DE GÉNÉRATION QUI TRANSFORME.'[33]

If the term 'realism' is to be retained in connection with these texts, it must be understood in terms of the totally new emphasis it finds in such formulations as the following :

'Le nouveau réalisme se pose d'abord comme une expérience nécessaire de l'écriture (et non du style) et de la rigueur. Trop souvent cette désignation masque une confusion faite entre naturalisme, ou vérisme, et réalisme. Zola, pas plus que Sartre, n'est un réaliste.[34]

'Le réalisme, ici, ce ne peut donc être la copie des choses, mais la connaissance du langage; l'oeuvre la plus "réaliste" ne sera pas celle qui "peint" la réalité, mais qui . . . explorera le plus profondément possible la *réalité irréelle* du langage.'[35]

[33] *Tel Quel, Théorie d'ensemble* (Paris, 1968), p. 393.
[34] Jean-Edern Hallier, 'De l'art sans passé', *Tel Quel* No. 6, Summer 1961, p. 43.
[35] Roland Barthes, *Essais critiques*, p. 164.

Instead of effacing itself before a 'Reality' projected as its precedent, language, in this emphasis, is grasped as specific locus of the articulation of the real, of its real-ization. The practice of writing, as was stressed above, can be defined exactly as a radical experience of language. This experience, however, is not to be understood as some decorative reference to language as the style of an author, as the inversion of representation into the expression of the individual (the first of the formulations given above is explicit on the need to avoid this confusion); what is in question indeed in this experience is a hesitation of our very conception of the 'author' as an originating moment of discourse.

That conception has, in fact, an essential corollary, *criticism*. Author and criticism have developed together over the last hundred and fifty odd years until the achieved situation of today when the institutionalization of 'literary criticism' (in faculties, journals, newspaper reviews, etc.) in replacement of the discipline of rhetoric (founded not on the 'author' but on the orders of discourse) depends on and sustains the author (enshrined in syllabi and examinations, interviews and television portraits). The task of criticism has been precisely the construction of the author. It must read the author in the texts grouped under his name. Style in this perspective is the result of the extraction of marks of individuality, a creation of the author and the area of his value. Criticism, in short, is the modern hermeneutics; the passage from God to Author. Never do we open out a problematic under the question 'Who speaks?' ('What is an author?'), instead we strip away what is spoken to reveal an identity, the source of the author in his *expression* through the text. Author and criticism thus constitute modes of limiting the order of discourse, of placing it in an area of identity, origin and expression in which the problem of language ('who speaks?') will have neither reality nor position.

Such a reality and a position are given in the activity of the texts of the practice of writing. What can it really mean to speak of the author as the source of a discourse? Far from being the unique creation of the author as originating source, every text is always (an)other text(s) that it remakes, comments, displaces, prolongs, reassumes. A text opens in and from that complex formation of modes of articulation that gives, as it were, the theatre of its activity, a series of settings always already there as its very possibility; as the setting of language is always there, without origin and elsewhere to any individual moment of discourse, always received

24

'such as it is'. In this perspective, Balzac's text may be said to come not from 'Reality', via the transcription of its secretary, nor, in an immediate sense, from him as full source; rather, he is written in it (in its inscription), an effect of the text, held in an empire of signs, imposed by orders of discourse that no more than he could provide a simple moment of origin. It is this whole problematic that is constituted in the writing of a text such as *Finnegans Wake* and that constitutes the point of its 'realism'.

The recognition of the difference between Joyce's text and the work of Balzac in relation to this shift in the possibility of the concept of 'realism' may be developed a little further here with reference to a remarkable description of Joyce's practice given by Jacques Derrida in the course of the introduction to his translation of Edmund Husserl's *Frage nach dem Ursprung der Geometrie* :

'[la tentative de James Joyce :] répéter et reprendre en charge la totalité de l'équivoque elle-même, en un langage qui fasse affleurer à la plus grande synchronie possible la plus grande puissance des intentions enfouies, accumulées et entremêlées dans l'âme de chaque atome linguistique, de chaque vocable, de chaque mot, de chaque proposition simple, par la totalité des cultures mondaines, dans la plus grande génialité de leurs formes (mythologie, religion, science, arts, littérature, politique, philosophie, etc.); faire apparaître l'unité structurale de la culture empirique totale dans l'équivoque généralisée d'une écriture qui ne traduit plus une langue dans l'autre à partir de noyaux de sens communs, mais circule à travers toutes les langues à la fois, accumule leurs énergies, actualise leurs consonances les plus secrètes, décèle leurs plus lointains horizons communs, cultive les synthèses associatives au lieu de les fuir et retrouve la valeur poétique de la passivité; bref, une écriture qui, au lieu de le mettre hors jeu par des guillemets, au lieu de le *"réduire"*, s'installe résolument *dans* le champ *labyrinthique* de la culture *"enchaînée"* par ses équivoques, afin de parcourir et de reconnaître le plus actuellement possible la plus profonde distance historique possible.'[36]

The passivity noted by Derrida is Joyce's response to the activity of language, to the plurality of ways of real-izing the world and the plurality of writings available and possible within a culture (*Ulysses* had already been constituted as a repertoire of forms of writing). Language is a source that can be continually worked, even at the

[36] Jacques Derrida, introduction to E. Husserl, *L'Origine de la Géométrie* (Paris, 1962), pp. 104–5.

level of individual words; such a working (and this is its value) running into the 'history' of dream and myth, into the very 'origins' of fiction. *Finnegans Wake* (which is announced as 'polyhedron of scripture') offers the *space* of a work always *'in progress'*, the scene of a play of language ('scribenery') and not, as in realist writing, the (intended) linear progression of a process of notation. The writing here is the mise-en-scène of limits and it is this reading of limits that founds the activity of the text. Words 'rise to the surface', are broken, remade, collided, persuaded together in a series of fragmentary fictions that join and part in a multiplicity of differing ways in every reading of the text. All the 'action' takes place, in the circulation through the labyrinthine mesh of languages, on the threshold of sense in the moment of its production, of the passage from night into day, from the ecstasy of sleep into the wakefulness of speech;[37] the moment of the opening of the play of repetition and difference, of the same and the other—'le seuil enfin au-dessus duquel il y aura différence et au-dessous duquel il y aura similitude',[38] the threshold, that is, of those articulations which, in the process of his self-realization, the subject must take as the real, ground of his very intelligibility: 'le réel, image fabuleuse sans laquelle nous ne pourrions pas lire.'[39] It is that image that becomes the fable of *Finnegans Wake* in its narrative of forms of sense, in the endless pluralization which is the basis of the attempt at totality described by Derrida. This totality, in contrast to that attempted by the limitless writing of Balzac which is defined in terms of the transcription of a whole Society ('j'aurai porté une société toute entière dans la tête'[40]), is a totality grasped in the movement of the endless process of fictions, read in the moment of a perpetual displacement of limits: every word plays against its limits, against that which it limits, limits which are transposed in the reinscription of different series of signs that is always to be reaccomplished in the text. At every word the text reads its own possibility, its own production ('Le langage se réfléchissant', in Mallarmé's phrase), trembling on the

---

37 'L'enfant,' wrote Mallarmé, 'abdique son extase' ('Prose', *Oeuvres complètes*, Pléiade edition, p. 57); a passage that may be glossed with this passage from an essay by the comparative psychologist F. J. J. Buytendijk, to which we shall have occasion to return later: 'L'animal n'a pas d'objets. Il ne fait que pénétrer *extatiquement* son environnement . . . L'homme, conclurons-nous, c'est pour ainsi dire, un animal qui s'étant frotté les yeux, regarde étonné autour de lui, parce qu'il aperçoit l'*autre*.' *L'Homme et l'Animal* (Paris, 1965), p. 82 (my italics).
38 Michel Foucault, op. cit., p. 11.
39 Roland Barthes, introduction to A. Gallien, *Verdure* (Paris, 1967), p. 12.
40 *Lettres à Madame Hanska* II, p. 374.

26

edge of unreadability ('usylessly unreadable'), its real being the fable of language and not that of the natural attitude which provides an area of the 'readable' that is precisely an unconscious demarcation of its own limits. These questions of reading and readability, of the making and remaking of meanings, are, indeed, at the very core of its project. 'Ce n'est que dans le langage poétique que se réalise pratiquement "la totalité" du code dont le sujet dispose. Dans cette perspective, la pratique littéraire se révèle comme exploration et découverte des possibilités du langage; comme activité qui affranchit le sujet de certains réseaux linguistiques (psychiques, sociaux); comme dynamisme qui brise l'inertie des habitudes du langage.'[41]

There is finally at the heart of *Finnegans Wake* a silence, a silence against which every multi-tiered word in that unfinishing text reverberates. Paradox is profitable these days and the paradox of a literature of silence has been formulated joyously many times. The paradox is curious but significant in its dissimulation of writing as speech, and in fact there is no paradox. A project of silence and of making silent has been variously conceived within the development of what, since the Romantic age, we have called 'literature'; a project of 'saying other', of, exactly, hesitation. 'La littérature? C'est pouvoir dire par quels signes notre réalité vient vers nous.'[42]

To value literature thus is not to value a particular programme (Joyce is here an example, not a pattern), but simply to record an emphasis that has been insistent at least since the work of Lautréamont and Mallarmé and which is a moment of consciousness of creation, transformation, death even.[43] This moment is always felt as

[41] Julia Kristeva, *Semeiotiké: Recherches pour une sémanalyse* (Paris, 1969), pp. 178–9.
[42] Jean-Pierre Faye, *Le Récit hunique* (Paris, 1967), p. 35.
[43] The term 'literature' is always a problem. Its history is fully described in Roger Escarpit's pamphlet *La Définition du terme 'littérature'* (Université de Bordeaux, Faculté des Lettres et des Sciences Humaines, 1961; now reprinted in *Le Littéraire et le Social*, ed. R. Escarpit, Paris, 1970, pp. 259–72). All that it is necessary to remember here is that our current usage of the term is of fairly recent origin, having been developed in the course of the nineteenth century, and that, at one level, its development increasingly characterizes the otherness of literature, its silence; the term quickly assimilating the stigmata of 'uselessness', 'futility', 'madness', and so on. There has, of course, also been an acceptable and accepted literature, relegated to a defined area of 'amusement', 'emotion', etc., and an official literature, which is less a particular pantheon of names—it can, after all, include, say, Joyce—than a mode of reading or rather non-reading, the principle of which is Human Nature, a mysterious and indefinable essence that is sometimes called, in a more 'modern' emphasis, Psychology. Human Nature, as will be seen, has figured heavily in the non-reading of the *nouveau roman*.

dangerous in the perspectives it opens on the production of ourselves and our reality and is resisted within the natural attitude, which at the extreme teaches literature as *mad* (*Finnegans Wake* becomes 'the aberration of a great man') or, with unconscious reason, as *useless*, by both of which, of course, it means *other than itself*. The relation of the experience of language and the idea of death was formulated by Hegel in the image of the first act of Adam ('der erste Akt') as the constitution of a mastery over things in the process of giving names which, in converting them into idealities for man, annihilates them in their existence ('sie als Seinde vernichtete').[44] If through this fiction can be grasped the moment of the appearance of the other, of difference, of silence (realized exactly in the opening of speech, in the babble of voices), of the death of negation and limitation, literature, as that term may be understood in the light of the practice of *Finnegans Wake*, may be seen as being constituted, utopianically, as the moment 'before', aiming to rejoin, to *know* that 'erste Akt', the reality of which is forgotten in the censorship of the particular language that knows itself as natural, direct re-presentation of 'Reality', remaining ignorant of the 'guilt' of its activity ('toute chose qu'on nomme n'est déjà plus tout à fait la même, elle a perdu son innocence'[45]). Such a literature, to the discomfort of the authority of the natural attitude the prime demand of which is that literature should unreflectingly repeat its taken-for-granted forms, will, in its silence, have nothing to say.

The recognition contained in the term 'utopianically' used above must be stressed; it is, indeed, a recognition that is the very force of the writing of *Finnegans Wake*. The idea of the 'erste Akt' can only ever be a fiction; innocence is always already lost (and already that formulation itself is caught up in the process of fiction). The practice of writing is not a lapse into the unreflective adoption of the fiction of some 'essence', but a constant activity of suspicion of language and forms, of their questioning and 'undoing'. Its silence is not the retrieval of some original depth untouched by any process of articulation, but the very movement of its activity, which in its effect of hesitation places writer and reader in the 'hollow' of the realization of the play of forms that opens 'Reality'; in what *Nombres* describes as 'la partie creuse et concave de l'édifice'.[46] The problem

44 G. Hegel, *Sämtliche Werke*, ed. G. Lasson Vol. XIX, I (Leipzig, 1932), p. 211.
45 J.–P. Sartre, *Situations II* (Paris, 1948), p. 72.
46 *Nombres*, p. 34.

is the reactivation of habitual inattention, the demonstration in the activity of the writing of the night that is the defining horizon of the daylight forms : 'Nous vivons dans le faux jour d'une langue morte aux significations bornées : nous manquons le jour dans la mesure où nous manquons la nuit que nous sommes. Mais nous ne sommes pas autre chose que ce mouvement nocturne et diurne du lisible et de l'illisible, en nous, hors de nous,—et cela nous ne voulons pas le savoir.'[47] The unease that is caused by *Finnegans Wake* and that demands the security of its definition as 'aberration' is exactly that it is a '*nightynovel*'.

The situation of the nouveau roman is post-Joyce : Joyce, that is, is a major element in its situation. To say this is not so much to suggest particular points of influence, though no doubt these could be traced if it were felt to be important to do so (continuity is the backbone of the natural attitude), as to stress the position of the nouveau roman in the general context of the shift in literary consciousness that has been described here as the practice of writing, and so to indicate that the nouveau roman functions not on the grounds of the natural attitude (so that the feeling of the loss of innocence is strongly in evidence : 'Nous sommes entrés dans l'ère du soupçon . . .'),[48] but as a questioning of that attitude in its work of research in and exploration of the premises and possibilities of the novel. Its situation is that work of textual reactivation in which the work of Joyce represents so important a stage. The 'Balzacian' novel thus stands for everything the nouveau roman is concerned to call into question and it is not surprising to find the destruction of that novel (of its 'innocence', and so of the whole form) consciously worked through in many examples of the nouveau roman, 'anti-novels' according to the famous description given by Sartre :

'Les anti-romans conservent l'apparence et les contours du roman; ce sont des ouvrages d'imagination qui nous présentent des personnages fictifs et nous racontent leur histoire. Mais c'est pour mieux décevoir; il s'agit de contester le roman par lui-même, de le détruire sous nos yeux dans le temps qu'on semble l'édifier, d'écrire le roman d'un roman qui ne se fait pas, qui ne peut pas se faire.'[49]

[47] Philippe Sollers, *Logiques*, p. 240.
[48] Nathalie Sarraute, *L'Ere du soupçon* (Paris, 1956), p. 59.
[49] J.-P. Sartre, 'Préface'; Nathalie Sarraute, *Portrait d'un inconnu* (Paris, 1948), pp. 7–8.

This 'undoing' of the novel poses problems of reading. In relation to expectations of reading defined within the natural attitude examples of the nouveau roman, as is intended, produce an effect of unreadability; they remain unavailable for consumption, which means, in fact—and this is the unease they cause—that they have to be *read*. The texts of the practice of writing open, be it obliquely, the possibility of what Roland Barthes has called, in opposition to the 'texte lisible' of realist writing, the 'texte scriptible'; the text continually to be rewritten, a perpetual provision of differences. Where the novels of realist writing are constituted as objects, writing being no more than the incarnation of a 'Sense', the representation of a 'Reality' that reading must disengage, these texts are a production, an attention to the play of the *signifiant*, thus remaining (and the process of *Finnegans Wake* is exemplary here) without centre, calling us, in Barthes' words, 'à traverser leur écriture d'une nouvelle inscription'.[50] What is presented is the text, which cannot be discarded for some represented presence; the novels of the nouveau roman, for instance, are not open to summary (whence the necessity for the recognition of the limitations of this present essay, which must hope to stay this side of the recuperation of these novels into the patterns of expectation): all the insistence is on the specificity of the text and the activity of its reading.

This insistence creates unease, and not merely (as is necessary) on the part of the custodians of Human Nature. There is little in the nouveau roman of what is generally understood, in the light of Sartre's famous essay on the nature of literature and the possibilities of the novel *Qu'est-ce que la littérature?*, by the term *engagement*. There is, for example, as has so often been pointed out, no 'analysis' or 'description' of the political situation in modern France, and there have been various criticisms of this 'lack of commitment' ranging from the simple abuse of the supporters of the mythical Human Nature (thus François Mauriac, and the tone is fairly indicative; 'Vous pouvez jouer aux osselets dans votre coin. Le poème en puissance, c'est au Vatican qu'il se manifeste.'[51]) to the serious assessments made from within the framework of traditional Marxist think-

50 Roland Barthes, 'Musica Practica', *L'Arc* No. 40, p. 17.
51 Cit. A. Delmas, *A la Découverte du nouveau roman* (Paris, 1965), p. 29. (Attempts are also made, of course, to retrieve the nouveau roman for Human Nature: thus J. A. G. Tans: 'Au coeur de ce qui a été souvent décrié à tort comme une révolution littéraire ahurissante et néfaste, nous avons vu à l'oeuvre l'esprit et le coeur français éternels.' *Romans lisibles et romans illisibles* (Groningen, 1963), p. 13.)

ing on literature.[52] These criticisms tend, however, to depend exactly on the premisses of realist writing, on the assumption of the 'Balzacian' novel as norm. François Mauriac objects because Robbe-Grillet does not somehow *represent* the Vatican Council (or, presumably, something Mauriac regards as of equal value) and this kind of Marxist criticism similarly objects to the fact that the nouveau roman does not represent the contradictions of bourgeois society. What, after all, is *Dans le labyrinthe* beside Vietnam? Sartre has said that he cannot read Robbe-Grillet in an underdeveloped country. The comment is copied into Claude Simon's text *Orion aveugle* in the speech made by a participant at a colloquium on the social function of the writer held in a Latin-American country:

'¡Me parece (Il me semble) que la única jerarquía posible (que la seule hiérarchie valable) es la jerarquía (c'est la hiérarchie) de los problemas y de las necesidades (des problèmes et des besoins) de los pueblos de nuestros países (des peuples de nos pays) y ninguna otra! (et rien d'autre!). ¡Me parece (Il me semble) que si estamos reunidos aquí (que si nous sommes réunis ici), es para discutir de esos problemas (c'est pour discuter ces problèmes) y no de los problemas académicos (et non des problèmes académiques) de una creación literaria (d'une création littéraire) con los cuales nuestros pueblos oprimidos (dont nos peuples opprimés) no tienen nada que hacer! (n'ont rien à faire!).'[53]

The writers of the nouveau roman, that is, remain aware of the problem in these terms even while insisting on the need for the notion of a writer's commitment to be understood at the level of the problems of writing posed in his practice. Such an insistence was made by Robbe-Grillet in the course of a conference held at Leningrad in 1963 in the very title of his communication: 'L'écrivain, par définition, ne sait où il va et il écrit pour chercher à comprendre pourquoi il écrit'.[54]

There are two points that may be made here in connection with this question of *engagement*. Firstly, in the same interview in which he made the remark concerning the impossibility of reading Robbe-Grillet in an underdeveloped country, Sartre also made, in continua-

[52] Cf. e.g. E. Lop and A. Sauvage, 'Essai sur le nouveau roman', *La Nouvelle Critique* No. 124, March 1961, pp. 117–135, No. 125, April, pp. 68–87, No. 127, June, pp. 83–107; C. Burgelin and G. Pérec, 'Le nouveau roman et le refus du réel', *Partisans* February 1962, pp. 108–118. Cf. also the remarks on the nouveau roman in a survey of new trends in foreign literature by Raïssa Orlova and Lev Kopelev, *Novy Mir* No. I/ 1959, pp. 219–230.
[53] Claude Simon, *Orion aveugle* (Geneva, 1970), p. 106.
[54] *Esprit*, July 1964, pp. 63–5.

tion of this line of thought, the famous statement to the effect that in the face of the death of a child *La Nausée* is useless : 'En face d'un enfant qui meurt, la *Nausée* ne fait pas le poids.'[55] But the death of a child is not really to be set against literature in this way in an either/or choice, for without literature that death is nothing : language and literature, as supreme moment of linguistic activity, define that death, realize its tragedy that we grasp not in spite of but because of literature, as the use of the term 'tragedy' suggests, because of our capacity to make and remake meanings.[56] Secondly, criticisms of the supposed non-commitment of the nouveau roman are based on the idea that commitment can be judged at the level of *content* and that what is to be challenged, therefore, is not the mode of writing, which is to be retained, but traditional realms of content which are to be replaced, this being the area of radical literary *engagement*. Nothing can be further from the truth in our contemporary society. The official 'Balzacian' novel can and does contain everything. Where once realism, historically, was a question of changing and extending subject-matter and was felt in this way to be radical (and attacked as such for this with charges of 'shocking realism'),[57] we now have, in this sense, total realism. To call a novel 'shocking' today is no longer a moral but a commercial judgement. Any subject, and the more 'shocking' the better, can be and is consumed in novels, including Vietnam and the death of a child. What is now radical—and this has been the 'scandal' of the nouveau roman—is an activity of reflection on this general writing, on the forms of intelligibility it sustains. To call a novel by Robbe-Grillet 'unreadable' has a precise ideological value that it is the precise aim of the writing of that novel to refuse. The activity of the nouveau roman is to be understood in the context of its situation which, thinking back to that remark by Sartre, is not that of an underdeveloped country but that of a society characterized by the relentless spread of what Sollers described as 'cette parole insidieuse, incessante, et qui semble toujours être là avant que nous y pensions', a discourse in which we are 'naturally' obliged to find ourselves and which needs perhaps to be denaturalized, read in its form-ations.

The commitment of the nouveau roman lies here, then, in its reading of the formation of the 'Balzacian' novel and in its insis-

55 'Jean-Paul Sartre s'explique sur *Les Mots*', *Le Monde*, 18 April 1964, p. 13.
56 This point has been developed in connection with Sartre's remark by Jean Ricardou in his fundamental *Problèmes du nouveau roman* (Paris, 1967), pp. 16–18.
57 Cf. Raymond Williams, *The Long Revolution* (London, 1961), p. 275.

tence on a work of research and exploration, on understanding the foundations of intelligibility (of ourselves, of our world) in a presentation to the reader of possibilities of reading in the realization of which he may read himself in his construction. 'Tout se passe comme si on conférait la réalité à n'importe quoi plutôt qu'au langage' :[58] the texts of the practice of writing operate a reactivation of the experience of that reality, as, for instance, in the practice of *Finnegans Wake*. The area of the reactivation accomplished by the nouveau roman, so often specifically located in terms of a work on the 'Balzacian' novel, is to be understood in relation to the ubiquity and unconscious assumption as natural of the form of that novel, even in the most private areas of self-awareness. The novel, as Sollers puts it in that passage cited earlier, is the manner in which society speaks itself; the nouveau roman takes as its aim the reading of the forms of that discourse.[59] The nouveau roman, as it can be defined within the situation of the practice of writing, is thus an essentially critical enterprise directed at a questioning of the assumptions of the 'Balzacian' novel and, through that, of the habitual forms in which we define or *write* our lives. It is precisely this questioning that has caused it to be received as subversive and repudiated in an often startlingly violent language. We must be clear why a critic claiming to speak in the name of human values in literature should be able to describe Robbe-Grillet's *La Jalousie* as 'un piège à cons'.[60]

This violence seems to be an answer to a violence that can be understood in the activity of reading proposed by the nouveau roman. Such a suggestion is tentative (we lack a real descriptive theory of reading), but certain points might be briefly and simply indicated. Of particular interest in this respect is the development within the general form of the 'Balzacian' novel (and Balzac himself, of course, participated in this development) of the genre of the detective novel which is, in some sort, the summa of the process of the naturalization of the 'Balzacian' novel. The purpose of the

---

[58] Philippe Sollers, *Logiques*, p. 245.
[59] Cf. the following observation by Roland Barthes: 'il n'est ou ne sera plus possible de comprendre la littérature "heuristique" (celle qui cherche) sans la rapporter fonctionnellement à la culture de masse, avec laquelle elle entretiendra (et entretient déjà) des rapports complémentaires de résistance, de subversion, d'échange ou de complicité (c'est *l'acculturation* qui domine notre époque), et l'on peut rêver d'une histoire—parallèle et relationnelle—du nouveau roman et de la presse du coeur.' *Essais critiques*, p. 262.
[60] Pierre de Boisdeffre, *La Cafetière est sur la table* (Paris, 1967), p. 92.

detective novel is to end; the body of the novel is no more than a massive parenthesis between violence and its solution (what Michel Butor has called the final 'explosion de la vérité'[61]). All the reading consists in the movement from the one to the other, and it would be wrong to see in this movement which might suggest a certain activity —the reader 'spots the clues'—anything more, finally, than a fundamental passivity. The reading depends on the assurance of the ending (an assurance guaranteed by the expectations of the genre which is carefully defined according to strict rules) that will fix the reading in a final full truth, thus defining the text as without plurality. It is the ending that the writing—the parenthesis between opening and close—takes as its function to hide, so that the reading is, in fact, no more than the progressive negation or removal of the writing in order to re-present the original truth hidden behind. This is the *comfort* of the detective story : it offers a deep confirmation of the non-problematic nature of reality in absenting writing before an ultimate untroubled truth. In this, the detective novel may be seen as the very type of the 'Balzacian' novel with its premiss of a realist writing that declares itself transparent before the fixed source of 'Reality'. Hence the extent to which examples of the nouveau roman have worked through an 'undoing' of the detective novel—instances would include, in their different ways, Butor's *L'Emploi du temps*, Claude Ollier's *La Mise en scène*, Robert Pinget's *L'Inquisitoire*, and, of course, supremely, Robbe-Grillet's *Les Gommes*. Hence too the feeling of a violence inflicted by the nouveau roman in the experience of reading that it proposes, a violence which is felt as a result of its troubling the expectations of reading and which calls forth the violent reactions of a Boisdeffre. But, as Jacques Derrida puts it, and here lies the area of the *research* of the nouveau roman : 'Parce que nous commençons à écrire, à écrire autrement, nous devons relire autrement.'[62]

The nouveau roman, it is often and angrily said, is the 'death of the novel'. Evidently this is true in so far as the nouveau roman is a critique of the accepted 'Balzacian' novel in the operation of a calling into question (a bringing to consciousness) of its taken-for-granted assumptions. (There is, of course, nothing to stop this critique of the 'Balzacian' novel in the practice of a contemporary writing going hand in hand with an appreciation of the actual work

61 *L'Emploi du temps* (Paris, 1956), p. 147.
62 *De la Grammatologie* (Paris, 1967), p. 130.

of Balzac himself, as is notably the case with Michel Butor who has devoted several studies to Balzac's work[63]). Equally, of course, the 'Balzacian' novel is endlessly repeated and consumed in our society —in Britain indeed realist writing has hardly been challenged since Joyce, the reality of whose work has been largely ignored—and this in a way, as Barthes has suggested in the passage quoted earlier in a note to this chapter, gives the functional situation of the nouveau roman, which exists precisely in the 'undoing' of that novel. Usually, for reasons that will be clear by now, the attack on the nouveau roman as assassin of the novel is followed by an attack on the nouveau roman as assassin of Man, as being anti-human. 'What life says or seems to say hardly concerns them', comments Henri Peyre, representatively, discussing the work of Robbe-Grillet, Butor and Nathalie Sarraute.[64] (Note the idea of a speaking source called 'life' whose Truths a novelist has merely to transcribe.) Here the nouveau roman shares the fate of the recent development of semiotic thinking which is similarly attacked as anti-human; witness, for example, the attack on what is understood under the heading 'structuralism'. And these attacks are right. Does not Claude Lévi-Strauss declare in *La Pensée sauvage* that the final goal of the human sciences is not to constitute man but to dissolve him?[65] Does not Jacques Lacan find man constituted in the orders of the *signifiant*? Does not Louis Althusser in his reading of Marx disengage the reality of 'cette *mise en scène* . . . ce théâtre qui est à la fois sa propre scène, son propre texte, ses propres acteurs, ce théâtre dont les spectateurs ne peuvent en être, d'occasion, spectateurs que parce qu'ils en sont d'abord les acteurs forcés, pris dans les contraintes d'un texte et de rôles dont ils ne peuvent en être les auteurs, puisque c'est, par essence, un théâtre sans auteur'?[66] The work of 'structuralism' has been precisely the breaking of the full 'I', the displacement of the subject in his mise-en-scène in the network of structures that open his

63 Cf. e.g. 'Balzac et la réalité', *Répertoire* (Paris, 1960), pp. 79–93. (Balzac has been important to the present discussion in the presuppositions of his writing, but it seems worth recognizing briefly here that the emphasis of this discussion has not meant to imply some kind of simple 'dismissal' of his novels. Engels, as is well enough known, talked of the *Sieg des Realismus* with regard to Balzac's novels, and it is tempting to extend this experience of reading, as confirmed in certain other nineteenth-century novels, in thinking a 'dialogism' particular to these texts and which may be read from the perspective of the practice of writing. Such a work, of course, will need to be accomplished elsewhere.)

64 Henri Peyre, *French Novelists of Today* (New York, 1967), pp. 362–3.

65 *La Pensée sauvage* (Paris, 1962), p. 326.

66 *Lire le Capital* (revised edition Paris, 1968), II, p. 71.

realization as subject. The radical force of this work is summarized by Derrida in a passage in which he characterizes two contrasting attitudes:

'Il y a . . . deux interprétations de l'interprétation, de la structure, du signe et du jeu. L'une cherche à déchiffrer, rêve de déchiffrer une vérité ou une origine échappant au jeu et à l'ordre du signe, et vit comme un exil la nécessité de l'interprétation. L'autre qui n'est plus tournée vers l'origine, affirme le jeu et tente de passer au-delà de l'homme et de l'humanisme, le nom de l'homme étant le nom de cet être qui, à travers l'histoire de la métaphysique ou de l'onto-théologie, c'est-à-dire du tout de son histoire, a rêvé la présence pleine, le fondement rassurant, l'origine et la fin du jeu.'[67]

The questioning of the fictions of 'source' and 'origin' is made through an attention to the reality of language, to forms of the articulation of division and difference, to structures (understanding structure as 'that which puts in place an experience for the subject whom it includes'). Our concept of the author and that of Man, of which the former is a particular expression, are interdependent with an elision of that reality. The attack on the second kind of thinking described by Derrida in the name of Humanism connects with the attacks on the nouveau roman made in the same terms, and it is indicative that two of the most brilliant writers on the nouveau roman have been centrally concerned in the main body of their work with the development of that second kind of thinking and have analysed, in different ways, the context of the defensive assumptions of Man, Human Nature, and so on. In *Les Mots et les Choses*, his 'archaeological' account of the varying and discontinuous epistemological fields of Western culture from the sixteenth century to the threshold of the modern age, Michel Foucault situates 'man' as a creation of recent history ('un simple pli dans notre savoir') and notes its dependence on a dispersion of language 'outside itself', as the transparent expression of a fixed and stable representation of 'Reality' to itself (as 'le double méticuleux, le miroir sans buée d'une connaissance qui, elle, n'est pas verbale . . .[le langage] se tient à une certaine distance de la nature pour en incanter par sa propre docilité et en recueillir finalement le portrait fidèle'[68]). In *Mythologies*, Roland Barthes describes the way in which a certain order of discourse, that of myth, functions in bourgeois society as the process

[67] *L'Ecriture et la Différence* (Paris, 1967), p. 427.
[68] *Les Mots et les Choses*, pp. 309-10.

of the transmutation of cultural meanings into 'natural' meanings, stabilizing historical consciousness in the definition of an absolute idea of the Human. It is hardly necessary to stress how that description can include the account given here of the realist writing of the novel all the function of which is precisely to present itself as natural, to absent itself as convention and form.

Foucault also notes a 'return of language' and the beginning of the disappearance of 'man', the subject dispersed into a plurality of possible positions and functions ('L'être du langage n'apparaît pour lui-même que dans la disparition du sujet'[69]) :

'Si ce même langage surgit maintenant avec de plus en plus d'insistance en une unité que nous devons mais que nous ne pouvons pas encore penser, n'est-ce pas le signe que toute cette configuration va maintenant basculer, et que l'homme est en train de périr à mesure que brille plus fort à notre horizon l'être du langage? L'homme s'étant constitué quand le langage était voué à la dispersion, ne va-t-il pas être dispersé quand le langage se rassemble? . . . l'homme a composé sa propre figure dans les interstices d'un langage en fragments . . .'[70]

This reappearance is grasped by Foucault, and here his analysis joins that made by Barthes in *Le Degré zéro de l'écriture*, in the development in literature of the experience of language marked by the work of a Mallarmé, a Roussel or a Joyce and which can be seen as a vital part of the context of the work of theory that is today undertaking 'man's' dissolution. It is this dramatic consciousness of language and forms of writing that characterizes the texts of what I have called the practice of writing, those texts that have 'fractured' the forms of the novel. The writer can no longer take language for granted, his *responsibility* lies in a reflexive consciousness, a *practice* of writing; in Mallarmé's decisive formulation, 'il suivra la méthode du langage (la déterminer). Le langage se réfléchissant.'[71] The 'anti-humanism' of the nouveau roman lies here in the responsibility of a work on the novel as a series of forms and so its de-construction as an area of the realization of the security of 'man' and of ourselves in his shadow—'Qui reconnaît-on en nous sinon un personnage de roman?'

It is also often said in a general emphasis—and the nouveau roman may then be taken as a symptom in this connection—that we are living in the period of the 'death of the book'. Such an

[69] Michel Foucault, 'La pensée du dehors', *Critique* No. 229, June 1966, p. 525,
[70] *Les Mots et les Choses*, p. 397.
[71] 'Notes', *Oeuvres complètes*, p. 851.

emphasis is, of course, best known as that of Marshall McLuhan, prophetic witness of the close of the Gutenberg era and the retotalization of fragmented man in the electronic media, but this is not the place for a detailed critical discussion of the myths of his work. What is interesting to draw here from the general emphasis is that the challenge to the novel—supreme Gutenberg product—which is made in the practice of writing determines not in some sense a 'death' of the book, but, on the contrary, exactly a revaluation of the book. It is the conception of the book that is changing, as can be read plainly enough in Joyce or Mallarmé: this is what must be thought through from the recognition formulated by Derrida: 'La fin de l'écriture linéaire est bien la fin du livre, même si aujourd'-hui encore, c'est dans la forme du livre que se laissent tant bien que mal engainer de nouvelles écritures, qu'elles soient littéraires ou théoriques.'[72] The change could be illustrated by considering the development of the work of Michel Butor. After a group of works exploring, in a process of self-elucidation, certain problems in the novel form ('Le roman tend nécessairement et doit tendre à sa propre élucidation'[73]), as, for instance, in *Degrés*, an essay in the accomplishment of 'une totalité à l'intérieur d'une description' through the attempt at a complete notation of the 'Reality' of an hour-long geography lesson in a French lycée that calls into question the realist premises of the 'Balzacian' novel in the very incompletion which it dramatizes, Butor seems to turn into fields of book composition, the texts of which demand new kinds of reading in an immediate and obvious way, as, for instance, in *Mobile* (published with a certain rightness in the same year as *The Gutenberg Galaxy*), a sort of kinetic construction in prose, a portrait of the USA using a literary equivalent of collage, with bits of speeches, advertisements, typographical artifices and so on, in the organization of which the reader must actively participate in *his* reading.[74] Yet to illustrate the change in these terms can also be misleading, for such an illustration tends to obscure, in its focus on composition achieved with the help of picture or typographical arrangement, the new presence of the book as *text* in the practice of writing and so, in its general implications, to imply that the change is felt most crucially in books

---

[72] *De la Grammatologie*, pp. 129–30.

[73] 'Le roman comme recherche', *Essais sur le roman* (Paris, 1969), p. 13.

[74] It is worth noting in this connection that much of Butor's work has, in fact, taken the form of collaboration with artists: e.g. (with G. Masurovsky) *Litanie d'eau* (Paris, 1964); (with J. Hérold) *Dialogues des règnes* (Paris, 1967). Claude Simon has also been interested in such work: cf. (with J. Miró) *Femmes* (Paris, 1966).

that somehow aspire to the condition of painting, which is far from being the impetus of the practice of the nouveau roman. As Sollers has put it : 'le lecteur . . . doit, non pas comme on le dit trop souvent, fabriquer un livre par sa lecture, mais devenir à chaque instant sa propre écriture—c'est-à-dire briser la parole qui en lui est parlée par les préjugés afin de juger lui-même sur pièces, d'accéder à sa propre *génération*.'[75] The 'brisure' is effected in the nouveau roman in its shattering of the passive readability of realist writing, consumed according to what McLuhan would call a 'lineal decorum';[76] a natural, transparent writing without trace received as no more than a copy of a presence to be reinstituted in a 'lecture *transcendante*'.[77] In its work on this readability, the nouveau roman thus refuses the book as object to refind the world as a series of systems of articulation onto the reading of which its activity of writing opens the reader : 'ce système de significations, qui est à l'intérieur du livre, va être une image du système de significations à l'intérieur duquel le lecteur est pris, dans toute sa vie quotidienne, et à l'intérieur duquel il est perdu.'[78] It is thus that these texts put on their pages 'du lecteur' and that they encompass the projection of the end of the book as object in the way that Derrida suggests. The projection, however, remains ceaselessly to be remade; the 'texte scriptible' is still to be accomplished; glimpsed obliquely ('tant bien que mal') in the very fact of this projection, it is conceived precisely in the book, in the drama of writing, against the natural representation of linear writing, against the fixity of stereotype and repetition. Here lies the area of the work of the nouveau roman.

So far I have referred without hesitation to 'the nouveau roman'. Many, however, writers and critics alike, would deny that there is any such thing and insist on the diversity of the bodies of work to which reference is made under that general heading. This insistence is justified and, given the context of the shift in literary consciousness that I have described as the practice of writing, the diversity is necessarily the case. If the individual novelists grouped together in terms of the idea of the nouveau roman can be seen as a group, it is simply in their common situation with regard to this shift; it is this that has been recognized in some sort in the characterization

---

[75] *Logiques*, pp. 242-3.
[76] *The Gutenberg Galaxy* (London, 1962), p. 201.
[77] Jacques Derrida, *De la Grammatologie*, p. 229.
[78] Michel Butor and Georges Charbonnier, *Entretiens avec Michel Butor* (Paris, 1967), p. 24.

of the nouveau roman as '*l'école du refus*'.[79] The nouveau roman is thus understood in terms of that reflexive consciousness, that work on and exploration of traditional premisses of the novel, which has been discussed above. It is in this connection that the term 'nouveau roman' retains its value and it is essentially in this connection that I shall use it here, very much, indeed, as Robbe-Grillet defines his use of the term at the beginning of *Pour un Nouveau Roman* :

'Si j'emploie volontiers, dans bien des pages, le terme de *Nouveau Roman*, ce n'est pas pour désigner une école, ni même un groupe défini et constitué d'écrivains qui travailleraient dans le même sens; il n'y a là qu'une appellation commode englobant tous ceux qui cherchent de nouvelles formes romanesques, capables d'exprimer (ou de créer) de nouvelles relations entre l'homme et le monde, tous ceux qui sont décidés à inventer le roman, c'est-à-dire à inventer l'homme.'[80]

My concern here is to present the situation of certain bodies of writing that have been generally grouped together (and rightly in so far as this grouping stresses their common situation in the practice of writing) as the nouveau roman.

Brief mention should be made, however, of what might be described as the 'social history' of the nouveau roman. (There is an important sociological study to be done one day of the reception of the nouveau roman.) It may be said to have found its essential beginnings in the nineteen-fifties. It is generally difficult to assign clear dates to literary 'movements' (that term is used here of the nouveau roman with all the qualifications implicit from the discussion of the idea of the nouveau roman in the preceding paragraph) and various dates can be argued for the 'birth' of the nouveau roman. Claude Simon was writing in the forties, as was Nathalie Sarraute whose *Tropismes* first appeared as early as 1939, although it received little attention at the time. It was in the fifties, however, that the idea of the nouveau roman was developed : it was then that the key novels and theoretical articles began to be written and that the nouveau roman began to dominate the French literary scene as a 'literary phenomenon'. The date of the first deliberate use of the term 'nouveau roman', after and in the midst of a whole host of other proposed terms (*roman blanc, anti-roman, anté-roman, pré-roman, roman expérimental, jeune roman, nouveau réalisme*, etc.), to desig-

[79] Cf. Bernard Pingaud's early article 'L'école du refus', *Esprit* Nos. 7–8, July-August 1958, pp. 55–9.
[80] *Pour un Nouveau Roman* (Paris, 1963), p. 9.

40

nate what was felt as a movement is again a matter for speculation; its first use may have been, as Jean-Pierre Faye suggests, by Maurice Nadeau in an article written in 1957.[81] What is certain is that it was, above all, the special number of the review *Esprit* published in July-August 1958 which fixed and confirmed the phenomenon of the nouveau roman.[82] A brief list of some of the main works up to this date may help to give a picture of the development : 1953—Alain Robbe-Grillet, *Les Gommes* (Prix Fénéon); Nathalie Sarraute, *Martereau*. 1954—Michel Butor, *Passage de Milan*. 1955—Robbe-Grillet, *Le Voyeur* (Prix des Critiques). 1956—Nathalie Sarraute, *L'Ere du soupçon*; Butor, *L'Emploi du temps* (Prix Fénéon); Robert Pinget, *Graal Flibuste*. 1957—Robbe-Grillet, *La Jalousie*; Claude Simon, *Le Vent*; Butor, *La Modification* (Prix Renaudot). 1958— Robert Pinget, *Baga*; Claude Ollier, *La Mise en scène* (Prix Médicis); Claude Simon, *L'Herbe*. This is the core of that body of work described by the July-August 1958 number of *Esprit* as the 'nouveau roman'.

It is not by chance that the above list is headed by Robbe-Grillet's first published novel for it was his work which to a large extent precipitated the definition and discussion of what was taken to be a new literary movement. Robbe-Grillet's early novels and the seminal articles devoted to them by Roland Barthes in the review *Critique*[83] acted, as it were, as the impetus and focus for the definition of the new activity in the novel form, and it was in terms of a consideration of those novels and, subsequently, of Robbe-Grillet's own theoretical essays that the general activity was grasped, no matter how misguidedly. Hence the assortment of terms for the supposed nouveau roman school—*l'école du regard, mouvement chosiste*, etc.—that were arbitrarily applied to describe collectively the work of Robbe-Grillet, Sarraute, Butor, Simon, Pinget, and various other writers.

It was in these terms that the nouveau roman was generally received and it was this reception, of course, that to a considerable extent created it as a literary phenomenon in that arena of literary gossip and scandal for which there is no real equivalent in England, lacking as it does the vast machinery of literary journalism avail-

[81] 'Nouvelles formules pour le roman', *Critique* No. 123–124, August-September 1957, pp. 707–22; cf. Jean-Pierre Faye, op. cit., p. 32.
[82] 'Le Nouveau Roman', *Esprit* No. 7–8, July-August 1958.
[83] 'Littérature objective', *Critique* No. 86–87, July-August 1954, pp. 581–91; 'Littérature littérale', *Critique* No. 100–101, September-October 1955, pp. 820–6. (Both articles are reprinted in Barthes's *Essais critiques*.)

able in France. The nouveau roman rapidly became *the* cause célèbre, the fashionable topic in debate, and it is in this context that the attacks, counter-attacks and endless pseudo-discussions are to be understood. It would be wrong to absolve the writers of the nouveau roman themselves from responsibility for this trivialization. Barthes was noting as early as 1959 that 'La complaisance du Nouveau Roman à se parler légèrement et ambitieusement à travers des dialogues inutiles et faux, contredit au caractère radical de son éthique littéraire, à la qualité de ses oeuvres véritables.'[84] Practitioners of the nouveau roman, and above all, as we shall see, Robbe-Grillet, have become fodder, in some cases willing fodder, for a journalism whose assumptions constitute everything which the *practice* of the nouveau roman is concerned to challenge in its thinking of literature.

This then is the context of the brief presentation of the nouveau roman to be attempted in the following pages, through the discussion of the work of four writers, Nathalie Sarraute, Alain Robbe-Grillet, Claude Simon, and finally Philippe Sollers. It is in the chapters devoted to Robbe-Grillet and Sollers that the bulk of the theoretical discussion is carried through. May it be stressed once more that no more is attempted here than the presentation of a particular moment in what I have called the practice of writing, simply a pre-text for reading the nouveau roman, whether it be in the work of the writers specifically discussed or in Pinget or Butor or whoever. This indeed is the point of the wager of such a presentation, of the risk of its writing, for it must seek to remain, as it were, perpetually 'by the side of' the work that is here in question, not constituting that work as object and opening a distance which it can span with an interpretive discourse, fixing a sense, but sliding itself ceaselessly before that work in an attempt to open into the reality of the experience of reading it proposes. The consciousness of the risk is most pressing in the final chapter on the work of Philippe Sollers and it is from that consciousness that this book was written; its aim is to stress the reality of the work of the nouveau roman in its practice of writing. In this connection, it seemed right to begin with the work of Nathalie Sarraute because in a real sense the *critical* problem of reading her novels pose is acute. To consider her novels is to go back to the evaluations of a traditional reading and the difficulties

---

84 'Tables rondes', *Les Lettres Nouvelles*, 25 March 1959, p. 52.

they raise in this context and to realize from these difficulties the kind of work being developed in her writing, that work the bases of which subsequent chapters will be concerned to define, resuming, demonstrating and extending that situation of the nouveau roman which the present chapter has been concerned to introduce.

2

Nathalie Sarraute

The publication in 1968 of Nathalie Sarraute's new novel *Entre la vie et la mort* confirmed the continuity of her work which extends along a clearly defined central line of pursuit. Her six novels to date, together with an initial collection of short prose pieces, the critical essays and studies and the radio plays, have a tightly integrated coherence of relationship. This body of work has been produced over a considerable period of time (some thirty-five years), but it is difficult as yet to point to any really adequate critical assessment of its achievement. The reasons for this are complex, and to a large extent the complexity stems from the work itself; from a certain ambiguity of approach suggested by it that, in work which can be so readily characterized in terms of its coherence, inevitably seems paradoxical. The problem posed by the novels, and here lies the difficulty of adequate assessment, is one of *reading*. It is with a consideration of that problem of reading that this chapter is concerned.

The habitual approach to Nathalie Sarraute's novels is made in the context of discussion of the nouveau roman. This context, which is evidently that of the present chapter, is vital. It can, however, also be misleading, as misleading as the concept of the nouveau roman itself which has been popularly defined with reference to certain theories of Alain Robbe-Grillet. If there are significant connections to be made between Nathalie Sarraute's work and that of Robbe-Grillet, they can be made only by considering the meaning of the two quite separate bodies of work in relation to their work on the novel form from within the shift in consciousness represented by the practice of writing, and not by discussing the one in terms of the other. It is perhaps salutary to recall that, while Robbe-Grillet's first novel appeared in 1953, Nathalie Sarraute published her *Tropismes* in its original form in 1939, *Portrait d'un inconnu* (parts of which had already appeared in *Les Temps Modernes*[1]) in 1948, and *Martereau* in 1953, the same year as Robbe-Grillet's *Les Gommes*.

Nathalie Sarraute's work can be seen, in fact, as standing at the opposite end of the spectrum to that of Robbe-Grillet, and she has herself defined their differing emphases : both of them attempt to seize a basic reality, but 'Cette réalité je la cherche dans les mouvements psychologiques à l'état-naissant, ce que j'ai appelé les "Tropismes". Robbe-Grillet la poursuit dans l'appréhension directe, sans recours aux moyens de la description traditionnelle de l'objet.'[2] As will be seen in the following chapter, it is open to doubt whether or not this is an adequate account of the purpose of Robbe-Grillet, who seems to hold not merely to the idea ascribed to him here by Nathalie Sarraute of the novel as the medium for cleansing, anti-anthropomorphic descriptions of objects, but also to the idea of the novel as medium for the representation of extreme subjectivity, and finally (the impetus of the writings of Raymond Roussel will be recognized here) of the novel as linguistic fiction, its realism, as Roland Barthes has insisted, lying essentially in its demonstration of the 'réalité irréelle' of language. Be this as it may, Nathalie Sarraute's own theory of the novel is fundamentally concerned with the novel as a representative, mimetic medium, a medium suitable in this respect for the psychological realism that she defines as the aim of her writings. She can speak of the novel in an almost Zolaesque manner as a laboratory for scientific research, and she has specifically rejected the conception of the novel in terms of a self-reflective linguistic structuration, what Robbe-Grillet has called 'le roman lui-même qui se pense' :[3]

'Je pense que toute exploration du langage qui ne comporterait pas, mieux, qui ne se justifierait pas par la création d'une substance inconnue, qui perdrait contact avec un ordre de sensations neuf, qui se contenterait de n'importe quel contenu, même naïvement banal,

---

[1] *Les Temps Modernes* I, No. 4, 1946, pp. 601–24.

[2] *Times Literary Supplement*, 13 March 1959, p. 145. Robbe-Grillet has indicated the degree to which he can assent sympathetically to Nathalie Sarraute's project in 'Le réalisme, la psychologie, et l'avenir du roman', *Critique* No. 111–112, August-September 1956, pp. 695–701.

[3] 'Pourquoi la mort du roman?' *L'Express*, 8 November 1955, p. 8.

indifférente à ce contenu et enfermée dans le miroitement du langage, ne pourrait pas échapper à l'esthétisme, à l'académisme.'[4]

Her idea of the novel is set out in the series of essays, written 'pour me justifier ou me rassurer ou m'encourager', collected in *L'Ere du soupçon*. The context of her work, as she there defines it, is less a recognized tradition than the creation of a new one depending on the conjunction of Dostoevsky and Kafka, of the 'roman psychologique' and the 'roman de situation'. Dostoevsky commands respect by virtue of the insights he gives the reader through his characters into the subconscious world that exists beyond the boundaries of the individual, into the realm of instinctive, impersonal movement rendered, for example, through the spasms and tortured antics of Fyodor Karamazov in Father Zossima's cell; and Kafka because of his portrayal of the violence in the seemingly ordinary and everyday and his concomitant emphasis on the impossibility of sustaining any longer the belief in the 'moi substantiel'; the aggressive individuality of the Romantic hero gives way to the empty anonymity of K, the name shrivels to an initial letter. The conjunction of Dostoevsky and Kafka in these terms brings us to the very heart of Nathalie Sarraute's work as she conceives it and so, necessarily, to the question of her attitude to psychology in the novel. In a now notorious passage of an essay in *L'Ere du soupçon* (p. 83)* she remarked that 'Le mot "psychologie" est un de ceux qu'aucun auteur aujourd'hui ne peut entendre prononcer à son sujet sans baisser les yeux et rougir'. The remark was made, however, in an essay the initial development of which, despite a certain complexity, is evidently ironical and indeed some few pages later the interest of the modern novel is described as its 'mise au jour d'une matière psychologique nouvelle' (p. 94). The stress falls on the 'nouvelle'; what

---

4 'La littérature aujourd'hui' (interview), *Tel Quel* No. 9, Spring 1962, p. 49. In a communication to the colloquium on avant-garde writing held at Loches in 1970, Nathalie Sarraute attacked those who 'voulant aller plus loin, cherchent à faire du roman une forme pure qui ne renverrait à rien d'autre qu'à elle-même, le texte se constituant à partir du seul langage et se contentant de ses jeux.' (Cf. *Le Monde*, 8 April 1970, p. 12.). It is more than possible that the writers she has in mind here are those of the *Tel Quel* group, though the characterization is totally inaccurate as a description of their work and might better fit certain statements made by Robbe-Grillet. The *reading* of Nathalie Sarraute's texts proposed at the end of this present chapter is based on the recognition, readable in her texts, of the text as work in and on language, this without reducing her work to some 'miroitement du langage'.

* Page references to major works given in the text in this and subsequent chapters relate to the original editions listed in the Select Bibliography at the end of this volume.

Nathalie Sarraute is keen to reject is a traditional approach of the 'psychological novel' :

'Qu'entendez-vous par psychologie? Si vous entendez par là l'analyse des sentiments, la recherche des mobiles de nos actes, l'étude des caractères, alors je crois qu'aujourd'hui une oeuvre romanesque non seulement *peut* ne pas être psychologique, mais encore qu'elle ne *doit* pas l'être.'[5]

If she clearly separates her work from that of Proust, it is in terms of the closeness of her focus on the inner dramas of the *present* moment and her endeavour to 'les faire revivre au lecteur dans le présent' (*L'Ere*, p. 98), in contrast to what she sees as the distance in Proust from such moments which are observed 'au repos, et comme figés dans le souvenir' (p. 97), and it is thus that she can regard Dostoevsky as a healthier influence. She fully acknowledges her debt to the achievement of the novelists who have preceded her; her work must be 'un petit pas plus avant dans l'exploration psychologique : là où de grands écrivains comme Dostoevsky, Proust et Joyce ont fait des pas de géant.'[6]

The nature of the 'matière psychologique nouvelle' that Nathalie Sarraute intends to render in her novels is explicit in the title of her first published work, *Tropismes*, for the concept of tropisms is at the centre of all her writings : 'Les tropismes ont continué à être la substance vivante de tous mes livres.'[7] Tropism is a term from plant physiology, defined by the *Oxford English Dictionary* as meaning, 'the turning of an organism, or a part of one, in a particular direction (either in the way of growth, bending, or locomotion) in response to some external stimulus, as that of light'. In the world of Nathalie Sarraute's novels the external stimuli are found in the ordinary everyday encounters between people, and take the form of the outwardly innocuous phrases of casual conversation. Man's external life, the public reality of these conversational encounters, is an inauthentic surface that masks a kind of Sartrean drama of conflict (the Preface to *Portrait d'un inconnu* belongs to the same period as *L'Etre et le Néant*), a continual attack on and flight from the other. This conflict is neutralized in a recognized middle ground of banality, of Heideggerian Gerede, a 'Grenzland zwischen Einsamkeit und

[5] 'La littérature aujourd'hui', p. 50.
[6] Letter to René Micha; cit. René Micha *Nathalie Sarraute* (Paris, 1966), p. 66.
[7] Preface to the Paris, 1964, edition of *L'Ere du soupçon*, p. 9. (The term 'tropism is' also used, in a different way, by the Austrian novelist Heimito von Doderer. Cf. the discussion of Doderer in Michael Hamburger's *From Prophecy to Exorcism* (London, 1965), pp. 131–9.)

Gemeinschaft', in Kafka's phrase. Beneath this neutralization of the surface world, however, lies the violent world of tropistic movement —'une matière étrange, anonyme comme la lymphe' (*Portrait d'un inconnu* (p. 72)—which Nathalie Sarraute refers to as the world of *sous-conversation*. Under every phrase of a banal conversation a drama of reception and response is taking place. Phrases from the surface world of conversation act as stimuli, setting in motion a swirl of tropistic movements in which people struggle back into the protective shelter of the next neutralized cliché, thus refurbishing the fabric of the conversational Grenzland or 'zone mitoyenne'. This drama is the immediate focus of Nathalie Sarraute's novels:

'these little movements never show themselves directly, they are always concealed within, they can only be guessed at from the surface, from conversation and from our actions, quite banal actions. And what interested me was to show what is hidden beneath these utterly banal words and actions.'[8]

She seeks not to create individual 'characters', but to render 'un même fond commun', or, as Gide put it in *Paludes*, 'l'histoire du terrain neutre, celui qui est à tout le monde'.[9] The feel of her work and the vision it embodies is summed up by this passage from Hugo von Hofmannsthal's dramatic prologue to Brecht's *Baal* :

'Our time is unredeemed; and do you know what it wants to be redeemed from? . . . The individual . . . Our age groans too heavily under the weight of this child of the sixteenth century that the nineteenth fed to monstrous size . . . We are anonymous forces . . . Individuality is an arabesque we have discarded.'[10]

If individuality is an arabesque to be discarded, then it is clear that similar treatment must be accorded to the conventional formal patterns of the novel. The consequences of Nathalie Sarraute's vision for her development of the novel form are of crucial importance here. The traditional concept of 'character', the Balzacian urge to '*camper* un héros de roman', is seen by her as totally false to the psychological realism she is seeking to achieve. 'Les personnages . . . ne parviennent plus à contenir la réalité psychologique actuelle' (*L'Ere*, pp. 70–1). To construct a novel in terms of characters is at once to push the focus exclusively toward the individual. Balzac gives the people in his novels names, occupations, houses, sets of

8 *Der Monat*, (interview) December 1963, p. 27.
9 *Paludes* (Paris, 1920), p. 62.
10 Cit. Martin Esslin, *Brecht: A Choice of Evils* (London, 1959), p. 29.

personal possessions, a full complement of external signs intended to fix their individuality for the reader. In Nathalie Sarraute's vision this individuality is seen as no more than a flimsy envelope covering the automatic flow of impersonal, anonymous tropistic movement, common to all men. The age of innocent belief in the firm, hard outlines of individual personality has given way to the age of suspicion; the well defined contours of the miserly Père Grandet to the shifting nonentity of the old man in *Portrait d'un inconnu* which, by virtue of its 'undoing' of the novel form, Sartre characterized in 1948 as an 'anti-roman'. As few people as possible are given names in Nathalie Sarraute's novels, and there is an absolute minimum of particularizing action: the reader is to be firmly dissuaded from reading them as traditional novels. 'Il faut . . . empêcher le lecteur de courir deux lièvres à la fois, et puisque ce que les personnages gagnent en vitalité facile et en vraisemblance, les états psychologiques auxquels ils servent de support le perdent en vérité profonde, il faut éviter qu'il disperse son attention et la laisse accaparer par les personnages . . .' (*L'Ere*, p. 71). Realism lies not in the slavish representation of the surface world but in the rendering of the deeper world beneath it which gives it its structure. Nathalie Sarraute is fond of quoting Paul Klee's statement to the effect that art does not reproduce what can be seen, it makes things visible.

These are the terms of her rejection of the traditional structures of the novel: how then can the novelist proceed? She acknowledges Ivy Compton-Burnett and Henry Green as pioneers[11] in the handling of the level of conversation, but the main difficulty lies inevitably in the rendering of the *sous-conversation*, and this difficulty has remained unresolved so far in the development of the novel:

'On n'a pas encore découvert ce langage qui pourrait exprimer d'un seul coup ce qu'on perçoit en un clin d'oeil : tout un être et ses myriades de petits mouvements surgis dans quelques mots, un rire, un geste.'
Le Planétarium, p. 39

Her answer is precisely the creation of such a language, depending on a set of images and imagistic expressions that can contain the movement of the *sous-conversation*. Any page from her novels is immediately recognizable because of this language with its series of recurring key terms. The people wear shells ('coquille', 'carapace') like the shells of turtles or snails, protection for the deadly struggle

---

[11] Though not necessarily as *influences*. She first read Ivy Compton-Burnett in 1950. (Cf. 'Virginia Woolf, ou la visionnaire du "maintenant," ' [interview] *Les Lettres Françaises*, No. 882, 29 June 1961, p. 3).

that takes place in the arena of conversation—'ils luttent front contre front, engoncés dans leurs carapaces, leurs lourdes armures' (*Portrait*, p. 48). Like serpents they twist, turn, writhe ('se tortillent'), spitting venom at one another, or else like octopuses attempt to grapple one another with tentacles. When some chance phrase shatters their defences, a repugnant sticky matter spurts out ('jaillit') from them and they flow into the anonymous current of tropistic movement, frantically attempting to clamber back into the security of banality, to escape from the darkness that has engulfed them : 'Tout s'éteint. Nuit noire. Où êtes-vous? Répondez. Nous sommes là tous les deux. Écoutez. J'appelle, répondez-moi. Juste pour que je sache que vous êtes toujours là. Je crie vers vous de toutes mes forces.' (*Les Fruits d'or*, p. 20). The overall central image pertaining to this world is that of the planetarium; people live as though in a planetarium, protected by the reassuringly smooth sham sky from the turbulence of the real one beyond it.[12] The basic urge is to huddle ('se blottir') under this sham sky, under the shelter of cliché, out of reach for the moment of the violence that is the dominant reality of this world : 'On vivait en pleine terreur,' someone remarks in *Les Fruits d'or* (p. 172). It is a world not without affinity with that of Ionesco's theatre where again everyday unthinking chatter masks a latent and essential violence capable of manifesting itself at any time.[13]

[12] This image is explicit only in the title of *Le Planétarium*, but it is a key image for Nathalie Sarraute herself from the very beginning of her work. In 1939 she collected a group of prose pieces under the title of 'Le Planétarium', but the volume was never published.

[13] It might be noted here that the idea of the inauthentic level of conversation is also central in Proust. Earlier I used the expression 'zone mitoyenne,' an expression that occurs in a crucial passage in which Bergson comments on what he sees as the inadequacy of language, its generalization, hence its banality: 'Nous nous mouvons parmi des généralités et des symboles . . . Nous vivons dans une zone mitoyenne entre les choses et nous, extérieurement aux choses, extérieurement aussi à nous-mêmes' (*Le Rire*, Paris, 1900, p. 158). The same distrust of language at this level is manifested and elaborated by the narrator of *A la recherche du temps perdu*, and both the similarity and the difference of the emphasis from that in Nathalie Sarraute's work can readily be grasped. For both novelists the level of conversation (in Proust 'causerie,' the realm of 'parole') is superficial and the task of the novelist is the rendering of a deeper level which involves a work on language (Proust's theory of metaphor, Nathalie Sarraute's creation of tropistic imagery), but of which the object, the nature of this deeper level, is essentially different in the two novelists. Where Nathalie Sarraute seeks the *anonymous*, Proust, as the quotation from Bergson will have already suggested, seeks the *individual* (and it is this that conversation masks); 'ce résidu réel que nous sommes obligés de garder pour nous-mêmes, que la causerie ne peut transmettre . . .' (III, p. 257). 'On a entre soi et chaque personne le mur d'une langue étrangère' (II, p. 522). Nathalie Sarraute's 'characters' are equally alone, but alone in their anonymity, and in a common language that stimulates the tropistic movements that unite them in separation.

Martereau is typical of Nathalie Sarraute's work, and in its deliberately explicit and subversive use of a named character (Martereau) affords a very clear insight into the recasting of the novel form her vision structures. The narrator of the novel is a hypersensitive young man with a highly attentuated grasp on his reality as an individual. He feels himself to be 'un jardin public livré à la foule' (p. 27), and this passive malleability makes him a peculiarly effective catalyst in the process of the revelation of the world of *sous-conversation*. It is the movements of this subterranean world indeed that fascinate him, and he takes a luxurious pleasure in observing them, 'C'est une véritable volupté que j'éprouve à les contempler' (p. 39). So much so that he sets up experimental situations in order to study the movements in all their aspects, and watches the results with 'l'excitation du savant qui voit son hypothèse hâtive confirmée par l'expérience' (p. 69). His field of observation is also the field in which he is himself a participant—his immediate family circle, consisting of his uncle, his aunt and their daughter. Together the four of them play a violent game of endlessly changing liaisons; now uncle, aunt and narrator against the daughter, now aunt and narrator against the uncle, and so on. The weapons they use in this internecine warfare are, of course, words, the seemingly harmless phrases of everyday speech that serve both as defence and as attack, as shield or as shot fired against the enemy. ('Ces mots, anodins en apparence—mais seuls les non-initiés pouvaient s'y tromper.' *Le Planétarium*, pp. 50–1.)

The action of the novel is the unceasing repetitive movement of the *sous-conversation* and the minimal 'plot' of the novel—the buying of a country house and the strategy employed in order to avoid embarrassing questions from the tax authorities with regard to the money used for its purchase—is unimportant except as the context of this action, as indeed the members of the family are important only as the terrain for a study of the anonymous world of tropistic undulation, for 'les états psychologiques auxquels ils servent de support.' Into the family circle comes Martereau, the only named 'character' in the book. The fact of the name is significant, for in Martereau the narrator discovers precisely a *character*, an individual contained within a firmly defined outline, 'un seul bloc' (p. 101), apparently master of the turbulent subterranean world into which the others ceaselessly dissolve, able to mould it into a hard and durable personal reality. 'Martereau ne "tique" pas. Ce n'est pas son genre : il n'a pas de ces mouvements rapides, cachés, un peu hon-

teux, aussitôt réprimés . . . Pas une ombre ne le traverse' (p. 133).
The narrator is filled with wonder at the sight of such a spectacle
and he derives a voluptuous contentment from the contemplation of Martereau's family photo album, which seems to epitomize his fixed solidity.[14] Martereau becomes for the narrator an island
of certainty in the sea of fluid anonymity that surrounds him; 'la
certitude, la sécurité se trouvent là' (p. 96). It is the uncle who introduces Martereau into the narrator's world, since he needs him for
the purposes of his attempt at tax evasion : Martereau is to buy the
country house in his name (note the importance even in the surface
action of Martereau as a *name*), thus shielding the uncle. Little by
little, however, Martereau's solidity begins to be called into question. Suspicion encircles him. Does he or does he not mean to acknowledge the uncle's ownership of the house, or will he try to keep
it for himself? He becomes a function of the guerilla warfare in
the family whose members group themselves into factions for or
against him. The firm outline of his character begins to blur until
he too flows into the same sea of anonymity as the others. As the
narrator ruefully remarks at the end of the novel, 'cela frémit en
lui, se soulève, bouillonne, tourbillonne, myriades de particules infimes, mondes qui gravitent, cela déferle de lui sur moi, ce que je
redoutais' (p. 285). The dissolution of Martereau is the essence of
the novel : the arabesque of individuality is discarded before the
very eyes of the reader to make way for, on Nathalie Sarraute's
terms, the more profoundly realistic study of the impersonal life.

The formal problem that Nathalie Sarraute faces in *Martereau*
lies in the structure of the narrative. In *L'Ere du soupçon* she argues
in favour of the first person singular narrative form, since with
such a form 'le lecteur est d'un coup à l'intérieur, à la place même
où l'auteur se trouve, à une profondeur où rien ne subsiste de ces
points de repère commodes à l'aide desquels il construit les personnages. Il est plongé et maintenu jusqu'au bout dans une matière
anonyme comme le sang, dans un magma sans nom, sans contours'
(p. 74). The 'je' functions, as it were, as a midway stage between
the author's voice and that of a Balzacian 'personnage', floating re-
sponsively on the swirling sea of tropistic movement. There is some
falling away from this conception in *Martereau* : the narrator is at
once a seismographic register of the *sous-conversation*, a role akin to

---

[14] Photographs have, of course, a quite opposite effect for Proust's narrator or for
Virginia Woolf's characters for whom they evoke not solidity but, on the contrary, the
passage of time.

that of the novelist herself and that involves him in the same problems of rendition that beset her ('je ne peux que retrouver par bribes et traduire gauchement par des mots ce que ces signes représentent', p. 34), and also situated within the world recorded to some extent as a definite individual, as the nephew caught in a particular action, minimal though it may be. There is considerable awkwardness about the status of the narrator and this awkwardness is felt especially in the context of a central device of Nathalie Sarraute's technique, the repetition of the same conversational scene over and over again in order to capture the movements of the *sous-conversation* underlying the outward responses of *all* the participants. It is not surprising that in *Le Planétarium* and, above all, in *Les Fruits d'or* Nathalie Sarraute modified this narrative form to a considerable extent, moving away especially from a central narrator figure. In *Les Fruits d'or* there are no named characters and no action; the book simply records the cocktail party small-talk that greets the appearance of a novel called 'Les Fruits d'or' and the myriad tropistic movements that eddy beneath it. The 'je' here becomes truly disengaged, passing from the present speaker to present speaker in the conversations, and while it may well be possible to identify one or two groups of speakers with some small degree of continuity, this is of negative importance : what is important is the *sous-conversation* which is here rendered completely within its own right. Anonymity has become the scope of the novel.

This definition of the scope of the novel in terms of the representation of autonomous impersonal experience poses crucial problems that have to be faced in any assessment of Nathalie Sarraute's work in connection with its relationship to the novel form, and certain obvious criticisms can be indicated readily enough from within the context of the novel form's history, a context which Nathalie Sarraute's theory can seem to justify. One can, then, question the value of her achievement. The exclusive focus on the impersonal intentionally works against the individual, denying the possibility of the creation of distinguishing patterns and perspectives. Furthermore, it involves a concomitant denial of time, and hence of narrative. Time is 'une eau dormante au fond de laquelle s'élaborent de lentes et subtiles décompositions' (*L'Ere*, p. 65). The novels are structured to portray an endless series of present moments ('what I am after is moments'[15]), the motionless movements in the stagnant pool of time :

15 *Der Monat*, p. 28.

thus the repetition of conversational scenes from every angle in order to render all the underlying movements, 'the moment whole', to use an expression of Virginia Woolf's.[16] The idea of meaningful development of time, the continuity of narrative, is necessarily missing from her novels, since all moments are the same at the level of *sous-conversation*. The sameness is contained in the language with its sets of recurring images and its sliding pronouns. It is worth calling to mind here a famous passage in a letter from Lawrence to Edward Garnett concerning Lawrence's intentions in the writing of *The Rainbow* :

'You mustn't look in my novel for the old stable *ego* of character. There is another *ego*, according to whose action the individual is unrecognisable, and passes through, as it were, allotropic states which it needs a deeper sense than any we've been used to exercise, to discover are states of the same single radically unchanged element. (Like as diamond and coal are the same pure single element of carbon. The ordinary novel would trace the history of the diamond—but I say, "Diamond, what! This is carbon!" And my diamond might be coal or soot, and my theme is carbon.)'[17]

Though Lawrence is evidently a very different novelist from Nathalie Sarraute (one might note in passing that sexual themes as such are almost totally absent from her novels), there is nothing in this passage taken at its face value with which she would disagree. Lawrence too is opposing 'character' with a deeper impersonal world, 'to whose action the individual is unrecognizable'; his 'carbon' parallels her 'matière étrange, anonyme, comme la lymphe'. Note also the dependence on terms drawn from biology common to both of them—Lawrence's 'allotropic states' matches Nathalie Sarraute's 'tropismes'.[18] Yet it is clear that Lawrence's novels *narrate* an exploration of the relationships that structure human reality between conscious and unconscious, male and female, individual and society, and so on. The intended theme may be carbon, but in the actual novels it is rather this set of *relationships*. It is this narrative significance that Nathalie Sarraute has deliberately abandoned in her

16 *A Writer's Diary*, ed. Leonard Woolf (London, 1953), p. 139.
17 *Collected Letters*, ed. H. T. Moore (London, 1962), I, p. 282.
18 The status of the term 'tropisme' in Nathalie Sarraute's theory can only be strictly metaphorical. The extension of the concept of tropisms from plant physiology to sessile animals even has been strongly contested, and the comparative psychologist F. J. J. Buytendijk has declared the concept to be totally lacking in interest for a consideration of man and the higher animals. (*L'Homme et l'Animal*, p. 88.)

novels and it has to be asked where lies the relevance or indeed the originality of what she has gained thereby with regard to the development of the novel form.

There is a moment in *Daniel Deronda* when the simple Rex Gascoigne, who is infatuated with Gwendolen, asks her how she would feel were he to leave Pennicote :

' "Should you mind about my going away, Gwendolen?"
' "Of course. Every one is of consequence in this dreary country," said Gwendolen, curtly. The perception that poor Rex wanted to be tender made her curl up and harden like a sea-anemone at the touch of a finger.' (I, VII).

The image in that passage, an example of what F. R. Leavis has well termed George Eliot's 'psychological notation',[19] might have come from the pages of a Nathalie Sarraute novel. It renders a tropistic movement, the inner hardening against the other, the automatic response on Gwendolen's part as she registers the perception, derived from the stimulus of his conversational phrase, that Rex wishes to be tender; it renders, in short, the *sous-conversation* below Gwendolen's 'Of course'. But the brief passage does a great deal more than this. It *distinguishes* Rex and Gwendolen. Gwendolen's character, her nature as an individual, emerges in the subtly positioned 'curtly' (note the carefully placed comma), and in the cruelly slighting answer to Rex. At the same time, her 'dreary country' commands a measure of assent, her England is sterile and deadening, she inhabits the same world that Esther Lyons rejects in *Felix Holt* because of its 'moral mediocrity' (Ch. XLIII). 'Dreary' gives the bored, spoilt, inactive life of Gwendolen, but relates also to the whole movement of the novel, to the theme of the need for a firm moral tradition, the need for the regeneration that is Daniel's quest. Similarly, 'poor' is both a fact about Gwendolen's character—this is her characteristic condescending dismissal of those she feels to be weaker than herself—and about Rex, who *is* 'poor' in his pathetic attempt to get Gwendolen to respond to his infatuation. The important point about this passage is its complexity of reference, a complexity that is properly narrative and that demands to be read in this way. George Eliot has the movement of the *sous-conversation* rendered, but in terms of its interaction with the temporal reality of the surface world, with individual and with social realities, the

[19] *The Great Tradition* (London, 1948), p. 102.

sum of these *interactions* being the significant form of the novel. It is this kind of *narrative realism* which, historically, has been a central distinction of the novel, and that is absent from Nathalie Sarraute's work. Has she not taken rather than, as she claims, one step forward, one step backward, since the rendition of *sous-conversation* can be read equally in the work of those novelists she acknowledges as the impetus for her advance; in that of Joyce ('Stephen, shielding the gaping wounds which the words had left in his heart, said very coldly: "I am not thinking of the offence to my mother".'[20]), and in that of Virginia Woolf whose novels indeed offer in many ways close parallels with Nathalie Sarraute's writings. Philip Walsh's insight with regard to the self in *Mrs Dalloway*, for instance, is very Sarrautian, down to the very imagery, and even to the concept of Gerede ('gossiping'):

'For this is the truth about our soul, he thought, or self, who fish-like inhabits deep sea and plies between obscurities, threading her way between the boles of giant weeds over sun-flickered spaces and on and on into gloom, cold, deep, inscrutable; suddenly she shoots to the surface and sports on the wind-wrinkled waves; that is, has a postive need to brush, scrape, kindle herself gossiping.'[21]

Raymond Williams has remarked, in a discussion of what has here been called narrative realism, that in *The Waves* 'all the furniture, and even the physical bodies, have gone out of the window, and we are left with voices and feelings, voices in the air',[22] and this description fits even more accurately *Les Fruits d'or*, where the 'extension' of Virginia Woolf in the narrowing of the focus to the impersonal movements of the present moment leaves the reader totally deprived of narrative contours.

---

[20] *Ulysses* (London, 1960), p. 8.
[21] Nathalie Sarraute has always rejected the parallel between her work and that of Virginia Woolf. 'Je crois que nos sensibilités sont vraiment à l'opposé l'une de l'autre' ('Virginia Woolf, ou la visionnaire du "maintenant" ', p. 3). And it is clear that the theme of time, crucial in Virginia Woolf (and which is finally behind Phillip Walsh's insight), is absent from her work where the focus on the present moment involves her 'characters' in a state of hyper-activity very different from the 'stream of consciousness' of, say Mrs Dalloway or Mrs Ramsey. (The differences are stressed in Ruby Cohn's 'Nathalie Sarraute et Virginia Woolf,' *Revue des Lettres Modernes*, 1964, No. 94–9). Nevertheless a close parallel between the work of the two novelists could be demonstrated, and the essential difference finally might well be found to lie in a reduction of narrative complexity in the novels of the later writer inherent in her minute study of the impersonal. The difference may then pose more relevantly a problem of reading, felt already with regard to Virginia Woolf as Williams' comment suggests.
[22] *The Long Revolution* (London, 1961), p. 279.

Williams helps to define a further element of the problem posed by Nathalie Sarraute's work when he comments on 'the strange case of the Virginia Woolf "charwoman" or "village woman"' whose entrance is accompanied by the 'sudden icy drop in the normally warm sensibility',[23] for something of the spirit of this can also be applied to Nathalie Sarraute. It is not, as Williams suggests of Virginia Woolf, that the world of the novelist herself is socially closed in this way, but that this kind of closure is to be found in the range of her novels. The narrator in *A la recherche du temps perdu* sees the works of any novelist as one total work, communicating one central insight, one special knowledge, and he takes Dostoevsky, as his example (III, p. 378). 'Cette beauté nouvelle et terrible d'une maison, cette beauté nouvelle et mixte d'un visage de femme, voilà ce que Dostoevsky a apporté d'unique au monde . . .' Were one thus to seek to characterize the unique contribution of Nathalie Sarraute's novels, would it not have to be in terms of her portrayal of the rarefied, narcissistic world of a particular section of the post-war Parisian *haute bourgeoisie*, the world and language of Passy and Auteuil? *Le Planétarium*, its characters maniacally coveting socially and aesthetically unimpeachable furniture and dreaming obsessively of possessing the perfect apartment, epitomizes this. The term 'character', it will be noted, has crept back into the picture, for the fact that her work can be seen in this way is to say of it, as Nathalie Sarraute herself has said of Proust's, that 'toutes ces particules se collent les unes aux autres, s'amalgament en tout cohérent . . . où l'oeil exercé du lecteur reconnaît aussitôt un riche homme du monde amoureux d'un femme entretenue, un médecin arrivé . . . une bourgeoise parvenue' (*L'Ere*, p. 84). The portrayal of the totally impersonal coexists with the portrayal of the particular social reality.[24] This points to a fundamental weakness in the theoretical writings, of which the dubious concept of tropism is a symptom. That *Le Planétarium*, in addition to the representation of fluid anonymity, also achieves the study of a specific social milieu is inevitable, for whatever the status of the *sous-conversation*, the very fact of the level of conversation

[23] *The Long Revolution*, p. 283.
[24] This insight is the foundation of the revaluation of her work by Sartre: 'elle croit atteindre par les échanges protoplasmiques qu'elle décrit, des relations interindividuelles et élémentaires, alors qu'elle ne fait que montrer les effets abstraits et infinitésimaux d'un milieu social très défini . . . ni l'individu n'est vraiment replacé dans le milieu qui le conditionne, ni le milieu dans l'individu: nous restons sur le plan indifférencié et illusoire de l'immédiat.' (*Les Ecrivains en personne*, ed. M. Chapsal, Paris, 1960, pp. 213–4.)

immediately involves a surface particularity, no matter how banal this may be kept : banality is not some unchanging absolute, but socially and hence historically defined. It is this lack of historical awareness that is so weakening in Nathalie Sarraute's theory : man is there seen as a fixed and absolute entity, not as relevantly situated in a particular social reality. This is the basis of the curious way in which she speaks in *L'Ere du soupçon* of the traditional psychological novel as having exhausted one aspect of man and of its therefore being necessary for the novel to turn to the study of another aspect, with the implication that one day all the aspects will have been covered and the novel will become redundant, and of the lack of interest shown in the theoretical writings in the relationship between conversation and *sous-conversation*, in the construction of the latter as opposed to its description. In this respect there is one vital area that is all the achievement of the novels, with regard to which, in an age of suspicion, the theoretical writings show a strange innocence— the area of language.

It is here that I want to return to the occasion mentioned at the beginning of the present chapter, the recent publication of Nathalie Sarraute's crucial novel, *Entre la vie et la mort*. This novel, while clearly continuous with those that precede it, manifestly achieves a kind of narrative realism and, simultaneously, in the very evidence of this achievement, suggests the shift of emphasis it entails from the traditional idea of this realism, thus offering, so to speak, a means of recasting the whole approach to Nathalie Sarraute's work, of recasting, that is, the reading of the novels.

Where *Les Fruits d'or* was the record, at the level of conversation, of the career of a finished novel in the world of literary gossip, *Entre la vie et la mort* relates, as it were, the preceding stage, the life and death struggle that is the creation of a novel. This theme gives the novel an immediate narrative coherence. By putting the creation, the writing, of a novel at the centre of her book, Nathalie Sarraute meaningfully narrates the interconnections of conversation and *sous-conversation*, of individual and collective, of conscious and unconscious. The same focus on tropistic movement and the same recurring modes of description are carried through from the earlier works, but they are now distinctly ordered round a central figure, the writer (whom Nathalie Sarraute warns the reader in a note on the cover not to try to build up into a 'hero'), and the eddying movements of the *sous-conversation* beneath the conversational world in which this central figure moves are given significance in their connection to the whole process that is his struggle to create. The opening page of the novel puts before us the writer and the activity of writing ('J'arrache la page . . . Je jette. Je prends une autre feuille.'), and the novel closes in the middle of his dialogue with 'la seule grande forme' to which he is giving life. The stuff of the novel is his creation, both in the sense of the book he is creating and in the sense of the creation of the writer himself, and the two senses are fused in the connections that the novel narrates. The writer's childhood sensations and memories—his first train journey, a teacher, the reactions of his mother and father to the acceptance for publication of his first book—interconnect with scenes of conversation in the style of those in *Les Fruits d'or*—a party given over to literary chit-chat, a visit the writer receives from a group of curious admirers. The changing liaisons in the violent world of conversation, such as were described above in the discussion of *Martereau*, are present here, but generally and essentially from the standpoint of the writer. It is he who is ranged against 'ils' throughout the book, flitting and reflitting rapidly from confrontation ('ils') to conversation ('vous') to alliance ('nous'), always to fall back into the isolation of confrontation ('je suis seul dans le camp ennemi', pp. 44–5), and always sustaining the dialogue with the form that is within him between life and death ('elle'). The coherence of the novel can thus be indicated in these terms in a manner reminiscent of that in which the coherence of *Daniel Deronda* could be indicated, but such terms are precariously inadequate; they stop short of the novel's reality, of which nevertheless the image is centrally present—*the practice of writing*.

That the theme of the novel has increasingly been the writing of the novel is often a subject of critical comment, and that such a theme is sterile—there is talk of the 'narcissism' of the novel—is easily and quickly said. Huxley's Philip Quarles in *Point Counter Point* toys with the idea of the novel within a novel within a novel within . . . , and there is a kind of clever gratuitousness in the display. *Entre la vie et la mort* is not, however, to be understood in this context, for what is here in question is, finally, less a novel about a novel, than the act of writing that is the novel and such a 'theme' (the term is properly impossible) is not sterile, but, on the contrary, of the most crucial importance : it is, in the definition of its focus at the level of the organization of language itself, the idea of the construction of the real, 'le "réel" (image fabuleuse sans laquelle nous ne pourrions pas lire).' The context in which *Entre la vie et la mort* is to be understood is that shift in the development of the novel form represented by the practice of writing. The situation of this shift, as was stressed earlier, is not to be grasped in traditional accounts of a change from Balzacian realism to psychological realism or whatever, but at the level of writing, the practice of which is now the experience of that practice; 'l'écriture (l'expérience radicale du langage) est une question de vie ou de mort'.[25] Philippe Sollers' phrase, *the radical experience of language*, expresses the essence of the realism of the novels representative of this shift, and the image of life and death follows with a lucid necessity. It is an image that is evident in differing forms in Roussel, Proust, Joyce, Robbe-Grillet (*Dans le labyrinthe*), Sollers himself (*Drame, Nombres*), and, of course, in the very title even of *Entre la vie et la mort*; an image of *limits*, the reality of which is structured and grasped precisely at the level of this radical experience of language, whether in, as for Roussel, an experience of writing mining what has been characterized as an 'espace tropologique',[26] in the research of Proust's novel that establishes, across a play of presence/absence, 'grand jour'/'obscurité', 'causerie'/'silence', and so on, that is its foundation, the text as the sole possible mode of presence, milieu of 'la seule vie par conséquent réellement vécue', in the attempt at totality in *Finnegans Wake*, in work on what might be called the syntax of the novel form as in *Dans le labyrinthe*, or in the activity of writing as here in Nathalie Sarraute's novel.

'Hérault, héraut, héros, aire haut, erre haut, R.0' (p. 28): the rhythm of the progression of words themselves. 'Des mots suintent en une fine trainée de gouttelettes tremblantes . . . se déposent sur le papier' (p. 242). But someone speaks, 'Héraut . . . -Mais qu'est-ce que tu marmonnes depuis une heure?' (p. 30); someone writes, 'Je reprends une nouvelle feuille . . . Sur la page blanche les mots, les phrases se forment. Miracle. Comment peut-on?' (p. 8). Words and their articulation are all the activity of the text, the principal movement of which lies in the pronouns. *Entre la vie et la mort* is a play of pronouns; play as a game, their regulated and active exchange; play as the full range of pronouns, je, tu, il, elle, nous, vous, ils, elles; play as a theatrical representation, their staging in the space of the writing that is in itself all the drama.

---

25 Philippe Sollers, *Logiques*, p. 73.
26 Cf. Michel Foucault, *Raymond Roussel* (Paris, 1963), ('Il ne veut plus doubler le réel d'un autre monde, mais dans les redoublements spontanés du langage, *découvrir* un espace insoupçonné et le *recouvrir* de choses encore jamais dites,' p. 25).

In a now famous essay on verbal categories and the Russian verb[27] Roman Jakobson characterizes various ways in which code and message in language can take themselves as objects of reference or 'overlap' one another. To summarize very schematically : 1) A message can send back to a message, as, for example, in reported speech, simultaneously a message within a message and a message about a message ('He told me he would come to tea'). 2) A code can run back in a circle into the code. Jakobson's example is the proper noun, 'la signification générale d'un nom propre ne peut se définir en dehors d'un renvoi au code. Dans le code d'anglais, "Jerry" signifie une personne nommée Jerry.'[28] 3) A message can refer to the code, overlapping with it, as, for example, in explanations of words or phrases, ('The word leveret means a young hare'). 4) Every linguistic code contains a special class of grammatical unities which Jakobson proposes to call *shifters* and the peculiar characteristic of which is that they cannot be defined other than with reference to a message.

It is this last category that is of interest here since it is as a shifter that Jakobson defines the pronoun 'je'. On the one hand, the sign 'je' is, as such, a *conventional* part of a particular code, the French language, and it changes following a change of code, becoming 'I', 'ego', 'ich' and so on, while on the other hand, 'je' cannot be defined other than with reference to the existential situation of its enunciation; code and message overlap :

'. . . . *Je* ne peut être défini qu'en termes de "locution", non en termes d'objets, comme l'est un signe nominal. *Je* signifie "la personne qui énonce la présente instance de discours contenant *je*". Instance unique par définition, et valable seulement dans son unicité.'[29]

The first person singular pronoun, far from belonging to the most elementary and primitive stratum of language, is described by Jakobson as one of the most complex and difficult-to-handle verbal signs, one of the latest and most troublesome acquisitions of the child and one of the first losses in aphasia.[30] Considering the other pro-

[27] *Shifters, Verbal Categories and the Russian Verb*: Russian Language Project, Dept. of Slavic Languages and Literatures (Harvard, 1957), p. 14 et seq. My references are of necessity to the more easily accessible version in Jakobson, *Essais de linguistique générale* (Paris, 1963), pp. 176–96.
[28] p. 177.
[29] Emile Benveniste, *Problèmes de linguistique générale* (Paris, 1966), p. 252.
[30] Cf. Jakobson, *op. cit.*, p. 180, and also 'Two aspects of language and two types of aphasic disturbances,' in *Fundamentals of Language*, pp. 53–82, *Essais de linguistique générale*, pp. 43–67.

nouns, it is evident that 'tu' is similarly a shifter, necessarily linked, as the French linguist Emile Benveniste has stressed in his extension of Jakobson's work, on an existential axis with 'je' (' "tu" est nécessairement désigné par "je" et ne peut être pensé hors d'une situation posée à partir de "je" ')[31] although on this axis 'tu' opposes 'je', 'comme la *personne non-subjective* en face de la personne *subjective* que "je" représente'.[32] The axis je/tu excludes the third person, which is, as it were, 'outside', so much so indeed that Benveniste questions the very idea of 'person' used in its respect. 'Nous' is 'je' plus 'non-je', whether 'toi', 'lui', 'elle', 'vous' or 'eux'; as such, it is a 'false' plural, a fact rendered by the change in sign found in most languages, je/nous, as opposed to a normal pluralization, je/jes : ' "nous" est, non pas une multiplication d'objets identiques, mais une *jonction* entre "je" et le "non-je", quel que soit le contenu de ce "non-je".'[33]

In the light of these distinctions from linguistics it is perhaps easier to read a page of *Entre la vie et la mort* (p. 11) :

' "Moi je n'ai rien à dire. Moi ça ne présente aucun intérêt ... Non, je vous en prie, ne vous moquez pas de moi ..." Tout ébouriffé, échauffé, je me dégage, je cours me réfugier parmi eux.

'Me voici de nouveau l'un d'eux, un chaînon anonyme. Nos yeux sont fixés sur lui. Nos regards appuient sur lui ... "Continuez. Dites-nous. Vous aviez déjà commencé ... Si on ne vous avait pas interrompu ... mais on a perdu assez de temps ... nous vous supplions ... Ne nous faites pas languir ..."

'Il se tait. Sous la pression de nos regards il rentre en lui-même, s'enfonce ...'

All the action here depends on the pronouns and the shifting series of axes moi/vous, je/eux, nous (je+eux)/lui, nous/vous, nous/lui. The problem, the *danger*, lies in the 'je'; 'je' in Nathalie Sarraute is always a risk from which 'nous' is the escape ('je cours me réfugier parmi eux'). 'Vous' (polite singular) is the moment of the slide into the problematic 'je' here under the fire of the phrase 'Dites-nous', and as such, in the face of 'nous', is the passage into solitude and otherness, the exclusion of 'il', 'Il se tait. Sous la pression de nos regards il rentre en lui-même, s'enfonce ...'

This is the play of Nathalie Sarraute's writing : where then is the unity of its action? The answer lies in the 'je', in the construction

[31] Benveniste, *op. cit.*, p. 228.
[32] *Ibid.*, p. 232.
[33] *Ibid.*, p. 233. (This summary is inevitably sketchy and the reader is asked to refer to Benveniste's essay '*Structure des relations de personne dans le verbe*,' pp. 225–36).

of the 'subject'. As a shifter 'je' is a moment at which the code of which it is a part overlaps with the message in which it is articulated, convention overlaps with existential relation. Within the given language, the milieu in which man constitutes himself as subject, 'je' is thus, as it were, the crucial and difficult point in that dialectic of *langue* and *parole*, code and message, defined by Saussure in the *Cours de linguistique générale*; a dialectic described by Merleau-Ponty from the point of view of the individual subject as follows:

'La parole est donc cette opération paradoxale où nous tentons de rejoindre, au moyen de mots dont le sens est donné, et de significations déjà disponibles, une intention qui par principe va au-delà et modifie, fixe elle-même en dernière analyse le sens des mots par lesquels elle se traduit.'[34]

This dialectic has a reality, though the status of this reality is not one of direct equivalence, at the level of the traditional distinction with regard to the novel between discourse and narrative, *discours* and *histoire*. Each term of this distinction has a set of grammatical categories appropriate to itself, notably verbal tenses and pronouns, 'je' and 'tu', for example, for the reasons indicated above in their description as shifters, evidently belonging to the realm of *discours*. In *Entre la vie et la mort*, however, the distinction is subverted: there is neither *discours* nor *histoire*, or, more exactly, the latter overlaps completely with the former in a practice of writing which sets its own image at the centre of the text, 'Je reprends une nouvelle feuille . . . Sur la page blanche les mots, les phrases se forment.' 'Je' sends back always to the present of the text before the reader; as 'je' of the conversation defined in the unique moment of its enunciation, textually held in the play of its limits, 'tu', 'il', 'elle', 'nous', 'vous', 'ils', 'elles', (attempts to construct a hero, comments Nathalie Sarraute in the cover note, will find 'un héros, fait de pièces disparates, qui peut difficilement tenir debout'); as 'je' of the writing the practice of which *is* the narrative, a narrative that is thus never 'finished' but ever present as the moment of its articulation, grasped 'entre la vie et la mort', 'C'est mort. C'est vivant. Et c'est mort' (p. 99). Writing that is the narrative is doubled by the narrative of the writing, the doubling fused in the pronouns:

'Il a pris pied de ce côté. Ici des mots postés partout montent la garde . . . ils s'approchent . . . Qu'y a-t-il? . . . Je la cherche, agité,

[34] *Phénoménologie de la perception* (Paris, 1945), pp. 445–6.

anxieux, partout où il est possible qu'elle se montre, qu'elle me fasse signe . . . de ces petits signes entre nous . . .

'Et tout à coup je les vois . . . Sur eux je me jette, je fouille, là je m'enfonce, tournant pour la suivre . . .

'Quand par moments je m'arrête, quand je cherche à m'orienter . . . où suis-je? où m'a-t-elle amené? . . . il m'arrive de percevoir venant de loin des chuchotements . . . Je reconnais des mots de là-bas . . . leurs mots . . .'

pp. 242, 252–3[35]

The doubling there helps to define the central quality of Nathalie Sarraute's text, its *hesitation*. Such a hesitation is not in the individual words themselves (there is no work on language in the sense that there is in *Finnegans Wake*), but, precisely, in the writing, 'les mots hésitants' (p. 242). The meaning is always direct, 'des mots de là-bas . . . leurs mots', but always, if the expression may be allowed, *hovered*, and it is the overlapping of *discours* and *histoire* that founds this hovering. Everything refers back to the context of its enunciation, to its representation in the space of the writing and is to be read, as the image of writing indicates, in this space, present as the moment of its dramatization in a practice of writing.

It is here that Barthes' definition of realism, to which reference was made in Chapter 1, is important. From the perspective of what Barthes analyses in *Le Degré zéro de l'écriture* as the growth of the consciousness of a 'problématique de l'écriture'[36] (within which the shift in the history of the novel called here the practice of writing may be understood), a contemporary realism is not to be cast in terms of the representation of things but in those of a knowledge of language, of a profound exploration of the 'réalité irréelle du langage'. This is not some call for 'irresponsible verbal pyrotechnics', but, on the contrary, a recognition of the reality of language and of the writer's responsibility with respect to that reality, a responsibility the consciousness of which is the basis of the work of a Mallarmé or a Joyce and which is the situation of the nouveau roman. Barthes' definition is at the level of writing itself, of what has here been characterized as the *practice* of writing, not at the level of a general rhetoric which serves as an *instrument* for *representing* an *exterior* reality. These novels that practise writing propose their own

[35] Cf. Philippe Sollers' *reading* of Marcelin Pleynet's *Comme*; 'pour approcher ce texte nous devons donc entendre par "nous" ou "eux": les mots; par "il": le langage; celui qui l'incarne fictivement; par "elle": la pensée, la page' (*Logiques*, p. 220).

[36] *Le Degré zéro de l'écriture* (Paris, 1953), p. 125.

rhetoric,[37] which is not the servant of expression but the activity of the novel, a grasping of limits within language itself, its theatralization as writing. The activity of writing, practised as such, transcends dialectically the limits it defines in that definition in which it is included, as Nathalie Sarraute's text is a *play* of pronouns in all the senses of that word. Here evidently is the problem of *reading*, for what a text such as *Entre la vie et la mort* demands is not the decipherment and recognition of a code or series of codes, as in Balzac where everything is a code that the writing is to read to the reader ('la table est le plus sûr thermomètre de la fortune dans les ménages parisiens. Une soupe aux herbes et à l'eau de haricots, un morceau de veau aux pommes de terre . . . Enfin tout trahissait une misère sans dignité'[38]), but the grasping of the code of the writing itself (language) as an area of activity (transformation) in the demonstration of its play (limits). There is the radical experience of language, in the reading, 'le lecteur est . . . à la place même où l'auteur se trouve' (*L'Ere*, p. 74), what Valéry meant perhaps when he described the ideal of literature as 'finir par savoir ne plus mettre sur sa page que du "lecteur".'[39]

Lucien Goldmann (writing before the publication of *Entre la vie et la mort*) has stressed Nathalie Sarraute's position at the close of an established tradition rather than at the start of a new one,[40] and an attempt was made in the first part of the present chapter to demonstrate the possibility of such an assessment. Her work can be described as an extension of that of Proust, Joyce and Virginia Woolf, in so far as the work of these novelists itself is described in traditional terms, and the extension which her work represents will then be seen as a discarding of the varied elements, the interconnection of which gave the narrative structure of the novels of her predecessors, in favour of a narrow, and theoretically dubious, focus on an area of impersonal and anonymous experience, from which narrative significance is inevitably absent. Yet such an assessment, in the light of *Entre la vie et la mort*, is deeply problematic; perhaps literally a *misreading* of the novels, a misreading which is a refusal to understand a fundamental change in the novel form, fundamental in a way that is not grasped by the idea of a change to 'psychological realism', and which the continuity of the large

---

[37] Cf. Gérard Genette, 'Enseignement et rhétorique au XXe siècle,' *Annales*, March, 1966, pp. 292–305.
[38] *La Comédie Humaine*, VI, 183.
[39] *Oeuvres* (Pléiade edition), II, 587.
[40] 'Nouveau roman et réalité,' *Pour une sociologie du roman* (Paris, 1964).

majority of novels published has masked. The continuity of these novels, whether 'social', 'psychological', 'documentary', or whatever, their *innocence*, is indeed a direct target of the nouveau roman in the reactivation of its research in the novel form. The practice of writing is the definition of Nathalie Sarraute's age of suspicion of the novel.

3

Alain Robbe-Grillet

Argument

'Je vous accorde que *Dans le labyrinthe* est finalement récupérable.
Si je pensais qu'il ne l'était pas, je ne continuerais pas à écrire; j'aurais
atteint mon but.'

ALAIN ROBBE-GRILLET

The novels of Alain Robbe-Grillet are to be read at the level of their
irretrievability, precisely, that is, at the level at which *reading* is
posed as a problem and explored as such. The activity of the Robbe-
Grillet text offers, to use one of Robbe-Grillet's own formulations, 'le
roman lui-même qui se pense'. This irretrievability profoundly
troubles a certain institutionalized conception of literature (which
judges the novels *unreadable*) and the unease provoked by Robbe-
Grillet's texts might be demonstrated across a whole spectrum of
critical reaction, ranging from outbursts of indignant hysteria to the
more serious attempts to retrieve these texts, of which Bruce Morrissette's *Les Romans de Robbe-Grillet* is perhaps the best example.
What is more crucial (and more surprising) is the attempt at retrieval to be found in the theoretical discourse of Robbe-Grillet himself, notably in the confusion of his *Pour un Nouveau Roman*, which
suggests a certain inability to assume the reality of his own texts
in exactly those terms in which they are most radical.

The theoretical discourse allows, in fact, the schematic postula-
tion of three Robbe-Grillets. The first is that of the famous article
'Nature, humanisme, tragédie'; the Robbe-Grillet whose project is

to realize a cleansing non-metaphorical, thus non-anthropomorphic, thus non-tragic description of the world of things, the *chosiste* Robbe-Grillet, leader of the supposed *école du regard*, to take up the terms coined in the heat of the critical reaction to his novels. *Les Gommes* might be read in these terms as the erasure of human meanings : Wallas, the detective 'hero' seeking desperately for meaning, discovers himself as the author of the crime in the very fact of his quest. The second Robbe-Grillet, the theoretical formulation of whose position is probably best read in the introduction to the *ciné-roman, L'Année dernière à Marienbad*, is the antithesis of the first : the Robbe-Grillet of extreme subjectivism. The reality of the novels in this perspective—a reality which is, as in the first, *representational*—is the screen of the mind of the central perceiving character, locus of the undifferentiated projection of images of perception and imagination, reality and fantasy, and no longer the redemptive neutrality of geometrical description, which indeed now becomes the function of paranoia. Morrissette, legitimately from within this perspective, reads *La Jalousie*, with the help of insights from Stekel, as a representation of the obsessional.

It is in relation to these two antithetical Robbe-Grillets that various critics have felt able to talk of the *phenomenological* foundation of Robbe-Grillet's theories. Such an assimilation is itself, however paradoxical this may seem, very often part of the operation of retrieval of a Robbe-Grillet text, for the idea of phenomenology on which it is based is generally extremely reductive, so that the accepted modes of thinking about literature are in no way challenged by its proposition. It is difficult to understand how such an assimilation could ever have been seriously proposed in connection with the theoretical writings, since such a key stress of phenomenology as the intentionality of consciousness is entirely absent from *Pour un Nouveau Roman*. This absence, in fact, permits the conception of mind basic to the second Robbe-Grillet which is, of course, essentially that of classical materialism, and equally the conception of scientific description basic to the first Robbe-Grillet which is again that of classical materialism and which in its taking-for-grantedness (its projection on the grounds of the natural attitude) neither Husserl, Sartre nor Merleau-Ponty could ever accept in these terms, demanding as it does, interrogation in the moment of the phenomenological reduction. Sartre, be it noted, has himself on occasion radically criticized Robbe-Grillet's theories in this respect. It is the absence of the intentional consciousness moreover that seems to allow an antithetical reversal of progress from the first to the second Robbe-Grillet : he can swing abruptly from the one isolated pole to the other—there is no relation between them.

The absence of consciousness allows concomitantly the absenting of language which poses no problem, for example, in 'Nature, humanisme, tragédie'. Purified of the human thickness of metaphor, language can be returned to an immediate instrumentality. In proportion, however, as language and its reality become a point of reflection in the theoretical writings (as, for instance, in the essay on Raymond Roussel in *Pour un Nouveau Roman*), appears the third Robbe-Grillet with reference to whom the most vital connections can be made with the project of the novel-texts. Here language is conceived in its reality as the milieu of production of meanings, a conception that at the level of the literary text posits the essence of that text not in terms of representation (Robbe-Grillet can even speak now of description as a project of destruction) but in terms of the demonstration of its movement. The demonstration is the conversion into play of forms of discourse. In the course of an ORTF television programme Robbe-Grillet commented : 'il [le romancier] parle, et en même temps il ne reste rien de ce qu'il dit puisque tout se détruit au fur et à mesure, comme si la seule chose intéressante était le mouvement de la parole, et non pas du tout ce qu'elle dit; c'est ce mouvement créateur d'une parole qui ne croit pas à autre chose qu'à ce qu'elle est en train de dire sur le moment.'

The activity of the text hovers or hesitates forms of discourse. It is a question for Robbe-Grillet of *reading* the production of the novel form (of grasping its intelligibility, of *forming* it as a *vraisemblable*), all the effort of which traditionally has lain in the effacement of its own production and the dispersion of its form(s) in the illusion of its direct representation of 'Reality'. Where the realist novel is realized in its repetition of the forms of the general social text, which sustains its continuity and provides the basis for the natural logic of its action, the text of a novel such as *Dans le labyrinthe* or *La Maison de rendez-vous* is founded in a play of variables in the demonstration of which the writing accomplishes a series of fixed variations (fixed in the *space* of the text presented as such), thus producing a kind of equilibrium of hovering significations. As Leibniz spoke of the 'geometral' of an object, so one could perhaps by analogy speak of *Dans le labyrinthe* as a 'scriptural'—the saturation of a series of propositions and relations in the practice of the writing.

It is in an attention to this practice of writing that Robbe-Grillet's novels can be *read* and it is such a reading that this chapter will attempt to prepare. The difficulty of such a preparation must be recognized, and foremost in this difficulty is the confusion manifested in the theoretical writings and outlined briefly above, a confusion attended by a certain glibness on the part of Robbe-Grillet, a facility that collapses the interrogation at the centre of his tentative (his practice) into the repetition of a set of tricks—his career as film-maker is perhaps symptomatic in this respect. It is at this point exactly that his work becomes so easily retrievable (think of the success of *Trans-Europ Express*). What is proposed here is, then, a preparation towards the possibility of reading the novel-texts on their own terms as experience of reading.

I

Elaboration

'Les théoriciens, c'était les autres . . .'
ALAIN ROBBE-GRILLET

'Je ne suis pas un théoricien du roman' : it is with this disavowal that Robbe-Grillet opens the collection of his major theoretical essays, together with some of his shorter review articles, published in 1963 under the title *Pour un Nouveau Roman*. In the brief account of the history of these theoretical writings that follows this somewhat paradoxical disclaimer, Robbe-Grillet insists on their *practical* impetus, on their direct application in a line of *research* in which 'creation' and 'criticism', those traditional antitheses of the thinking that reproaches Robbe-Grillet for not writing like Balzac, are fused in a single purpose—the exploration of 'les problèmes de l'écriture' (*Pour un Nouveau Roman*, p 11). If Robbe-Grillet disclaims any pretension to the constitution of a theory of the novel ('Ces textes ne constituent en rien une théorie du roman . . .', ibid., p. 9), it is clear nonetheless that his insistence on the creative importance of his criticism in the *research* that, rather than a *theory*, characterizes the nouveau roman ('*Le Nouveau Roman n'est pas une théorie, c'est une recherche*', ibid., p. 114) gives the writings collected in *Pour un Nouveau Roman* central prominence. The body of theoretical writings extends, however, far beyond the confines of that volume—embracing the articles omitted there, the introduction to the *ciné-roman*, *L'Année dernière à Marienbad*, the presence of Robbe-Grillet in his film *Trans-Europ Express*, the mass of short journalistic pieces, interviews, communications at conferences, and so on, and finally the novels themselves.

There are at least two sets of difficulties that face anyone attempting to come to terms with the problem of reading Robbe-Grillet. One set of difficulties is relatively minor, and concerns the degree to which Robbe-Grillet, whether because of the 'scandal' of the first novels, the fashionable success of his collaboration with Resnais in *L'Année dernière à Marienbad*, or more recently the preoccupation with erotic imagery marked by *Trans-Europ Express* and his latest film *L'Eden et après*, has always been the focus of intense journalistic interest. In the face of a barrage of interviews and various other forms of attention from press and television, he has often reacted with a kind of playful wit that serves to turn the tables on his interlocutors. This wit, moreover, does not spare more scholarly targets. Witness, for example, the *prière d'insérer* he wrote for the cover of Bruce Morrissette's *Les Romans de Robbe-Grillet* to the effect that the book perhaps revealed more about the person conducting the discussion than about the object under discussion.[1] Witness again a passage in an essay by Maurice Lecuyer, *Réalité et imagination dans Le Grand Meaulnes et Le Voyeur*. Lecuyer apparently sought from Robbe-Grillet himself direct information with regard to the 'influences' on *Le Voyeur*, Robbe-Grillet's second published novel, and was rewarded with the names of Kafka, Sartre, Queneau and, lastly, that of a certain Hallier, author of *Les Aventures d'une jeune fille* of which Lecuyer unsuspectingly records that he has been unable to find any trace.[2] Jean-Edern Hallier's novel of that title was in fact published in 1963, some eight years, that is, *after* the publication of *Le Voyeur*. There are, indeed, connections to be made between the two books in terms of an attempt to describe certain emphases and tendencies of the contemporary French novel, but not in terms of the plotting of influences for their own sake; a point that Robbe-Grillet neatly makes by inverting the concept of influence that Lecuyer proposes. It is clear that Robbe-Grillet's statements, and especially those made in interviews, need to be considered carefully and related to their level of operation that is

[1] Bruce Morrissette, *Les Romans de Robbe-Grillet* (Paris, 1963).
[2] Maurice Lecuyer, *Réalité et imagination dans Le Grand Meaulnes et Le Voyeur* (Rice University Studies, Vol. 51, No. 2, Spring 1965), p. 51.

sometimes fundamentally strategic rather than directly theoretical.

The second and major set of difficulties poses a much more considerable problem, which is at the heart of the problem of *reading* Robbe-Grillet. 'Jamais, en somme, la confusion ne semble avoir été plus forte', concluded Philippe Sollers at the close of his review of *Pour un Nouveau Roman*,[3] and as we read the articles collected there and Robbe-Grillet's various other statements of intention, confusion can indeed seem everywhere. To some extent this confusion is a chronological difficulty, for, although there are no clear-cut divisions, certain emphases are radically modified in the course of the development of the theoretical writings and certain successive central lines of interest emerge clearly in this perspective. In this development, furthermore, Robbe-Grillet has undoubtedly been influenced by some of his critics, an influence that he has not always fully understood in its theoretical implications in his own subsequent critical formulations. The articles devoted by Roland Barthes to Robbe-Grillet's first two published novels furnish the most striking example of such an influence, but there are other less evident examples, the essays of Jean Ricardou, for instance. The confusion is not, however, to be explained completely in terms of the progressive development of Robbe-Grillet's thinking. The theoretical emphases shift radically, but they are all to be found together in Robbe-Grillet's writings from the very start and the confusion has to be recognized as endemic to a great many of Robbe-Grillet's theoretical statements.

To note this confusion is now not enough; it is necessary to understand it, to follow through the development of the theoretical writings even in their difficulties and confusions, together with the novels (as 'un double jeu d'accords et d'oppositions', *Pour un Nouveau Roman*, p. 11), in the exploration of literature, of writing, that Robbe-Grillet attempts in his work. It may be noted in this connection that despite such disavowals of theoretical purpose as that with which he opens *Pour un Nouveau Roman*, Robbe-Grillet himself has put considerable value on that aspect of his work represented by that volume. He has even tended in the past at times to judge not the critical work against the novels, but vice versa, the novels against the critical work. Thus in 1958 he noted 'un parallélisme assez lâche' (ibid., p. 46) between the two faces of his work and went on

[3] *Tel Quel* No. 18, Summer 1964, p. 94.

to stress that *if his novels had failed* to follow the directions indicated by the theoretical formulations this was not to be taken as implying some error in the latter; and in a debate that same year he spoke of his novels as lagging behind his intentions, rather than postulating the gap as created by the inadequacy of the intentions.[4]

The importance attached to the criticism both by Robbe-Grillet and by his critics and explicators is the context of the continual distortion of the reality of the novels and the radical experience of reading they propose. The distortion has been brought about by the explanation of the novels outside the terms of that experience, their *retrieval*. The problem of retrievability was raised by Robbe-Grillet in the course of an interview in 1959 with regard to the retrievability of *Dans le labyrinthe* : 'Je vous accorde que *Dans le labyrinthe* est finalement récupérable. Si je pensais qu'il ne l'était pas, je ne continuerais pas à écrire; j'aurais atteint mon but.'[5] What has to be seen is that that retrievability has been operated above all by and thanks to Robbe-Grillet himself, the context of the operation being the confusion of the theoretical writings which has blocked access to the experience of the novels and provided the terms of various explanations. Robbe-Grillet, that is, has not always been contemporary with himself. What follows is, therefore, a long examination of Robbe-Grillet's writings in order to re-find that experience, to re-situate the novels. The course of this examination may well cause surprise, as for instance in its questioning of the assimilation of Robbe-Grillet's theories within the perspective of phenomenology and its use of just that perspective to criticize those theories. This procedure is not intended to deny the possibility of any relation between Robbe-Grillet's work and existential phenomenology (though it will become clear that this is not here regarded as ultimately the most pertinent way of understanding Robbe-Grillet's writing), but rather as a critique of certain presuppositions in Robbe-Grillet's theoretical work and the unquestioning general acceptance of these presuppositions as 'phenomenological', an acceptance which guarantees the phenomenological explanation of the novels. The aim will be to de-centre this phenomenological perspective. What is attempted here then, may it be stressed again, is a reading of the theoretical writings in order to open the way for the real experience of reading proposed by the novels.

4 'Révolution dans le roman?', *Le Figaro Littéraire*, 29 March 1958, p. 9 ('mes livres sont *en retard* sur mes intentions').
5 Interview, *L'Express*, 8 October 1959, p. 33.

II

'After so many things that I could no longer enumerate, the nails, the frog, the sparrow, the bit of wood, the pole, the nib, the lemon peel, the cardboard box, etc., the chimney, the cork, the arrow on the ceiling, the gutter, the hand, the hands, etc., etc., the lump of earth, the bedsprings, the ash-tray, bits of wire, toothpicks, pebbles, the chicken, warts, gulfs, islands, needles, etc., etc., ad nauseam, here was this teapot popping up like a jack-in-the-box without rhyme or reason, extra, gratis, and for nothing, like a fifth wheel on a coach, an ornament of chaos. I had had enough.'

WITOLD GOMBROWICZ, *Kosmos*

Robbe-Grillet dates his début as a 'theoretician' of the novel from 1955/1956[6] when, stimulated by his impatience with the reception of his first two published novels *Les Gommes* and *Le Voyeur* (1953 and 1955), he accepted the invitation of *L'Express*, at that time a daily newspaper, to write a series of brief articles under the general title of 'Littérature d'aujourd'hui'.[7] He had, in fact, done some brief book reviews in the previous two years for *Critique* and *La Nouvelle Nouvelle Revue Française*,[8] but these are hardly ever more than short descriptions of the works under review, and it is, as Robbe-Grillet himself comments, only with the *Express* articles and, above all, with the two essays 'Une voie pour le roman futur' (1956[9]) and 'Nature, humanisme, tragédie' (1958[10]) that he sounds a distinct, independent theoretical note.

[6] Cf. *Pour un Nouveau Roman*, p. 8.
[7] 'Il écrit comme Stendhal . . .', 25/10/1955, p. 8; 'Pourquoi la mort du roman?', 8/11/55, p. 8; 'L'écrivain lui aussi doit être intelligent', 21/11/55, p. 10; 'Les français lisent trop', 6/12/55, p. 11; 'Littérature engagée, littérature réactionnaire', 20/12/55, p. 11; 'Réalisme et révolution', 3/1/56, p. 15; 'Pour un réalisme de la présence', 17/1/56, p. 11; 'Kafka discrédité par ses descendants', 31/1/56, p. 11; 'Le réalisme socialiste est bourgeois', 21/2/56, p. 11.
[8] *Critique* 1953: 'Samuel Beckett, auteur dramatique', No. 69, pp. 108–14; 'Eugène Ionesco *Théâtre*', No. 73, pp. 564–5; 'Joë Bosquet, le rêveur', No. 77, pp. 819–29; 1954: 'Robert Pinget: *Mahu ou le matériau, Le renard et la boussole*', No. 80, pp. 82–5. *Nouvelle Nouvelle Revue Française* 1953: reviews of James Hanley, *Le tourbillon*, April, pp. 728–9; I. Silone, *Une poignée de mûres*, May, pp. 917–8; Pierre Gascar, *Les Bêtes*, July, pp. 141–4; Jean-Luc Déjean, *Les voleurs de pauvres*, December, pp. 1103–4; 1954: reviews of Pierre Gascar, *Le temps des morts*, January, pp. 137–8; Jean Duvignaud, *Le piège*, April, pp. 716–8; Jacques Brenner, *Daniel ou la double rupture*, Henry Green, *Amour*, May, pp. 902–4, 907–9; Italo Svevo, *La conscience de Zéno*, July, pp. 138–41; Jean Cayrol, *L'espace d'une nuit*, July-August, pp. 317–9; M. de M'Uzan, *Les chiens des rois*, October, pp. 724–5.
[9] *La Nouvelle Nouvelle Revue Française*, July 1956, pp. 77–84.
[10] Ibid., October 1958, pp. 580–605.

The theory (and in 'Nature, humanisme, tragédie' it most ex- ✱
plicitly *is* a theory) in these early writings, which is present to a lesser
extent in the later ones, has a point of departure which is, in intention at least, a philosophical one : the definition of a new humanism
resting on a necessary awareness, with which man must learn to
come to terms, of that (limited) part of existence that can properly
be called human. Literature enters the argument at its conclusion
as a mode of breaking down traditional false assumptions and
demonstrating this new awareness. The awareness is based on the
recognition that the world quite simply *is* : it does not *mean* anything, it is just *there*, and any attempt to attach a meaning to it
in human terms, to give some 'profondeur' to its solid existence, is
dangerously misguided. 'Or le monde n'est ni signifiant ni absurde.
Il *est* tout simplement' (*Pour un Nouveau Roman*, p. 18). The world
is in no way to be regarded as existing *for* man; it has no complicity with him whatever. 'L'homme regarde le monde, et le monde
ne lui rend pas son regard' (ibid., p. 53). Things are things, and are
not to be contaminated by attempts to appropriate them into a
world of human significance. 'Les choses sont les choses et l'homme
n'est que l'homme' (ibid., p. 47). The only 'quality' of things is the
fact of their presence; 'les choses *sont là*. Leur surface est nette et
lisse, intacte, sans éclat louche ni transparence' (ibid., p. 18). Traditional humanism, however, has been based on the contrary assertion
of man's supremacy, on an anthropomorphism that has tried to
relate the world inextricably and *essentially* to man. In the process
of this appropriation things have been sullied and dirtied and the
être-là of the world is lost behind a veil of false assumptions and
abusive metaphors. Reviewing Jean Cayrol's *L'Espace d'une nuit*,
Robbe-Grillet attacks 'des constructions symbolistes qui nient la
réelle présence des êtres et des choses.'[11] The point about metaphor
is crucial for Robbe-Grillet and it brings literature into the forefront
of the discussion. One key way in which he sees this false anthropomorphism establishing itself is, in fact, through language and, in
particular, through the use of metaphor. Metaphor is for Robbe-
Grillet to be seen as a means of creating a deceitful solidarity by
positing analogies between the human and the non-human world
which it unites in its process. 'La métaphore, en effet, n'est jamais
une figure innocente' (*Pour un Nouveau Roman*, p. 48), its guilt
lying in the attempt it implies to establish 'un rapport constant

[11] *La Nouvelle Nouvelle Revue Française*, July-August 1954, p. 319.

entre l'univers et l'être qui l'habite' (ibid., p. 49).[12] To talk of a village 'squatting' low in a valley is a subtle way of humanizing the world, of bringing it under human dominion by throwing over it a network of human meanings, and is thus, concludes Robbe-Grillet, a vicious abuse of language. There is a need for a determined and fundamental *cleansing* of literary language, 'rien ne doit-il être négligé dans l'entreprise de nettoyage' (ibid., p. 52).

This attack on metaphor amounts, in the terms in which it is made, to an attack on the major emphasis of literary language during the last two hundred years: on the foundations of Romanticism (Wordsworth speaks of 'the spirituality with which I have endeavoured to invest the material universe, and the moral relation under which I have wished to exhibit its most ordinary appearances',[13] Hegel of the restlessness of the Romantic Spirit, 'Der Geist arbeitet sich nur so lange in den Gegenständen herum, so lange noch ein Geheimes, Nichtoffenbares darin ist'[14]), on the Symbolist transmutation of material reality (Ezra Pound speaks of Yeats 'dawdling around Notre-Dame', pausing 'to admire the symbol with Notre-Dame standing inside it',[15] and the latter in a poem like 'Coole Park and Ballylee' conducts a veritable hunt for symbols in the natural world; 'Another emblem there!', he cries at one point in the poem on sighting some swans[16]), on Proust's insistence on the *essen-*

---

[12] The anthropomorphic foundation of metaphor was noted by Vico in the *Scienza Nuova* ('la maggior parte dell'espressioni d'intorno a cose inanimate sono fatte con trasporti del corpo umano e delle sue parti e degli umani sensi e dell'umane passioni', II. III. 2: G. Vico, *Opere*, Verona, 1957, p. 172) and is regarded by modern semantics as a major category of metaphorical expression (cf. Stephen Ullmann, *Semantics: An Introduction to the Science of Meaning*, Oxford, 1962, p. 215). Roland Barthes has, in fact, described a use of metaphor as a mode of *dissociation* in Chateaubriand's *La Vie de Rancé*: 'On croit communément que l'effort littéraire consiste à rechercher des affinités, des correspondances, des similitudes et que la fonction de l'écrivain est d'*unir* la nature et l'homme en un seul monde (c'est ce que l'on pourrait appeler sa fonction synesthésique). Cependant la métaphore, figure fondamentale de la littérature, peut être aussi comprise comme un puissant instrument de disjonction; notamment chez Chateaubriand où elle abonde, elle nous représente la contiguïté mais aussi l'incommunication de deux mondes, de deux langues flottantes, à la fois solidaires et séparées, comme si l'une n'était jamais que la nostalgie de l'autre . . . Chez Chateaubriand, la métaphore ne rapproche nullement des objets, elle sépare des mondes . . . est toujours nostalgique; tout en paraissant multiplier les échos, elle laisse l'homme comme *mat* dans la nature . . .' ('La voyageuse de nuit'; Chateaubriand, *La Vie de Rancé*, Paris, 1965, 'Collection Le monde en 10/18', pp. 16–17). Even such a disjunctive use of metaphor would remain guilty in Robbe-Grillet's eyes in so far as it is an instrument of nostalgia and not of the calm statement of separation. (Cf. his criticism of Camus discussed below.)

[13] *Wordsworth: Poetry and Prose*, ed. W. M. Merchant (London, 1955), pp. 873–4.

[14] *Sämtliche Werke*, ed. H. Glockner, Vol. 13 (Stuttgart, 1928), p. 231.

[15] Canto 83, *The Cantos of Ezra Pound* (London, 1954), p. 563.

[16] *Collected Poems* (London, 1950), p. 275.

tial necessity of the relations defined in the process of metaphor ('la vérité ne commencera qu'au moment où l'écrivain prendra deux objets différents, posera leur rapport . . . et les enfermera dans les anneaux nécessaires d'un beau style'[17]), on André Breton's equally strong, though differently founded, insistence on the necessity of metaphor and his quest for the significant (Breton uses photographs in *Nadja* in order to avoid the very description Robbe-Grillet will propose as the basic task of literature : 'L'abondante illustration photographique a pour objet d'éliminer toute description—celle-ci frappée d'inanité dans le *Manifeste du Surréalisme*'[18]), on, in fact, more or less the whole range of post-Romantic literary activity. The particular cases that Robbe-Grillet actually takes up for criticism in his discussion of the sullying by metaphor of the pure existence of things in the world are both more expected and more subtle than the examples just given to indicate the extent of his attack : more expected since the cases he takes up are those of novelists, and so are related directly to his immediate practical interests, more subtle since, instead of the more obvious examples from the Romantics' uses of metaphor, the examples on which he chooses to comment are Balzac and the Realist novel, Camus and Sartre.

If the world of objects seems to be firmly *there* in the *Comédie Humaine*, this is, finally, an illusion, Robbe-Grillet insists, since it is there only in so far as it 'doubles' or reflects the characters : it is simply 'le double de l'homme lui-même'.[19] Things are important in the Balzacian novel only in that they *signify*; they themselves are lost under the weight of meaning they are made to carry—'Un simple bouton de gilet peut signifier richesse, puissance, satisfaction'.[20] Georges Poulet has commented that 'chez Balzac, le monde des apparences a une importance à la fois extraordinaire et nulle. Il est une "traduction matérielle de la pensée", c'est-à-dire un langage. Et comme tout langage, il a pour office de disparaître en faisant apparaître ce qu'il exprime.'[21] This is put more directly in the

---

[17] *A la recherche du temps perdu*, III, p. 889.
[18] *Nadja* (Paris, 1963), p. 6. (Even the photographs are not intended as cleansing presentations of objects. Mikel Dufrenne notes: 'Avec *Nadja*, Breton fait la chasse aux signes, il photographie un gant ou une terrasse de café comme les Romains eussent photographié un vol de corbeaux ou les entrailles d'une victime.' 'Mal du siècle?' *Revue d'Esthétique*, Vol. 17, Fascs. III and IV, August-December 1964, p. 205).
[19] Alain Robbe-Grillet, 'Conférence', *Revue de l'Institut de Sociologie de Bruxelles*, 1962/1963, p. 444.
[20] Alain Robbe-Grillet, 'Révolution dans le roman?', p. 7.
[21] Georges Poulet, *Etudes sur le temps humain II: La distance intérieure*, (Paris, 1952), p. 175.

characterization of the Balzacian narrator at the opening of the short *Facino Carne*, who by dint of his careful schooling in the streets of Paris can seize directly the meaning underlying the things that surround him : 'Chez moi l'observation était déjà devenue intuitive . . . *elle saisissait si bien les détails extérieurs qu'elle allait sur le champ au-delà*'.[22] The wealth of detail that constitutes a description in a Balzac text has for its final purpose a self-effacement before the social meaning that it is its function to signify. The objects in Madame Marneffe's bedroom in *La Cousine Bette* are so many *signs* that the novelist will read to the reader : 'un petit Dunkerque assez bien garni' and 'des jardinières en porcelaine chinoise luxueusement montées' signify the presence of a lover of a certain standing and a certain kind of social existence.[23] What is understood historically as Realism in literature is anything but realism in the sense, in which Robbe-Grillet intends the term, of the presence of things in and for themselves without human significance. Nor does the Naturalism of, say, Zola, to whom Robbe-Grillet has sometimes been (erroneously) related, offer any improvement in this connection since from Robbe-Grillet's point of view it proposes exactly the same kind of inauthentic (non-)presence of objects. Zola's definition of description demonstrates this clearly enough : 'Je définirai donc la description : Un état du monde qui détermine et complète l'homme.'[24] Things and characters are in a relation of correspondence, the former being no more than an extension of the latter, their 'double', exactly the *relation* Robbe-Grillet wishes to break—'l'homme est complété par ses vêtements, par sa maison, par sa ville, et sa province'.[25]

The criticism made in *Pour un Nouveau Roman* in this context of

---

[22] *La Comédie Humaine*, VI, p. 66 (my italics).

[23] Ibid., p. 182. The characteristic of the Balzacian description is not so much, as is commonly believed, exaggeration, but rather an *overabundance of sense*. Martin Turnell cites the famous description of the Pension Vauquer in *Le Père Goriot* and comments with regard to the following sentence, 'Pour expliquer combien ce mobilier est vieux, crevassé, pourri, tremblant, rongé, manchot, borgne, invalide, expirant' (ibid, II, pp. 851–2) : 'It is clearly an example of Balzac's attempt "to go one better".' (*The Novel in France*, London, 1950 p. 225.) In fact the fault of the sentence (if fault there is) is rather an excess of sense: the chair must signify the whole dilapidation of poverty that in the central contrast of the novel is to be juxtaposed, in the journey Rastignac daily makes from the one to the other, with the splendour of the Faubourg Saint-Honoré. In a kind of extended transfer the chair receives all the features of Goriot and his miserable existence even, finally and proleptically, his death ('expirant'). The balance between object and sign in Balzac's novels is precariously held.

[24] Emile Zola, *Le Roman expérimental* (Paris, 1928) p. 299.

[25] Ibid., p. 228.

Camus and Sartre is more cautious than that levelled against the Balzacian novel, yet is effectively, on Robbe-Grillet's terms, equally damaging. Camus's *L'Etranger* is in very many ways a clear point of departure both for the nouveau roman in general and for Robbe-Grillet in particular, and above all in its forging of what Barthes describes as 'un degré zéro de l'écriture'.[26] Sartre's description of Camus' style in the course of an early review of *L'Étranger* reads indeed precisely as a description of the use of language demanded by Robbe-Grillet :

'Un naturaliste du XIXe siècle eût écrit : "Un pont enjambait la rivière". M. Camus se refuse à cet anthropomorphisme. Il dira : "Au-dessus de la rivière il y avait un pont". Ainsi la chose nous livre-t-elle tout de suite sa passivité. Elle *est là*, simplement, indifférenciée.'[27]

Sartre also notes, however, that at certain points in his work Camus is false to this principle and is led to 'faire de la poésie'.[28] It is these points that Robbe-Grillett takes up in his criticism of *L'Etranger*. If for Camus's absurd man 'il ne s'agit plus d'expliquer et de résoudre, mais d'éprouver et de décrire' on the basis of an 'indifférence clairvoyante',[29] and if the first fifty or so pages of *L'Etranger* do seem to be written in a language cleansed of deceitful metaphor, yet finally the vision of the book can be seen to depend on the assertion of analogies between human and non-human and metaphor reappears as a dominant factor in the writing. In the key scene in which Meursault kills the Arab on the beach, the sun is an active presence, active in what is felt as its relentless implacability. The sun is *blamed* for the murder, and Robbe-Grillet comes to the conclusion that :

'L'absurde est donc bien une forme d'humanisme tragique. Ce n'est pas un constat de séparation entre l'homme et les choses. C'est une querelle d'amour, qui mène au crime passionnel. Le monde est accusé de complicité d'assassinat.'
Pour un Nouveau Roman, p. 58

The conception of the novel outlined by Camus in *L'Homme ré-volté* could only confirm Robbe-Grillet's judgement, for, instead of

26 Roland Barthes, *Le Degré zéro de l'écriture*, p. 109.
27 J.–P. Sartre, *Situations I* (Paris, 1947), p. 119.
28 Ibid., p. 120.
29 Albert Camus, *Essais* (Pléiade edition), p. 174.

there being defined as the means of a simple recognition of separation, the novel is seen exactly in terms of the quarrel between man and the world to which Robbe-Grillet objects in *L'Etranger*, as a simultaneous posing of and challenge to the world; 'Le roman naît en même temps que l'esprit de révolte et il traduit, sur le plan esthétique, la même ambition'.[30] In similar fashion Robbe-Grillet also locates a dubious emergence of metaphor in Sartre's *La Nausée*, commenting that '*l'existence* s'y caractérise par la présence de distances intérieures . . . la *nausée* est un penchant viscéral malheureux que l'homme ressent pour ces distances. Le "sourire complice des choses" s'achève en un rictus : "Tous les objets qui m'entouraient étaient faits de la même matière que moi, d'une espèce de souffrance moche" ' (*Pour un Nouveau Roman*, p. 61).[31]

In this context Kafka (to whom he constantly refers as a source for an authentic contemporary writing) is especially significant for Robbe-Grillet as a point of comparison, even in the very way in which his work has been subjected to an operation of retrieval. Kafka, '*avant tout* un écrivain réaliste',[32] in whose work things everywhere assert their irrefragable presence, has been traduced by the zeal of his (so-called) admirers who in the face of this obstinate presentation of the world of things have responded by attempting to reappropriate his work into their world of myth, symbol and comfortable meaningfulness. In Kafka, a ladder is a ladder, but for his admirers this *être-là* of the thing itself is unacceptable and deeply disquieting : the ladder must thus be made to lead somewhere, to Heaven, for example, or to wherever else is required. They seek significance behind the things that proliferate in the pages of Kafka's novels, but, insists Robbe-Grillet, there is no 'behind', no 'depth' of hidden meaning : 'Le monde visible est bien chez lui le monde

[30] Ibid., p. 662.
[31] After the criticism of Sartre in 'Nature, humanisme, tragédie', Robbe-Grillet also goes on to criticize the work of the poet Francis Ponge in these same terms. Ponge, a volume of whose poems is entitled *Le Parti pris des choses*, does indeed speak of presenting things as 'les muettes instances qu'elles font pour qu'on les parle, à leur valeur, et pour elles-mêmes—en dehors de leur valeur habituelle de signification,—sans choix, et pourtant avec mesure, mais quelle mesure: la leur propre' (cit. Sartre, *Situations I*, p. 260), but there is an attendant recognition of the all-pervading presence of man: 'Il y a toujours *du* rapport à l'homme . . . on ne peut aucunement sortir de l'homme' (cit. Sartre, ibid. p. 256). The aim of speaking the real presence of things is effected in Ponge by what Robbe-Grillet sees as the erection of a network of mirroring metaphors that once more found a humanization of the world of things: 'tranquilles, domestiquées, elles regardent l'homme avec son propre regard' (*Pour un Nouveau Roman*, p. 62).
[32] 'Kafka discrédité par ses descendants'.

réel'.[33] *Les Gommes*, Robbe-Grillet's first published novel, might be seen as a recovery of the irretrievability of Kafka's work. The reference is, in fact, explicit: Wallas, the special-agent 'hero' of *Les Gommes*, takes a room at the opening of the book in an 'obscur bistro de la rue des Arpenteurs' (p. 5), and the memory of Kafka's *Das Schloss* and the arrival in the village of K, the land-surveyor, in its opening pages, is immediately present in the reference given in the name of the street, 'la rue des *Arpenteurs*'.[34] Sent to solve a crime, to *survey* the scene and make meanings, Wallas finds meaning everywhere and nowhere; nowhere but in himself as man, the final criminal, always everywhere eagerly seeking signs and symbols (as Wallas seeks the rubbers that derisively refuse to appear, as the confident reader catches at the references to the Oedipus myth that run through the book and which in their obviousness and irrelevance are similarly derisively mocking), constantly attempting to rape objects (Wallas' wandering progress through the town in the course of the day is an itinerary of such rape) that present, finally, no more than a solid surface for the perusal of the eye. All expectations of meaning are to be erased.

Robbe-Grillet's concern then is for the establishment of a literature that will be faithful to the one certain fact about the world— 'le simple fait qu'il est là' (*Pour un Nouveau Roman*, p. 38):

'Puisque c'est avant tout dans sa présence que réside sa réalité, il s'agit donc, maintenant, de bâtir une littérature qui en rende compte.'
Ibid, pp. 21–2

Instead of the continued creation of a universe of meanings, whether psychological, social, functional or whatever, it is necessary to re-establish the world in the solid immediacy of its presence. 'Dans les constructions romanesques futures, gestes et objets seront *là* avant d'être *quelque chose*' (ibid., p. 20). The need, in the face of the heritage of Balzac and the final inadequacy of Camus and Sartre, is for a fundamental *cleansing* of man's vision, which at the level of the activity of literature involves, as has been suggested already, the necessity of redeeming language from metaphor and all the in-authentic solidarity it implies: 'C'est donc tout le langage littéraire

[33] Ibid.
[34] 'ich der Landvermesser bin', announces K on his arrival at the village inn at the opening of *Das Schloss*, which in the standard French translation of Alexandre Vialatte becomes, of course, 'je suis l'arpenteur'.

qui devrait changer' (ibid., p. 23). Here lies the central function of *description* in Robbe-Grillet's theory :

'Décrire les choses, en effet, c'est délibérément se placer à l'extérieur, en face de celles-ci. Il ne s'agit plus de se les approprier ni de rien reporter sur elles.'
Ibid., p. 63

Formal geometrical description is the means by which objects are to be placed before the reader in their pristine state, unsullied by the distortion of any endeavour to draw them into complicity with the world of human meanings. The essence of description is thus, for Robbe-Grillet, *limitation*. Description is the careful definition of the absence of any Balzacian 'au-delà' :

'Enregistrer la distance entre l'objet et moi, et les distances propres de l'objet (ses distances *extérieures*, c'est-à-dire ses mesures), et les distances des objets entre eux, et insister encore sur le fait que ce sont *seulement des distances* (et non pas des déchirements), cela revient à établir que les choses sont là et qu'elles ne sont rien d'autre que des choses ... Il y a désormais refus de *toute* complicité.'
Ibid., p. 65

By training an agronomic engineer, Robbe-Grillet never ceases in his interviews to emphasize his scientific background,[35] and in particular his grounding in the method of scientific observation : 'l'observation scientifique consiste à décrire *sans interpréter, à ne jamais donner une signification* aux choses'.[36] Strict scientific observation and description of the world of surface is, therefore, all important in Robbe-Grillet's cleansing project, and vision is thus its key mode for the rendition of, to borrow a phrase from Wallace Stevens, 'the cleanliness of a heaven/That has expelled us and our images'.[37] It is here, precisely in their appeal to man's vision, that the importance for the contemporary novel of photography and the cinema is crucial. The photographic or cinematographic image forces man to see things in and for themselves; 'Le récit filmé nous tire hors de notre confort intérieur vers ce monde offert' (*Pour un Nouveau Roman*, p. 19) :

'Dans le roman initial, les objets et gestes qui servaient de support à l'intrigue disparaissaient complètement pour laisser la place à leur

---

[35] 'Je suis de formation purement scientifique'; 'Alain Robbe-Grillet—géomètre du temps', (interview) *Arts*, 20–26 March 1953, p. 5.

[36] (Interview) *Revue de Paris*, January 1959, p. 132.

[37] 'Notes towards a Supreme Fiction,' *Collected Poems* (London, 1955), p. 381.

seule signification : la chaise inoccupée n'était plus qu'une absence ou une attente, la main qui se pose sur l'épaule n'était plus que marque de sympathie, les barreaux de la fenêtre n'étaient que l'impossibilité de sortir . . . Et voici que maintenant on *voit* la chaise, le mouvement de la main, la forme des barreaux. Leur signification demeure flagrante, mais au lieu d'accaparer notre attention, elle est comme donnée en plus; en trop, même, car . . . ce qui apparaît comme essentiel et irréductible à de vagues notions mentales, ce sont les gestes eux-mêmes, les objets, les déplacements et les contours, auxquels l'image a restitué d'un seul coup (sans le vouloir) leur *réalité*.'
Ibid., p. 19

The image reveals things in an inhabitual presence : now they are *there*. The lesson for the novelist is obvious for Robbe-Grillet: optical description ('la description optique', ibid., p. 65) is the function of the cleansing power of vision ('le pouvoir laveur du regard', ibid., p. 66), the way to the deanthropomorphization of the world and the restitution of its chaste presence. In passing, Robbe-Grillet recognizes the final impossibility of 'l'objectivité au sens courant du terme—impersonnalité totale du regard' (ibid., p. 18), but the central character of the works of the projected new realism is described as follows :

'l'oeil de cet homme se pose sur les choses avec une insistance sans mollesse : il les voit, mais il refuse de se les approprier, il refuse d'entretenir avec elles aucune entente louche, aucune connivence, il ne leur demande rien; il n'éprouve à leur égard ni accord ni dissentiment d'aucune sorte. Il peut, d'aventure, en faire le support de ses passions, comme de son regard. Mais son regard se contente d'en prendre les mesures; et sa passion, de même, se pose à leur surface.'
Ibid., p. 48

Les Gommes is a refusal of psychology—'un roman descriptif et scientifique'.[38]
The refusal of the anthropomorphic appropriation of the world is presented in terms of a refusal of its *tragedization*. Robbe-Grillet is acknowledgedly indebted to Roland Barthes here, and at the head of his essay 'Nature, humanisme, tragédie', he places the following quotation from Barthes :

'La tragédie n'est qu'un moyen de recueillir le malheur humain, de le subsumer, donc de le justifier sous la forme d'une nécessité, d'une sagesse ou d'une purification : refuser cette récupération et rechercher

[38] 'Alain Robbe-Grillet—géomètre du temps'.

les moyens techniques de ne pas y succomber traîtreusement (rien n'est plus insidieux que la tragédie) est aujourd'hui une entreprise nécessaire.' Ibid., p. 45[39]

As D. H. Lawrence, thinking of Arnold Bennett's 'resignation', put it, 'Tragedy really ought to be a great kick at misery'.[40] Barthes is objecting to tragedy as a mode of *resolution through resignation* of problems of suffering, objecting to the *naturalization* or *essentialization* of the contradictions of particular historico-social situations, a process which is seen by Barthes as basic to bourgeois culture[41] and to which the refusal of tragedy in Brecht (whose theatre Barthes through his work in the review *Théâtre populaire* was instrumental in introducing in France) is a direct response. For Robbe-Grillet, traditional humanism operates just this kind of false essentialist tragedization of the world, positing essential relationships between man and the world in the inevitable contradictions resulting from which is created a tragic reaction—nausea, the absurd, or whatever —which in its absolution (in both senses) of the contradictions inherited in the posited relationships effects a denial of man's freedom. To refuse *communion* with the world is to refuse tragedy :

'Refuser notre prétendue "nature" et le vocabulaire qui en perpétue le mythe, poser les objets comme purement extérieurs et superficiels, ce n'est pas—comme on l'a dit—nier l'homme; mais c'est repousser l'idée "pananthropique" contenue dans l'humanisme traditionnel, comme probablement dans tout humanisme. Ce n'est, en fin de compte, que conduire dans ses conséquences logiques la revendication de ma liberté.' Ibid., p. 52

The critique of what Robbe-Grillet refers to as the essentialist conceptions of man does indeed link him at one level not simply to the work of Barthes but to that whole focus of contemporary research that has called into question the received notions of Man, Human Nature, and so on.[42] More directly, however, Robbe-Grillet has seen

---

[39] In fact, Robbe-Grillet misquotes Barthes slightly In the article in *Arguments* from which the passage is taken the last words read 'est aujourd'hui une entreprise singulière, et quels qu'en soient les détours "formalistes"', nécessaire' ('Il n'y a pas d'école Robbe-Grillet', *Arguments* No. 6, February 1958, p. 7.)

[40] *Collected Letters* I, p. 150.

[41] Vid. below pp. 180 ff.

[42] When Foucault writes: 'Réconfort cependant, et profond apaisement de penser que l'homme n'est qu'une invention récente, une figure qui n'a pas deux siècles, un simple pli dans notre savoir, et qu'il disparaîtra dès que celui-ci aura trouvé une forme

himself, albeit vaguely, and has been seen by others a good deal more definitely as connected with existentialism and phenomenology as these were developed in France in the years following the war. Robbe-Grillet expresses this connection simply in terms of his opposition of the notion of the essential to the reality of the existential, but there is, of course, more to existential phenomenology than that and quoting Heidegger at the head of a brief article.[43] This 'more' has been assumed for Robbe-Grillet by various critics in what are often extremely general terms. Bruce Morrissette, despite the radical critique of behaviourism represented by *L'Etre et le Néant* and *Phénoménologie de la perception*, speaks of an 'optique phénoménologique' in Robbe-Grillet's work *supported by* behaviourism.[44] Renato Barilli, basing his argument exclusively on the introductory chapter of *L'Etre et le Néant*, finds for Robbe-Grillet's writings 'un fond théorique constitué par la doctrine phénoménologique' but is hard put to account for the radical differences between Robbe-Grillet's theoretical presuppositions and *La Nausée*.[45] The most extended argument is that set out by Olga Bernal in her study of Robbe-Grillet in which she relates his work to phenomenology in terms of the *epoché* and the phenomenological enterprise of the description of 'the presence of things to consciousness' (more accurately, of phenomena as the correlates of the acts which intend them).[46] Three things are clear here : firstly, that Robbe-Grillet started writing at a time when the ideas of existential phenomenology and especially the ideas of Sartre were very much in the air and that he shares, almost inevitably, certain general orientations of the philosophical work at this level, as the occurrence of certain terms and expressions in his theoretical writings (the Heidegger quotation amongst others) indicates; secondly, that from a certain point of view the novels *are* available for discussion in the light of certain

nouvelle' (*Les Mots et les Choses*, p. 15), the conception of *l'homme* he is there discussing is that essentialist conception at the basis of the bourgeois mythology analysed by Barthes, and there is no need to stress the tonal relation between Foucault's statement ('réconfort cependant . . .') and Robbe-Grillet's stress on the necessity for the abandonment of humanisms centred on essentialist conceptions of man.
[43] Cf. *Pour un Nouveau Roman*, p. 95.
[44] Bruce Morrissette, *Les Romans de Robbe-Grillet* p. 40.
[45] Renato Barilli, 'De Sartre à Robbe-Grillet' in *Un Nouveau Roman? Recherche et tradition*, ed. J. H. Matthews: *La Revue des lettres modernes* Nos. 94–9, 1964, pp. 105–28 (the quotation is from p. 106).
[46] Olga Bernal, *Alain Robbe-Grillet: le roman de l'absence* (Paris, 1964), 'Introduction'. For a dissociation of the novels from phenomenological description, other than in the most general terms, see Enzo Paci, 'Robbe-Grillet, Butor e la fenomenologia', *Aut, Aut* May 1962.

aspects of existential phenomenology, though not, finally, in a very rigorous or pertinent way—it is possible, that is, to cover the novels more or less with its discourse; thirdly, and it is this that will concern us here in the task of clarification, Robbe-Grillet's theories as set out above are open to a radical and correct critique from the very standpoint of the premisses of existential phenomenology on which they are claimed to be based.

III

'zu den Sachen selbst.'

EDMUND HUSSERL

'Otez l'homme, les choses ne sont plus ni loin ni près, elles ne sont plus' :[47] Sartre's acid comment on Robbe-Grillet's theories is crucially indicative. At the centre of Sartre's *La Nausée* is the experience, or rather the consciousness, of existence : '*J'étais* la racine du marronnier. Ou plutôt j'étais tout entier conscience de son existence',[48] comments Roquentin at exactly the moment in *La Nausée* to which Robbe-Grillet objects in 'Nature, humanisme, tragédie'. The *static* nature of Robbe-Grillet's conception of man's realization of the world forces itself on the attention. Man and things are face to face in a situation of total stasis : things are there, and man's relation to them is merely ocular, passively contemplative. Marx referred to this kind of conception as that of non-dialectical materialism, that materialism he criticized in the first thesis on Feuerbach :

'The chief defect of all hitherto existing materialism (including that of Feuerbach) is that the thing, reality, sensuousness is conceived only in the form of the *object of contemplation*, but not as *sensuous human activity, practice* [*sinnlich menschliche Tätigkeit, Praxis*], not subjectively.'[49]

The view Marx criticizes there is precisely that underlying a peculiarly revealing passage of 'Nature, humanisme, tragédie' :

'L'homme saisit son marteau (ou une pierre qu'il a choisie) et il frappe sur un pieu qu'il veut enfoncer. Pendant qu'il l'utilise ainsi, le marteau (ou le caillou) n'est que forme et matière : son poids, sa surface de

---

[47] Madeleine Chapsal, *Les Ecrivains en personne*, p. 215.
[48] J.-P. Sartre, *La Nausée* (Paris, 1948), p. 167.
[49] *Marx-Engels Werke*, Vol. 3 (Berlin, 1959), p. 5.

frappe, son autre extrémité qui permet de le saisir. L'homme, ensuite, repose l'outil devant soi; s'il n'en a plus besoin, le marteau n'est plus qu'une chose parmi les choses : hors de son usage, il n'a pas de signification.'

Pour un Nouveau Roman, p. 53

There are several things to be noted here : that man is seen as in a casually *immediate* relationship with a world of things, with a world of absolute givens, from which relationship the terms *culture* and *society* have been suppressed or forgotten; that, in accordance with the absence of these terms, Robbe-Grillet habitually treats everything external to the individual as totally non-significant, to be picked up and put down as required without involving any degree of relation, transformation, interaction, production, or whatever; that, finally and inevitably, man too is seen as an absolute given, *l'homme* being employed in the argument in exactly the same kind of static way as in those essentialist conceptions of man that Robbe-Grillet sees himself as opposing.[50] It is salutary to note that what Robbe-Grillet describes in this passage as the right relation of man to the world, in which the awareness of the presence of things is firmly held, is seen in *La Nausée* as exactly the reverse. Describing his revelation in the park (*'J'étais* la racine du marronnier . . .'), Roquentin writes, thinking of his old blind and inauthentic attitudes :

'Même quand je regardais les choses, j'étais à cent lieues de songer qu'elles existaient . . . Je les prenais dans mes mains, elles me servaient d'outils, je prévoyais leurs résistances. Mais tout ça se passait à la surface . . . Et puis voilà : tout d'un coup, c'était là, c'était clair comme le jour : l'existence m'était soudain dévoilée.'[51]

Marx's *sensuousness* is apprehended here rather than in the *contemplation* proposed as authentic by Robbe-Grillet. Roquentin would have to see the relation posited as right by 'Nature, humanisme, tragédie' as precisely that of the 'natural attitude', as that, indeed, of the inauthentic, self-centred bourgeois society of Bouville encountered in all its idiotic complacency in front of the church on that unforgettable Sunday morning, as that the shattering of which, in the individual case of Roquentin himself, is the record

---

[50] Robert Champigny notes, 'Quant au mot "homme", il tend à se comporter à la manière d'un nom de personnage mythique . . .'; *Pour une Esthétique de l'essai* (Paris, 1967), p. 59.
[51] *La Nausée,* pp. 161–2.

of the journal that is *La Nausée*. There is a fundamental opposition to be grasped here between Robbe-Grillet's vision and that of existential phenomenology, an opposition the grounds of which may be explored directly in terms of the critique of Robbe-Grillet's theories that can be presented from the standpoint of existential phenomenology.

Phenomenology, in Sartre's words, plunges man back into the world.[52] The source of this restitution of 'le monde des artistes et des prophètes; effrayant, hostile, dangereux, avec des havres de grâce et d'amour'[53] is to be found in the work of Edmund Husserl and the nature of the impact of that work can probably best be understood if two traditional ways of thinking about man in the world, against which it was a reaction, are borne in mind. On the one hand, in the materialist emphasis, man had been seen as the result of a complex of physical, physiological and sociological influences which determined him from the outside, rendering him an essentially passive object in the material universe. On the other hand, in the idealist emphasis, man's mind had been regarded as a constituting source, his world a creation from out of himself, which, in the transcendental religious connection generally attached to such idealism, could be essentially linked to a prime constituting source called God or the Absolute Idea or whatever (a position Sartre has referred to as that of a 'philosophie alimentaire'[54]). Inner and outer, subjective and objective, ideal and material, and so on, are the antitheses created in the development of these two ways of thinking about man in the world, and in terms of which they conduct their arguments. It was this antithetical conflict that Husserl challenged as false with a central insight, that of the *intentionality of consciousness*, rejecting Lockean materialism with its concept of the mind as a fundamentally passive register of stimuli that bombard it from the external world and equally rejecting the idealist concept of the mind as the source of the objects it knows which thus exist 'in' consciousness alone. In place of the separate antithetical poles, Husserl posited the idea of relationship. Out of the sensible world the perceiving subject constructs a meaningful whole, but it is only in terms of this construction that the subject can know himself. Consciousness is always consciousness *of* something, it is an intentional act, in which alone can the perceiving subject grasp himself through the objects conscious-

---

[52] 'Ils [les phénoménologues] . . . ont replongé l'homme dans le monde'; *La Transcendance de l'ego*, ed. S. Le Bon (Paris, 1965), p. 86.
[53] *Situations I*, p. 34.   [54] Ibid., p. 31.

ness intends. It is the intentional act itself that realizes the subject and object dimensions, which Husserl refers to as the noetic and noematic aspects of intentionality, but neither can somehow be seen as more 'real' than the other, which would be to deny the intentional nature of consciousness and fall back into a reductive idealism or materialism.

Reality may be understood thus as the creative or dialectical relationship of subject and object realized in the intentional act that is consciousness. We have learnt, however, the traditional subject/object antithesis and we live what Husserl calls the *natural attitude* ('natürliche Einstellung'). Our reality is socially stabilized and objectified as Reality *tout court*, and within this stabilization we project a whole series of objective or natural sciences designed to know that neutral material world in which we find ourselves. We take our world for granted, a stance which Husserl describes as follows :

'I find ever present and confronting me a single spatio-temporal reality of which I myself am a part, as do all other men found in it and who relate to it in the same way. This "reality", as the word already indicates, I find *existing out there and I receive it just as it presents itself to me as something existing out there [als daseiende vor und nehme sie, wie sie sich mir gibt, auch als daseiende hin]*. "The" world as reality is always there : at the most it is here and there "other" than I supposed it, and should it be necessary to exclude this or that under the title "figment of the imagination", "hallucination", etc., I exclude it from this world which in the attitude of the general thesis is always the world existing out there. It is the aim of the *sciences issuing from the natural attitude* to attain a knowledge of this world more comprehensive, more reliable, and in every respect more perfect than that offered by the simple information received from experience, and to resolve all the problems of scientific knowledge that offer themselves upon its ground.'[55]

The central purpose of *phenomenology* is to go beyond this natural, taken-for-granted attitude (almost, as it were, 'before' it, as Husserl investigates the origins of mathematical science), and to describe what presents itself to consciousness as it presents itself, to investigate phenomena as the correlates of the acts which intend them, to describe and account for the construction of the natural attitude. Husserl's moto was 'zu den Sachen selbst', by which must be under-

---

[55] *Ideen zu einer reinen Phänomenologie und phänomenologischen Philosophie; Gesammelte Werke*, Vol. III, ed. W. Biemal (The Hague, 1950), p. 63.

stood the return to the intentional objects of consciousness in its intentionality.

The method for this return to things themselves was defined by Husserl as one of phenomenological reduction, of *epoché*, the suspension or 'bracketing out' of the taken-for-granted grounds of the natural attitude in order to attend to the intentional activity of consciousness. The French philosopher Paul Ricoeur has given, in the introductory chapter to his translation of Husserl's *Ideen*, an excellent account of the existential reality of the phenomenological reduction, the terms of which are worth careful consideration in relation to the discussion of Robbe-Grillet's theories :

'Je pense que chacun est invité à retrouver en soi ce geste de dépassement : j'oserai ainsi esquisser pour moi-même le sens "existentiel" de la thèse du monde : je suis d'abord oublié et perdu dans le monde, perdu dans les choses, perdu dans les idées, perdu dans les plantes et les bêtes, perdu dans autrui, perdu dans les mathématiques; la présence (qui ne sera jamais reniée) est le lieu de la tentation, il y a dans le voir un piège, le piège de mon aliénation; je suis dehors, diverti. On comprend que le naturalisme soit le plus bas degré de l'attitude naturelle et comme le niveau où l'entraîne sa propre retombée; car si je me perds dans le monde, je suis déjà prêt à me traiter comme chose du monde. La thèse du monde est une sorte de cécité au sein même du voir; ce que j'appelle *vivre* c'est me cacher comme conscience naïve au creux de l'existence de toutes choses : "im natürlichen Dahinleben lebe ich immerfort in dieser Grundform alles aktuellen Lebens" . . . Ainsi l'ascèse phénoménologique est une vraie conversion du sens de l'intentionnalité qui est d'abord *oubli* de la conscience et se découvre ensuite comme *don* . . . La réduction est le premier geste libre, parce qu'il est libérateur de l'illusion mondaine. Par lui je perds en apparence le monde que je gagne véritablement.'[56]

Increasingly in Husserl's thinking the idea of the phenomenological reduction carried with it a form of transcendentalism. The *epoché* invoked a 'transcendental egology'; a realm of pure nonintentional consciousness was postulated as remaining after the putting into suspension of the contents of consciousness. This 'transcendental Ego' is for Husserl that which is left over as 'phänomenologisches Residuum zürück als eine prinzipiell eigenartige Seinsregion'.[57] In the *Cartesianische Meditationen* of 1929, Husserl des-

56 'Introduction du traducteur'; E. Husserl, *Idées directrices d'une phénoménologie* (Paris, 1950), p. xx. (For the quotation from Husserl, see *Ideen*, p. 60.)
57 *Ideen*, p. 72.

cribes the Ego as a fully constitutive force, and the intentional relationship can be seen to be lost in a position which is apparently solipsist, though Husserl himself would have denied this. The final paragraph of the work concludes :

'The Delphic motto, γνῶθι σεαυτόν, has gained a new significance. Positive science is a science lost in the world. I must lose the world by *epoché* in order to regain it by a universal self-examination. "Noli foras ire", says Augustine, "in te redi in interiore homine habitat veritas".[58]

The phenomenology that is important here is the existential phenomenology derived in France from the impetus provided by Husserl's insights. Sartre's first major published work, *La Transcendance de l'ego: Esquisse d'une description phénoménologique* (1936), was a direct critique of Husserl's idea of the transcendental Ego and an attempt, as it were, to salvage the authentic phenomenological concepts in his work. Sartre contends that if it is the Ego that constitutes objects then its resulting non-intentional status, its status as an essence *before* consciousness, results in solipsism and the final incomprehensibility of consciousness. He insists on a return to the non-egological Husserl. The Ego must be made a part of the phenomenological reduction—'le Je transcendant doit tomber sous le coup de la réduction phénoménologique'[59]—so that it too, along with all other objects, stands outside consciousness and is thus an object of consciousness like other objects :

'L'Ego n'est ni formellement ni matériellement *dans* la conscience : il est dehors, *dans le monde,* . . . comme l'Ego d'autrui.'[60]

Consciousness becomes a stream, a spontaneity, a nothing, in the sense that nothing is 'in' consciousness, but rather everything is outside consciousness, grasped in its intentional acts, as an object *of* consciousness. Consciousness and the world are given simultaneously, defined in the intentional act that realizes them in relationship, the one with the other. As Sartre puts it in an early essay, 'Une idée fondamentale de la philosophie de Husserl : l'ntentionnalité' :

'la conscience est claire comme un grand vent, il n'y a plus rien en elle, sauf un mouvement pour se fuir, un glissement hors de soi; si, par impossible, vous entriez "dans" une conscience, vous seriez saisi par un tourbillon et rejeté au dehors, près de l'arbre, en pleine poussière, car

[58] *Cartesianische Meditationen,* ed. S. Strasser, *Gesammelte Werke* Vol. I (The Hague, 1950), p. 183.
[59] *La Transcendance de l'ego,* p. 37.
[60] Ibid, p. 13.

la conscience n'a pas de "dedans"; elle n'est rien que le dehors d'elle-même et c'est cette fuite absolue, ce refus d'être substance qui la constitue comme une conscience.'[61]

Husserl's theory of the intentionality of consciousness becomes a fully existential theory, and this is the basis of the definition of man's freedom. The self is the result of its being in the world : it is nothing essentially, it becomes as it exists. In Sartre's famous formulation, *existence precedes essence*. Merleau-Ponty, commenting on that conclusion to the *Cartesianische Meditationen* cited above, writes : 'Il n'y a pas d'homme intérieur, l'homme est au monde, c'est dans le monde qu'il se connaît'.[62] Bearing these emphases in mind, Robbe-Grillet's theoretical formulations can now be examined and radically challenged in their two major areas of contention, their conception of man's being in the world and their conception of the nature of language.

Robbe-Grillet defines man's freedom in terms of the recognition of the distance that separates him from the world in which he finds himself : man is man and things are things. This emphasis, however, becomes exactly that separation of subject and object into two non-communicating poles that is the point of reaction for the phenomenological insight into the intentionality of consciousness. Symptomatically, the concept of consciousness is absent from the pages of *Pour un Nouveau Roman*, its place being occupied by the sense of man's vision as the basic mode of his being in the world. Where for Sartre and Merleau-Ponty man takes possession of himself-and-his-world ('Je suis à moi, en étant au monde'[63]) in the intentional acts of consciousness, for Robbe-Grillet man looks at the world as if from across a void. Where Robbe-Grillet's conception of man's freedom depends on the recognition of necessary rigid separation, Merleau-Ponty's is defined in exactly opposite terms as the realization of the creative dialectical relation between man and the world :

'Qu'est-ce donc que la liberté? Naître, c'est à la fois naître du monde et naître au monde. Le monde est déjà constitué, mais aussi jamais complètement constitué. Sous le premier rapport, nous sommes sollicités, sous le second nous sommes ouverts à une infinité de possibles. Mais cette analyse est encore abstraite, car nous existons sous les deux rapports *à la fois* . . . Je ne peux manquer la liberté que si je cherche

---

61 *Situations I*, pp. 32–3.
62 M. Merleau-Ponty, *Phénoménologie de la perception*, p.v.
63 *Phénoménologie de la perception*, p. 466.

à dépasser ma situation naturelle et sociale en refusant de l'assumer d'abord, au lieu de rejoindre à travers elle le monde naturel et humain.'[64]

The basic term is not the world nor the perceiving subject, but the relationship between them, outside of which the isolated terms have no meaning, yet it is in these same isolated terms that Robbe-Grillet's supposedly existential-phenomenological arguments are always finally couched. Speaking of the dangers of the use of metaphor, Robbe-Grillet comments that under its effect 'je ne saurais plus retrouver l'origine de rien. La majesté se situait-elle d'abord en moi, ou devant moi? La question elle-même perdrait son sens' (*Pour un Nouveau Roman*, p. 50). Yet the question is anti-phenomenological in its assumptions, and posed in these terms its inadequacy at the level of existential experience is precisely the point of Sartre's and Merleau-Ponty's critiques.[65] Commenting on the concept of intentionality in Husserl, Sartre writes:

'Voilà que, tout d'un coup, ces fameuses réactions "subjectives", haine, amour, crainte, sympathie, qui flottaient dans la saumure malodorante de l'Esprit, s'en arrachent: elles ne sont que des manières de découvrir le monde. Ce sont les choses qui se dévoilent soudain à nous comme haïssables, sympathiques, horribles, aimables. C'est une *propriété* de ce masque japonais que d'être terrible, une inépuisable, irréductible propriété qui constitue sa nature même—et non la somme de nos réactions subjectives à un morceau de bois sculpté. Husserl a réinstallé l'horreur et le charme dans les choses.'[66]

That metaphor should play a crucial role in Roquentin's realization of his experience of the existence of the chestnut-tree root in *La Nausée* is thus no surprise, for the point of the revelation is not the establishment of a distance between himself and things, this indeed being precisely the comfortable attitude to which, at the beginning of his diary, he describes himself as longing to return ('Les objets,

---

[64] *Phénoménologie de la perception*, pp. 517, 520.

[65] Cf. Mikel Dufrenne, 'la vie intentionnelle n'est pas la vie d'une conscience constituante, elle est le lieu où se noue l'accord de la conscience et du monde. Ce qui est constituant, c'est cet accord même.' *Jalons* (The Hague, 1966), p. 266.

[66] *Situations I*, p. 34. Cf. *L'Etre et le Néant* (Paris, 1948); IV, II, III, pp. 690–708, 'De la Qualité comme Révélatrice de l'Etre': 'Sans aucun doute, le sens "humain" du *poisseux*, du *visqueux*, etc. n'appartient pas à l'en-soi. Mais les potentialités non plus, nous l'avons vu, ne lui appartiennent pas et pourtant ce sont elles qui constituent le monde. Les significations *matérielles*, le sens humain des aiguilles de neige, du grenu, du tassé, du graisseux, etc., sont aussi *réelles* que le monde, ni plus ni moins, et venir au monde, c'est surgir au milieu de ces significations.' p. 691.

cela ne devrait pas *toucher*, puisque cela ne vit pas. On s'en sert, on les remet en place, on vit au milieu d'eux : ils sont utiles, rien de plus'[67]), but the realization of the nature of existence, of that contingency of which he and the chestnut-tree root are both elements (*De trop*, le marronnier, là en face de moi un peu sur la gauche . . . Et *moi . . . moi aussi j'étais de trop*'[68]).

Central then to existential phenomenology is the awareness, in Merleau-Ponty's words, that 'le monde est non pas ce que je pense, mais ce que je *vis*',[69] and not, as Robbe-Grillet would express it, 'ce que je *vois*', a conception that gives the possibility of his ideas of language and vision as static neutral modes for inspecting and recording the world out there across the void.[70] Man, who in the emphasis of an existential phenomenology is a creative presence open to the world and exactly in that openness realizing (in both senses of the word) the world, becomes in Robbe-Grillet's account a spectator, whence the misguided project of cleansing the world of meanings.

'Parce que nous sommes au monde, *nous sommes condamnés au sens*.'[71] Man is in creative relationship with the world, the relationship of consciousness, in the intentional acts of which he takes possession of himself-and-his-world. Furthermore, he is born into a situation, and this situation is not an immediate, that is, unmediated, relation to some absolute natural Reality. As Sartre expresses it :

'pour nous, l'homme se définit avant tout comme un être "en situation". Cela signifie qu'il forme un tout synthétique avec sa situation biologique, économique, politique, culturelle, etc. . . . . On ne peut le distinguer d'elle car elle le forme et décide de ses possibilités, mais inversement, c'est lui qui lui donne son sens en se choisissant dans et par elle.'[72]

Man is born into history, into a particular *social* reality, a totalization created by and creating the individuals that compose it in a

---

[67] *La Nausée*, p. 23.

[68] Ibid., p. 163.

[69] *Phénoménologie de la perception*, p. xii (my italics).

[70] It is perhaps worth noting here that there is a problem with regard to the position accorded to vision by Husserl in his phenomenology of perception; see the discussion of Paragraph 41 of the *Ideen* by Gérard Granel in his *Le Sens du Temps et de la Perception chez E. Husserl* (Paris, 1968), pp. 229–40. The problem entails a problem of description and of language, recognized as such by Husserl himself in the appeal (as Leibniz before him) for the fixing of meanings in some *univocal* (i.e. non-equivocal) language.

[71] Ibid., p. xiv (my italics).

[72] *Réflexions sur la question juive* (Paris, 1946), p. 76.

continuous dialectical process. In Marx's words, 'Society is the unity of being of man with nature—the naturalism of man and the humanism of nature both brought to fulfilment'.[73]

It is the concept of *society* that is missing from 'Nature, humanisme, tragédie'. Man is a spectator gazing across the void that separates him completely from a world of things that may be casually picked up and put down as need be without any kind of significant relationship being involved. The concept of utility invoked by Robbe-Grillet in the passage cited above is, however, an immediate critique of this point of view.[74] The hammer, or the stone as hammer, is a means of changing the world, or, to put it another way, of giving the world significance, as indeed is language, and it is believed that language and the use of tools made a simultaneous appearance in the history of the development of man, contemporaneous modes of human activity, of what has been called 'le procès proprement humain par lequel les hommes donnent du sens aux choses'.[75] The absence of awareness of this process is, in fact, the natural attitude and it is exactly on the grounds of the natural attitude, which is never called into question, that Robbe-Grillet's theories are built. Olga Bernal in her study of Robbe-Grillet finds a methodological doubt at the basis of his theoretical writings similar to that at the basis of those of Sartre,[76] but it is only necessary to try to grasp the following comment by Iris Murdoch on *La Nausée* in relation to 'Nature, humanisme, tragédie' to become quickly aware of the real difference between the two, everything that falls under the range of Roquentin's doubt being held unreflexively in the latter as a self-evident truth :

'Roquentin experiences the full range of the doubt ... He feels doubts about induction (why not a centipede for a tongue?) and about classification (the seagull), distress at the particularity of things and the abstractness of names (the tramway seat, the tree root).'[77]

[73] *Marx-Engels Gesamtausgabe*, I. 3 (Frankfurt, 1932), p. 116.

[74] Robbe-Grillet's account depends on a 'chronology' that is the reverse of Sartre's: 'Le rapport originel des choses entre elles . . . c'est donc le rapport d'*ustensilité* . . . La chose n'est point d'abord chose pour être ensuite ustensile; elle n'est point d'abord ustensile pour se dévoiler ensuite comme chose: elle est *chose-ustensile*. Il est vrai, toutefois, qu'elle se découvrira à la quête ultérieure du savant comme purement *chose*, c'est-à-dire dépouillée de toute ustensilité . . . le résultat d'ailleurs de cette quête scientifique, c'est que la chose elle-même, dépouillée de toute instrumentalité, s'évapore pour finir en extériorité absolue.' *L'Etre et le Néant*, pp. 250–1.

[75] Roland Barthes, *Essais critiques*, p. 218.

[76] Olga Bernal, op. cit., p. 9.

[77] Iris Murdoch, *Sartre: Romantic Rationalist* (Cambridge, 1953), p. 13.

The terms of Roquentin's doubt—classification, language, scientific reason—are the terms of Robbe-Grillet's security, and we might bear in mind at this point, to stress the fundamental difference, his insistence on the neutral sufficiency of scientific description, of that scientific description that Sartre and Merleau-Ponty insist must be *included* in the phenomenological reduction.[78] It is in this context that the key elements in Robbe-Grillet's theory of vision and language can properly be estimated.

Vision for Robbe-Grillet, as has been seen, is the instrument (or potential instrument) of a non-anthropomorphical perception of, and hence relation to, the world by virtue of its uninvolving registration of the distances that separate man and things: 'Le regard apparaît aussitôt dans cette perspective comme le sens privilégié . . . La description optique est en effet celle qui opère le plus aisément la fixation des distances.' (*Pour un Nouveau Roman*, p. 65). Vision is crucially important for its cleansing possibilities ('le pouvoir *laveur du regard*') and the authentic mode of the demonstration of these possibilities is geometrical description, the careful recording of the distances established by the passive gaze of man the spectator. This type of thinking depends on the suppression of any kind of existential-phenomenological perspective, in the light of the insights of which Robbe-Grillet's thesis here that geometrical description 'revient à établir que les choses sont là et qu'elles ne sont rien d'autre que des choses . . . il y a désormais refus de *toute* complicité' (ibid.) can only be seen as profoundly self-deceptive. That perspective entails not the supposedly passive and unattached gaze in which Robbe-Grillet places all his faith, but the here and now of the lived project of the body which is simultaneously an opening to the world and the possibility of its appearance, a realization of the world, as has been said, in both senses of the word; Merleau-Ponty thus writes:

'La chose et le monde me sont donnés avec les parties de mon corps, non par une "géométrie naturelle", mais dans une connexion vivante comparable ou plutôt identique à celle qui existe entre les parties de mon corps lui-même.'[79]

Dynamic relation replaces separation. Instead of, as it were, arriving in a preconstituted space and peering at it from the margin of

[78] Cf. below p. 102.
[79] *Phénoménologie de la perception*, p. 237.

his existence, man is seen at the centre of the space that is *his* world, the condition of which is precisely the orientation of the body in its project :

'Tout nous renvoie aux relations organiques du sujet et de l'espace, à cette prise du sujet sur son monde qui est à l'origine de l'espace.'[80]

In these terms geometrical description is not to be considered as some kind of neutral instrument for some non-anthropomorphical expression of the world-in-itself : 'La nature n'*est* pas de soi géométrique.'[81] Robbe-Grillet's supposed neutral description runs back into the function of the body :

'Le corps propre est le troisième terme, toujours sous-entendu, de la structure figure et fond, et toute figure se profile sur le double horizon de l'espace extérieur et de l'espace corporel.'[82]

Developing the work of Oscar Becker, Merleau-Ponty thus insists on precisely the 'anthropomorphical' signification of geometrical description as Robbe-Grillet understands it :

'Quand je dis qu'un objet est *sur* une table, je me place toujours en pensée dans la table ou dans l'objet et je leur applique une catégorie qui convient en principe au rapport de mon corps et des objets extérieurs. *Dépouillé de cet import anthropologique le mot "sur" ne se distingue plus du mot "sous" ou du terme "à côté de".*'[83]

Robbe-Grillet talks of cleansing objects from human contamination by taking *their* measurements (*Pour un Noveau Roman*, p. 65), but 'un objet en lui-même n'a aucune grandeur' :[84]

'Dans l'espace *lui-même* et sans la présence d'un sujet psycho-physique, il n'y a aucune direction, aucun dedans, aucun dehors.'[85]

Robbe-Grillet's refusal of all complicity is meaningless : the end of all complicity could only mean the end of man (in the literal sense), his *absence*, but, Sartre comments, the absence of man is the absence of things. No thing is present in the sense in which Robbe-Grillet

[80] Ibid., p. 291. [81] Ibid., p. 69.
[82] Ibid., p. 117.
[83] Ibid., p. 118. (my italics).
[84] Ibid., p. 56n. [85] Ibid., p. 236.

speaks of presence : 'l'être en-soi nous échappe totalement'.[86] There is a 'gap' or 'delay' between the in-itself and the thing known in which precisely the world of things is realized.[87] The very concept of the *object* wavers in this perspective and is to be rethought, as it is, for example, in the work of Bachelard which recentres knowledge in the terms of a *project* : 'Au-dessus du *sujet*, au-delà de *l'objet* immédiat, la science moderne se fonde sur le *projet*';[88] 'l'objet ne saurait être désigné comme un *objectif immédiat*; autrement dit, une marche vers l'objet n'est pas initialement objective. Il faut donc accepter une véritable rupture entre la connaissance sensible et la connaissance scientifique;'[89] 'les objets scientifiques sont ce que nous les faisons, ni plus ni moins . . . Nous *réalisons* par degrés notre pensée scientifique.'[90]

The critique which has been offered here from the standpoint of existential phenomenology (as represented by Merleau-Ponty's *Phénoménologie de la perception*) of Robbe-Grillet's theories of geometrical description offers a focal example of what is a general absence of existential-phenomenological insight in his work with regard to the whole question of the nature of perception, an absence epitomized in the simple phrase 'le pouvoir laveur du regard'. The emphasis in Merleau-Ponty's work on the project of the body as 'l'instrument général de ma compréhension',[91] is necessarily opposed to the static idea of man as *a spectator* in the world :

'le système de l'expérience n'est pas déployé devant moi comme si j'étais Dieu, il est vécu par moi d'un certain point de vue, je n'en suis pas le spectateur, j'y suis partie, et c'est mon inhérence à un point de vue qui rend possible à la fois la finitude de ma perception et son ouverture au monde total comme horizon de toute perception.'[92]

[86] *L'Etre et le Néant*, p. 695.
[87] Cf. Gérard Granel, op. cit., pp. 254–5: 'Des "choses présentes", telles que la description les prend avec évidence pour point de départ, sont de pseudo-choses déjà imperceptiblement descellées de la retenue avec laquelle de choses *sont*. Ainsi descellées, elles sont mises-en-avant, chacune pour soi et les unes à côté des autres, en sorte que leur communauté ne peut plus être comprise que comme un ensemble de "rapports", que ce soient les rapports objectifs ou les rapports intentionnels. Mais des choses n'ont pas des "rapports". Elles n'ont *d'abord pas*, en effet, ce type d'existence et de présence-sur-le-devant que la description leur suppose quand elle commence par l'évidence des "choses présentes".' (Granel's explicit reference to Husserlian description but, mutatis mutandis, applies exactly to that of Robbe-Grillet.)
[88] Gaston Bachelard, *Le Nouvel Esprit scientifique* (Paris, 1934), p. 11.
[89] *La Formation de l'esprit scientifique* (Paris, 1938), p. 239.
[90] *La Dialectique de la durée* (Paris, 1936), p. 63.
[91] *Phénoménologie de la perception*, p. 278.
[92] Ibid., p. 350.

The concept of vision as the instrument by which man takes optical stock of a world of given forms 'out there' is nothing but the classic thesis of materialism that existential phenomenology seeks to correct. Materialism depends, as Merleau-Ponty puts it, on its ' "hypothèse de constance", c'est-à-dire . . . de la priorité du monde objectif',[93] an assumption that relegates man's perceiving attention to the world to the status of a sterile passivity :

'L'attention est donc un pouvoir général et inconditionné en ce sens qu'à chaque moment elle peut se porter indifféremment sur tous les contenus de conscience. Partout stérile, elle ne saurait être nulle part *intéressée*.'[94]

But just as Robbe-Grillet's description of distances is a significant articulation of the world, so, generally, perception in its attention to the world is construction of the world it grasps :

'Faire attention, ce n'est pas seulement éclairer davantage des données préexistantes, c'est réaliser en elles une articulation nouvelle en les prenant pour *figures*.'[95]

Perception *articulates* a world in which man finds himself and which is found only in this articulation. 'Parce que nous sommes au monde, nous sommes condamnés au sens.' It is the attention of human perception that brings the world into existence :

'La chose et le monde n'existent que vécus par moi ou par des sujets tels que moi, puisqu'ils sont l'enchaînement de nos perspectives, mais ils transcendent toutes les perspectives parce que cet enchaînement est temporel et inachevé.'[96]

Vision, the act of seeing, is thus not, as in the materialist emphasis to which Robbe-Grillet must be seen to assent in the central thesis of this period of his theoretical work (that of 'Nature, humanisme, tragédie'), merely a passive recording of the world, but a prime mode of its creative realization, of bringing it into existence. This, indeed, was a central recognition for Marx :

'The eye has become the human eye, just as its object has become the human object, an object that is social, human, derived from man

[93] Ibid., p. 34.
[94] Ibid.
[95] Ibid., p. 38 ('The figures of perception/as against/the figures of elocution', Charles Tomlinson, *American Scenes* (London, 1966), p. 44).
[96] Ibid., pp. 384–5.

and destined for man. In this way *the senses have become directly, in practice, theoreticians.*[97]

The idea of *culture*, of the whole way of life of a society, the term Robbe-Grillet suppresses in order to operate the schema of individual subject—distance (the void traversed by the gaze of the individual) —world of things (the dashes representing points of separation) reappears here as, to take up a phrase from a passage from Marx quoted previously, the naturalism of man and the humanism of nature both brought to fulfilment. Perception involves a process of social learning, is developed in the terms of a social intelligibility. Bachelard stressed this in rejecting the notion of the spectator, of the child suddenly opening his eyes onto the immediate spectacle of the world; 'L'enfant naît avec un *cerveau inachevé* et non pas, comme le postulat de l'ancienne pédagogie l'affirmait, avec un *cerveau inoccupé*. La société achève vraiment le cerveau de l'enfant; elle l'achève par le langage, par l'instruction, par le dressage.'[98] The notion of the eye as simply a camera is rejected, as in the following passage by the biologist J. Z. Young who can, in fact, be seen as developing Marx's idea of the 'human eye' :

'The visual receiving system in its untrained state has only very limited powers. We are perhaps deceived by the fact that the eye is a sort of camera. Contrary to what we might suppose, the eye and the brain do not simply record in a sort of photographic manner the pictures that pass in front of us. The brain is not by any means a simple recording system like a film . . . Many of our affairs are conducted on the assumption that our sense organs provide us with an accurate record independent of ourselves. What we are now beginning to see is that much of this is an illusion, that we have to learn to see the world as we do . . . In some sense we literally create the world we speak about . . . The point is to grasp that we cannot speak simply as if there is a world around us of which our senses give true information. In trying to speak about what the world is like we must remember all the time that what we see or what we say depends on what we have learned; we ourselves come into the process.'[99]

It is this *process* that is missing from the thinking of Robbe-Grillet, for whom seeing seems to be precisely the immediate illumination of a set of essentially constituted things 'out there in the

[97] Cit. L. Kolakowski, *Marxism and Beyond* (London, 1969), p. 67.
[98] *La Philosophie du non* (Paris, 1940), p. 128.
[99] Cit. Raymond Williams, *The Long Revolution*, p. 17.

world' waiting for man to turn his recording gaze upon them, rather than the process of the achievement of the articulations of perception in the transformation of horizon into figures or forms. Plunged into the world, man has, comments Merleau-Ponty, 'une liberté d'indifférence'[100] and the world he knows is created humanly out of that liberty. By cultural and social learning-processes his attention is developed, limited, as Young indicates, to only a fraction of the stimuli the world offers. Facets of the sensible world present themselves as indeterminate possibilities taken up and grasped as present (presented) by the intentional acts of consciousness, which determines them through the generalized resources of its sedimented experience of the world, resources to which the major contribution is made by language. Merleau-Ponty describes this process in his *Phénoménologie de la perception* in terms which directly oppose those of the characteristic formulations of 'Nature, humanisme, tragédie', replacing the refusal of all complicity by the idea of relationship as the central reality and necessity of man's being-in-the-world :

'la chose est le corrélatif de mon corps et plus généralement de mon existence dont mon corps n'est que la structure stabilisée, elle se constitue dans la prise de mon corps sur elle, elle n'est pas d'abord une signification pour l'entendement, mais une structure accessible à l'inspection du corps et si nous voulons décrire le réel tel qu'il nous apparaît dans l'expérience perceptive, nous le trouvons chargé de prédicats anthropologiques. Les relations entre les choses ou entre les aspects des choses étant toujours médiatisées par notre corps, la nature entière est la mise en scène de notre propre vie ou notre interlocuteur dans une sorte de dialogue. Voilà pourquoi en dernière analyse nous ne pouvons pas concevoir de chose qui ne soit perçue ou perceptible. . . La chose ne peut jamais être séparée de quelqu'un qui la perçoive, elle ne peut jamais être effectivement en soi parce que ses articulations sont celles même de notre existence et qu'elle se pose au bout d'un regard ou au terme d'une exploration sensorielle qui l'investit d'humanité. Dans cette mesure, toute perception est une communication ou une communion . . . comme un accouplement de notre corps avec les choses.'[101]

The cause of the blindness to the reality of the relationship here described is attributed by Merleau-Ponty to the deeply rooted preassumptions of materialism with its neat antithesis of the object-in-

100 *Phénoménologie de la perception*, p. 39.
101 Ibid., pp. 369–70.

itself and the subject-in-himself as pure consciousness,[102] the belief that things are things and man is man and never the two shall meet except through the inspection of vision, as Robbe-Grillet puts it.[103] The 'phenomenological' theories of Robbe-Grillet rest, in fact, firmly within the natural attitude. This, indeed, is the meaning of his (symptomatic) appeals to science for the methodological endorsement of his theories, to that science which Husserl, followed by Sartre and Merleau-Ponty, insisted had to be suspended in the *epoché*. For phenomenology 'la science classique est une perception qui oublie ses origines et se croit achevée', the function of the *epoché* being precisely to 'déjouer la ruse par laquelle elle se laisse oublier comme fait et comme perception au profit de l'objet qu'elle nous livre et de la tradition rationnelle qu'elle fonde'.[104] It is in these terms that the lines of a phenomenological critique of Robbe-Grillet's theory of geometrical description were sketched above, a theory based on the forgetting of its premises and its rationalization within the natural attitude as immediate representation of the Real. Robbe-Grillet provides a perfect example of what Sartre characterizes as a writer 'qui a commencé par un doute méthodique; mais . . . a refusé de mettre la science en question',[105] who comes down finally with what Merleau-Ponty calls the *non-dialectical postulate,* 'Being is'.[106] That critics have been able to find a methodological doubt basic

102 Cf. ibid., p. 370.
103 It is to be noted that when Robbe-Grillet does acknowledge the final impossibility of 'l'impersonnalité totale du regard', he still remains within the terms of this kind of naïve materialism, for it is not the immediacy of vision and world that is then put into question, but merely, as it were, the limited range of projection of a particular individual immediate vision, a kind of literal version of Henry James's idea of point-of-view and the 'house of fiction', which later becomes the basis of the second major emphasis in Robbe-Grillet's theories, the total subjectivity of the *nouveau roman*. There is a passage in Georges Matoré's *L'Espace humain* which seems to indicate the result that might be expected from this appeal to the 'pouvoir laveur du regard' and the recognition of the impossibility of an 'impartialité totale du regard' complex in just these terms, in, that is, the *multiplication* of immediate but limited centres of cleansing vision, but, as will be seen, neither theoretically nor in the novels does Robbe-Grillet actually follow this course: 'un regard peut être soit pur, vide, neutre, soit chargé (du sens, d'attention, etc.). Dans le premier cas, le mot est employé surtout au pluriel: ces *regards* impliquent non une vision strictement personnelle, émanant d'un foyer unique, mais un éclairage braqué en faisceau sur l'objet à examiner; ainsi se trouve réalisée une synthèse de vues nombreuses, simultanées ou successives, recouvrant cet objet d'une manière qui, plus complexe et étendue, est donc mieux informée et plus objective que celle dont se contenterait un observateur ne disposant que d'un *point de vue* limité.' (Paris, 1962, p. 116.)
104 *Phénoménologie de la perception*, p. 69.
105 *Situations I*, p. 259.
106 *Résumés de cours* (Paris, 1968), p. 65.

to Robbe-Grillet's work which connects him directly with existential phenomenology is, to say the least, surprising. Robbe-Grillet's explicit opposition to *La Nausée* in 'Nature, humanisme, tragédie', moreover, reveals at once the very separation of his theories from this kind of phenomenological thinking, for he is there obliged to take Sartre to task for calling into question the very geometrical descriptions on which his own theories depend.[107] The experience of existence for Roquentin is simultaneously the experience of the inessentiality of human articulations :

'En vain cherchais-je à *compter* les marronniers, à les *situer* par rapport à la Velléda, à comparer leur hauteur avec celle des platanes : chacun d'eux s'échappait des relations où je cherchais à l'enfermer, s'isolait, débordait. Ces relations (que je m'obstinais à maintenir pour retarder l'écroulement du monde humain, des mesures, des quantités, des directions) j'en sentais l'arbitraire; elles ne mordaient plus sur les choses.'[108]

All the terms most cherished by Robbe-Grillet (*compter, situer, hauteur, mesures, directions*) here fall within the extent of Roquentin's doubt.

The doubt extends, as Iris Murdoch indicates, even to language itself : 'Les choses se sont délivrées de leurs noms. Elles sont là, grotesques, têtues, géantes et ça paraît imbécile de les appeler des banquettes ou de dire quoi que ce soit sur elles.'[109] Directly linked to Robbe-Grillet's non-phenomenological conception of the nature of perception in these theories is, in a kind of mutual dependence, his non-phenomenological conception of language. The attack on metaphor is directed against the solidarity it establishes between man and the world through the operation of analogy, and the attack concludes with the insistence that the refusal of analogy must be total : 'rien ne doit-il être négligé dans l'entreprise de nettoyage. En y regardant de plus près, on s'aperçoit que les analogies anthropocentristes (mentales ou viscérales) ne doivent pas être mises seules en cause. *Toutes* les analogies sont aussi dangereuses.' (*Pour un Nouveau Roman*, p. 52). The abusive use of metaphor and the 'adjectif global et unique, qui tentait de rassembler toutes les qualités internes, toute l'âme cachée des choses' in the literature Robbe-Grillet will challenge can be summed up in the following terms :

107 Cf. *Pour un Nouveau Roman*, pp. 60–1.
108 *La Nausée*, p. 163.
109 Ibid., p. 159.

Le mot fonctionnait ainsi comme un piège où l'écrivain enfermait univers pour le livrer à la société' (ibid., p. 22). Trap or not, however, this is the very reality of language. Language *is* social : it operates a particular *découpage* of the sensible world, *articulating* out of the plenitude of being a human world in which man realizes himself. It is a mode of human activity : Merleau-Ponty talks of 'le geste linguistique' and relates language inextricably to the body's lived project. Like work, language is a way of structuring a reality, a central expression of man's creativity. Jacques Lacan has commented that it is the world of words that creates the world of things,[110] and Sartre declares, 'je suis langage'.[111] Language defines my reality but is also my project; I am born into a language that is the field of my activity :

'La parole est donc cette opération paradoxale où nous tentons de rejoindre, au moyen de mots, dont le sens est donné et de significations déjà disponibles, une intention qui par principe va au-delà et modifie, fixe elle-même en dernière analyse le sens des mots par lesquels elle se traduit.'[112]

A language is a mode of perception, of realization, a way of seeing the world and of learning to see it in the process which J. Z. Young characterizes as fundamental in the development of perception.

As in his conception of perception in the sense of vision, so too in his conception of language it is just this idea of *process* that is absent from Robbe-Grillet's theory, an absence which, again, depends on the suppression of any idea of culture. After the eradication of metaphor, language which as metaphor is a trap, that is, a way of humanly realizing the world, will become a cleansing instrument, like vision, for recording the world without any sort of anthropomorphic appropriation. Yet in its very nature language is metaphorical in the sense that it systematically realizes the world in human terms (as Robbe-Grillet comes to recognize in the third of his theoretical emphases : 'tout langage est, d'une façon ou d'une autre, *métaphorique*.')[113] The innocent relationship Robbe-Grillet wishes to establish is nonsense : 'Parler c'est agir : toute chose qu'on nomme, n'est déjà plus tout à

---

[110] *Ecrits* (Paris, 1966), p. 276 ('C'est le monde des mots qui crée le monde des choses').
[111] *Situations I*, p. 237.
[112] *Phénoménologie de la perception*, pp. 445–6.
[113] 'Procès à Robbe-Grillet', *Clarté* No. 39, December 1961, p. 9.

104

fait la même, elle a perdu son innocence.'[114] The logical conclusion of Robbe-Grillet's desire to refuse all contamination of the world with human significance is not to cleanse language of metaphor, but to stop using language. The critique of analogy and language itself leads to exactly the same aporia as the critique of human relation to things, summarized in Sartre's comment that if man is removed things are neither nearer nor farther away, they simply no longer are. That Robbe-Grillet feels no compulsion to take stock of these implications of his position is not surprising for, as in his theory of 'le pouvoir laveur du regard', he rests firmly within the natural attitude, within the classic materialist view of language (which, paradoxically, is the refusal of any materiality to language). In the natural attitude language is taken for granted by its speaking subjects as natural : it is the language through which they come to know themselves and is fully internalized and lived spontaneously; it is as natural as they are. Words 'stick' to things. Language is complete and perfect, fully and naturally at one with 'Reality'. Just as attention to vision can cleanse man's conception of the world in the neutral instrument vision offers for the inspection of the Reality, 'out there', so language, in Robbe-Grillet's argument, can be pared of metaphor and left as an instrument for passively recording the information derived from the immediate inspection of the world operated by the original instrument of vision. The eye inspects and then language records—the very natural attitude which existential phenomenology suspends in the *epoché*, the illusion in Sapir's words that 'one adjusts to reality essentially without the use of language and that language is merely an incidental means of solving specific problems of communication or reflection'.[115] The paring away of metaphor is a programme for a kind of final degree of conventionality, for the naïvest realist writing ('Quand donc le roman prétend au "réalisme", il prétend s'en tenir à l'observation naïve et à ce que permet d'enregistrer de cette observation le langage ordinaire.'[116]), for an attempt to reduce the specific presence of language, an attempt in which the proper noun figures as the potential mode of

---

[114] J.–P. Sartre, *Situations II*, p. 72. Cf. John Lyons, op. cit. p. 457, 'the vocabulary as a whole . . . is not only "anthropocentric" (organized according to general human interests and values), but "culture-bound" (reflecting the more particular institutions and practices of different cultures).'

[115] *Selected Writings of Edward Sapir*, ed. David G. Mandelbaum (Berkeley and Los Angeles, 1951), p. 162.

[116] Valéry, *Oeuvres* II, p. 802.

the absence of language by virtue of its supreme referential quality in the natural attitude.[117]

The conceptions of language and perception go together and the relation between Robbe-Grillet and classic materialism can be demonstrated a little more clearly with the help of Michel Foucault's 'archaeology' of the grounds of knowledge of the classical age in *Les Mots et les Choses*. At the core of the classical experience of language is the act of *naming*, the critique of abstraction and generalization in terms of a realism the aim of which is the naming of things in a moment of critical clarity ('où les choses elles-mêmes seraient nommées sans brouillage'[118]), in which language disappears :

'On peut dire que c'est le Nom qui organise tout le discours classique; parler ou écrire, ce n'est pas dire les choses ou s'exprimer, ce n'est pas jouer avec le langage, c'est s'acheminer vers l'acte souverain de nomination, aller, à travers le langage, jusque vers le lieu où les choses et les mots se nouent en leur essence commune, et qui permet de leur donner un nom. Mais ce nom, une fois énoncé, tout le langage qui a conduit jusqu'à lui ou qu'on a traversé pour l'atteindre, se résorbe en lui et s'efface.'[119]

The space of this sovereign act of naming can be no other than 'le pur tableau des choses'.[120] History is not narration or the revelation of signification, but *transcription* : 'L'âge classique donne à l'histoire un tout autre sens : celui de poser pour la première fois un regard minutieux sur les choses elles-mêmes, et de transcrire ensuite ce qu'il recueille dans des mots lisses, neutralisés et fidèles.'[121] History is

---

117 Cf. Michel Foucault's description of the role of the proper noun in the classical age: 'Or le nom propre dans ce jeu, n'est qu'un artifice: il permet de montrer du doigt, c'est-à-dire de faire passer subrepticement de l'espace où l'on parle à l'espace où l'on regarde, c'est-à-dire de les refermer commodément l'un sur l'autre comme s'ils étaient adéquats.' (*Les Mots et les Choses*, p. 25). We might recall Saussure's emphasis that 'le signe linguistique unit non une chose et un nom, mais un concept et un image acoustique' (*Cours de linguistique générale*, Paris, 1922, p. 98). It might also be noted here that there is a project for cleansing language to be found in Sartre, and when Sartre writes that 'la fonction d'un écrivain est d'appeler un chat un chat' (*Situations II*, p. 304) there is some reason to think that Robbe-Grillet's later programme in 'Nature, humanisme, tragédie' is there fore-echoed. In fact, however, Sartre's project involves the reestablishment of a language capable of serving as an instrument of *engagement*, of grasping a historical situation: 'Si nous voulons restituer aux mots leurs vertus il faut mener une double opération: d'une part un nettoyage analytique qui les débarrasse de leurs sens adventices, d'autre part un élargissement synthétique qui les adapte à la situation historique,' (p. 305).

118 *Les Mots et les Choses*, p. 133.

119 Ibid.

120 Ibid., p. 143.   121 Ibid.

106

neither the readable nor the comprehensible, but the visible. The purification of perception is a fully developed methodology; Foucault describes the 'privilège presque exclusif de la vue, qui est le sens de l'évidence et de l'étendue . . . Et encore, tout n'est-il pas utilisable dans ce qui s'offre au regard : les couleurs, en particulier, ne peuvent guère fonder de comparaisons utiles. Le champ de visibilité où l'observation va prendre ses pouvoirs n'est que le résidu de ces exclusions : une visibilité délivrée de toute autre charge sensible et passée de plus à la grisaille.'[122] This visibility has a composition that will ring familiar—'lignes, surfaces, formes, reliefs',[123]—and the crux of its operation is the development of a *natural* history, the immediate transcription of the given world of things 'de mots appliqués sans intermédiaire aux choses mêmes'.[124] No surprise perhaps that the programme of 'Nature, humanisme, tragédie' can be characterized in just these terms even down to the attack on metaphor : what is it, after all, but the reinstatement at a literary level of natural history, of the programme of Linnaeus? 'Toutes les similitudes obscures, dit Linné, ne sont introduites qu'à la honte de l'art.'[125]

The visible, which in these terms *is* the natural, is to replace for Robbe-Grillet the significant and humanly mediated. The general thesis of the natural attitude replaces the phenomenological urge to 'saisir le *sens* du monde ou de l'histoire à l'état naissant',[126] in the undertaking of which perception and language fall under the inspection of the *epoché*. Naïve materialism is substituted for the recognitions of dialectical materialism, and, taking the following passage to refer to Robbe-Grillet instead of Feuerbach, we may note Marx's critique of 'Nature, humanisme, tragédie' :

'He does not see how the sensuous world around him is not a thing given direct from all eternity, remaining always the same, but the product of industry and the prevailing state of society; and, indeed . . . an historical product . . . Even the objects of the simplest "sensuous certainty" are given him solely through social development, industry and commercial intercourse. The cherry-tree, like the majority of fruit-trees, was, as is well known, only a few centuries ago transplanted by *commerce* into our zone, and therefore only by this action

<hr />

122 Ibid., p. 145.
123 Ibid.
124 Ibid., p. 143.
125 Ibid., p. 146.
126 *Phénoménologie de la perception*, p. xvi.

of a definite society in a definite age has it become "sensuous certainty".'[127]

Intelligibility and visibility go hand in hand. Reality is to be *read* in its human, social construction. Existential phenomenology aims at the history of this construction in its description not of some immediately visible natural 'Reality', but of the realization of a reality through the intentional acts of consciousness.

There can be no real doubt now of the crucial importance of the concept of the visible and the notion of the cleansing power of vision in Robbe-Grillet's theories at this period; an importance manifested in the very contradictions that these ideas are forced to hold. Visibility in these terms is the mode of reduction, if not, for Robbe-Grillet, of resolution, of the problem of the *other*. Man *brings* 'otherness' into the world just as, and because, his realization as man depends on a context of limits, on a context of social organization. It is the tragic implications of this that Robbe-Grillet wishes to refuse through the programme set out in 'Nature, humanisme, tragédie' and the principal artifice of that refusal is to be the cleansing power of vision. If everything is visible in itself under the inspection of the eye able to recognize in this inspection the absolute and necessary separation between individual and world of things, then the problem of otherness (that Camus, for example, could experience in terms of the absurd) will disappear. There is no *other* : Robbe-Grillet simply states that man is man and things are things. If there is no *trace* of human meaning, then the other is nowhere traced in the sensible world; everything is, in a sort of infinite tautology, to be seen and accepted. The emphasis on visibility neces-

[127] *Marx-Engels Werke*, Vol. 3, p. 43. Barthes notes, 'tout ce qui est donné à l'homme est *déjà* humain, jusqu'à la forêt et au fleuve que nous traversons lorsque nous voyageons'; *Essais critiques*, p. 218. Robbe-Grillet's theories might, in fact, be assimilated to that mythical discourse defined by Barthes in his *Mythologies*, the function of which is precisely the occultation of history as Nature (cf. below, pp. 191ff.) : 'Le mythe est constitué par la déperdition de la qualité historique des choses: les choses perdent en lui le souvenir de leur fabrication. Le monde entre dans le langage comme un rapport dialectique d'activités, d'actes humains: il sort du mythe comme un tableau harmonieux d'essences. Une prestidigitation s'est opérée, qui a retourné le réel, l'a vidé d'histoire et l'a rempli de nature, qui a retiré aux choses leur sens humain de façon à leur faire signifier une insignifiance humaine,' (p. 251). It might perhaps be mentioned here that in comments on his recent novel *Projet pour une révolution à New York* (Paris, 1970) Robbe-Grillet now defines his activity exactly in terms of a response to the *mythology* of his society, speaking no longer of a world of things but, as Barthes in *Mythologies*, of a world of *signs*; 'je me trouve assailli par une multitude de signes dont l'ensemble constitue la mythologie du monde où je vis . . .' (*Le Nouvel Observateur* 26 June 1970). Cf. the discussion below of *Dans le labyrinthe*.

sarily involves the denunciation of intelligibility, precisely the point of differentiation, of the trace of human meanings, the world no longer seen but *scene*. Any system of differences, language, for example, is a contamination, hence Robbe-Grillet's insistence on the need for the cleansing of language, the metaphoric (paradigmatic) structure of which must be transformed, somehow, into a representational transparence *of which the trace is the visible*, which is guaranteed by the out-there that it does no more than mirror. Paradoxically, it is through the visibility of the other that the other is to be refused. This programme is based through and through on misconceptions. The world of objects, as has been seen, exists through and as the articulation of the human :

'L'animal n'a pas d'objets. Il ne fait que pénétrer extatiquement son environnement . . . Se distancier de cet environnement, le concrétiser en un monde, c'est un acte que l'animal ne saurait réaliser, pas plus qu'il n'est capable de transformer les centres de résistance, limités par ses émotions et impulsions, en objets. L'homme . . . c'est pour ainsi dire, un animal qui, s'étant frotté les yeux, regarde étonné autour de lui, parce qu'il aperçoit l'*autre*, parce qu'il a en face de lui un monde qui lui fut donné en don inexplicable.'[128]

Inexplicable, that is, in the natural attitude, where it is, precisely, simply visible, but, as Buytendijk stresses, intelligible in the fact of human presence. Language is the space of this presence. Hence the difficulty of Robbe-Grillet's theory of visibility. Visibility is to be the guarantee of the absence of human presence in the world and thus the mode of the refusal of tragedy, but this visibility depends on the once and for all absolute presence of 'the World' for inspection, verified by a language of which it is the foundation or trace (the trace of the noun will be the object and the noun will disappear without trace, transparent to the object), a dependence which suppresses the reality of language which is itself the space in which the world is realized. Hence the double negation on which Robbe-Grillet's theories depend and which is exactly that of the natural attitude as it is described by the existential phenomenology with which Robbe-Grillet has been so often linked : the negation of the activity of consciousness and the negation of the reality of language. Hence too, finally, the way in which the theory found in the emphasis of 'Nature humanisme, tragédie' will shift to its opposite, and the 'objective' become the 'subjective' theory, for it is this absence of any

---

[128] F. J. J. Buytendijk, *L'Homme et l'Animal*, p. 82.

term of relation (consciousness or language) which makes that shift possible.

IV

'La théorie est toujours insuffisante.'

ALAIN ROBBE-GRILLET

It was in terms of the theories that receive their central statement in 'Nature, humanisme, tragédie' that the attacks against Robbe-Grillet's programme for the novel and against his novels were mounted. Reasonably enough in the light of the general statement of the theory that has been described above, two expressions were coined to characterize Robbe-Grillet and the 'school' of which he was vaguely and inaccurately supposed to be the moving spirit—*chosiste* and *l'école du regard*. The attacks themselves, which were generally of a startling ineptitude, centred round *things*, the red rag to the bull who charged in the name of *l'âme humaine*. The quintessential definition of everything for which Robbe-Grillet stood, in the theory and in the novels, became the opening sentence of the short text 'Trois visions réfléchies', published in the *Nouvelle Nouvelle Revue Française* in April 1954 and later reprinted in *Instantanés*; 'La cafetière est sur la table.' (*Instantanés*, p. 9.)[129] The thing is placed 'out there' in all its *Dinglichkeit*, the coffee-potness of the coffee-pot left intact; thus was the sentence read in the light

---

[129] As late as 1967 Pierre de Boisdeffre, in the title of a good example of the inept attacks provoked by the nouveau roman, *La Cafetière est sur la table* (Paris, 1967), could take this same sentence both as expressive (and in this self-evidently ridiculous) of the nature of Robbe-Grillet's work and as expressive of the nature of the nouveau roman in general. It is worth pointing out that the basic 'quality' of these attacks, apart from their inaccuracy (at all levels; Boisdeffre attributes a very famous statement of Flaubert's to Benjamin Constant, op. cit., p. 20) and, as noted in Chapter I, a certain brutality of language, is the demand for *repetition*: what is desired is not in any sense a new novel but a repeat performance of the old. 'Nous n'avons vu surgir depuis la guerre ni un nouveau Bernanos, ni un nouveau Céline, ni un nouveau Giono, encore moins un autre Proust ou une seconde Colette' (ibid., p. 44), concludes Boisdeffre, wistfully surveying the nouveau roman. Similarly J. B. Barrère, who conducts most of his attack by talking about Hugo and Gide; but then Barrère's demands for the novel, and this is typical of the style of these attacks, amount to a plea for light relief flavoured with the happy minimum of reflection: 'le lecteur . . . attend quelque chose de différent de sa propre existence, qui ait du relief et soit capable de l'exalter. Un peu de conscience est bon, trop déroute ou dégoûte.' *La cure d'amaigrissement du roman* (Paris, 1964), p. 69.

of the general notions of Robbe-Grillet *chosiste*. Robbe-Grillet could be dismissed as a kind of arch-Naturalist : if Balzac had painted men, women and things and Zola had submitted men and women to things,[130] here was Robbe-Grillet establishing a world in which things were not only dominant but almost the only participants. Robbe-Grillet's novels were thus a priori unreadable and so unread. Had they been *read* in the terms they themselves proposed, this kind of attack could never have been made even despite the confusion of Robbe-Grillet's own theoretical pronouncements.

Consider for a moment the following passage :

'Chez Milan, au coin de la rue de Beaujolais. Petite boutique percée de tous côtés de grandes portes et fenêtres, demi-voilées de petits rideaux blancs étriqués, sales, qui ont la prétention de cacher un tas de choses qu'ils ne cachent pas. Même dans l'intérieur, appliquée à une porte-fenêtre, une armoire en glaces, également voilée de petits rideaux blancs, contenant des suspensoirs. A gauche, en entrant dans la boutique, à hauteur d'épaule, sept ou huit planches appliquées au mur. Sur une planche, une burette en fer blanc à huile, une assiette, sur laquelle il y a une vieille croûte de pain et une fourchette et un couteau sales; plus loin, un bol en faïence; plus loin, trois à quatre assiettes les unes sur les autres. Au fond, le comptoir : une petite lampe de cuivre sans abat-jour; à droite du comptoir, du côté des assiettes, panneaux en noyer avec cadre sculpté, bordure de vigne vierge avec des bouquets de grains. La fissure de la rainure de l'armoire, qui doit contenir des choses inconnues : une branche de buis bénit. Derrière le comptoir, portes et fenêtres voilées toujours de petits rideaux blancs trop courts. Une petite porte dans la partie supérieure semble indiquer l'endroit où couche le commis de Milan. A côté, une échelle pendue au mur. Dans la boutique, une chaise en paille avec une couverture de velours d'Utrecht rouge, sur laquelle se prélasse un chat café-au-lait ardent. Un escabeau en bois et une assiette par terre, qui contient de la pâtée.'
Edmond and Jules Goncourt, *Journal*[131]

It is this mode of writing that might have been expected as the necessary development from the theories of 'Nature, humanisme, tragédie'. Here the writing is deliberately absent, the purpose of the passage is confined entirely to a notation of the real 'out there'. Its space is that of name and position or distance, and language is reduced to the zero degree of indication, literally a pointing : 'Au fond,

---

130 'Balzac dit qu'il veut peindre les hommes, les femmes et les choses. Moi . . . je soumets les hommes et les femmes aux choses.' E. Zola, *Oeuvres complètes*, Vol. 8 (Paris, 1927), p. 357.
131 ed. R. Ricatte, Vol. I (Monaco, 1956), p. 228.

le comptoir', 'Derrière le comptoir, portes et fenêtres'. The verb as
point of relation and human action has disappeared, and the verb
être has been rendered redundant by the solid presence of the scene
seen out there to which the names point : 'Chez Milan, au coin de
la rue de Beaujolais. Petite boutique.' The scene of the writing
is expelled as far as possible from the writing and the minimalization
of syntax (organization) is the movement of this exteriorization. The
writing is no more than a mirror : the organization of the passage is
outside itself in the seen and its status is thus strictly taxonomic, it
lists, it literally takes stock of the shop. Effectively, the writing here
operates to the maximum a kind of *repression of the signifié*, con-
founding meaning and thing in an extended process of ostensive
definition. Syntax creeps back only as the qualification of detail, 'Un
escabeau en bois et une assiette par terre, *qui contient de la* pâtée';
the real connections are exterior, 'A gauche', 'sur une planche', 'plus
loin'. Nouns, the names of things, abound to do justice to the scene,
over forty-five direct uses of nouns to name the elements of its composition, and their abundance indicates the self-conscious inability
of the writing, aware of its inadequacy. Nouns proliferate in front
of the scene as seen which in its limitlessness always escapes the
writing that can thus only follow in a ceaseless process of notation.
In the impossibility of *ending*, the writing simply halts. Where the
writing does define limits to its notation, it is precisely in terms of
visibility. 'La fissure de la rainure de l'armoire, qui doit contenir
des choses inconnues : une branche de buis bénit'; between the two
elements seen and noted, the unknown and unnotable because un-
seen. The aim of the passage is exactly to write, in its most immediate
vision, the scene as seen, as it presents itself to the eye.

The mode of writing employed by Robbe-Grillet in his novels
differs radically from that employed by the Goncourt brothers in
this passage from their *Journal*. Certainly 'descriptions' might be
read in, say, *Le Voyeur* or *La Jalousie* that seem to connect to and
directly develop the programme of cleansing description proposed
in 'Nature, humanisme, tragédie', as, for example, the descriptions
of the banana plantation in the latter novel, with the exact enumera-
tion of the trees. It is evident in any *reading* of the novels, however,
that these descriptions are so many elements in a very careful *composition*. Each description forms a 'discursive point' in the combination and repetition of which, with a play of variations in the repeti-
tions, the novel is accomplished. These descriptions are deliberately
defined as elements of fiction : the description of the house in *La*

Jalousie can be varied, the number of rooms changed from repetition to repetition. It is difficult to conceive of the description of the shop in the Goncourts' passage being varied, its aim being exactly the representation of a scene outside itself which guarantees its veracity. Robbe-Grillet's 'descriptions' demand to be read as elements in a composition finding their meaning there in its structure (though, as will be seen, another realist account, in addition to that of the *chosiste* reading and again aided by Robbe-Grillet himself, will be advanced to *explain* them) and something of this experience of reading will be presented later in this chapter in a brief discussion of *Dans le labyrinthe*.

The structural significance of the 'descriptions' in Robbe-Grillet's novels makes it difficult to cite a single passage here for immediate comparison with that cited from the Goncourts' *Journal*, but something of the contrast between the two modes of writing may perhaps be demonstrated in a consideration of the famous (or notorious) description of the tomato slice in *Les Gommes* :

'Un quartier de tomate en vérité sans défaut, découpé à la machine dans un fruit d'une symétrie parfaite.

'La chair périphérique, compacte et homogène, d'un beau rouge de chimie, est régulièrement épaisse entre une bande de peau luisante et la loge où sont rangés les pépins, jaunes, bien calibrés, maintenus en place par une mince couche de gelée verdâtre le long d'un renflement du coeur. Celui-ci, d'un rose atténué légèrement granuleux, débute, du côté de la dépression inférieure, par un faisceau de veines blanches, dont l'une se prolonge jusque vers les pépins—d'une façon peut-être un peu incertaine.

'Tout en haut, un accident à peine visible s'est produit : un coin de pelure, décollé de la chair sur un millimètre ou deux, se soulève imperceptiblement.'

Les Gommes, p. 151

Here, instead of a notation of the real, there is a process of writing, an *activity* of description, a figure of the accomplishment of the text. The name is here the beginning of the writing and not its culmination : 'Un quartier de tomate . . .', the name and then the description. The description, moreover, and in this it accomplishes a function in the general thematic of the text, has to be read as modification : its process is the passage from perfection ('en vérité sans défaut') to imperfection ('un accident à peine visible'). (It ought to be noted in passing that the description neither limits itself to the visible nor to the non-anthropomorphic, as witness such terms as *accident*, *coeur*, etc.). The tomato is no more than an itinerary of the writing that in the achievement of this particular point of the text provides at once an element in the experience of reading worked for by the text (the description of the tomato disrupts the reading because of its apparent *textual* insignificance; it is unconnected to what precedes or follows) and also an element, an image, in the general thematic of the book which is organized entirely round a 'gap' that is figured in this description of the tomato with its production of an accident in its very process ('un accident à peine visible s'est produit'); the 'gap' in which is produced the accident of the death of Dupont, killed by Wallas sent to investigate his murder.

v

'Mais je n'ai pensé qu'à y mettre de la subjectivité!'
ALAIN ROBBE-GRILLET

The problem of reading posed by the novels offered in the very terms of its posing an easy and ready solution that Robbe-Grillet himself had no difficulty in himself apparently accepting, if not actually inspiring. If description in Robbe-Grillet's novels does not name the object in all its smooth object-ness, but, in its minute itinerary, pushes the object into the realm of the composition of the writing, finally destroying it, as the tomato slice is flawed in the passage of the writing, what can be the explanation? The answer comes 'naturally': far from objectively and neutrally presenting objects in and for themselves, quietly cleansed of human significance, the writing uses objects in the representation of the *discourse of the obsessional*.[132] Robbe-Grillet, champion of extreme objectivity, becomes the writer of extreme subjectivity; the innocence of description becomes the guilt of paranoia, and the process of explaining the novels can be set in motion. It would be difficult to date exactly this shift in emphasis with regard to Robbe-Grillet's own formulations of his intentions and of the object of the research in what he understood as the nouveau roman, but 1959 would be roughly accurate to the limited extent to which Robbe-Grillet's theoretical positions

---

[132] Cf. Didier Anzieu, 'Le discours de l'obsessionnel dans les romans de Robbe-Grillet', *Les Temps Modernes* No. 233, October 1965, pp. 608–37.

are available to this kind of chronological description.[133] The crucial exposition of the new theoretical emphasis is the introduction to the *ciné-roman*, *L'Année dernière à Marienbad* published in 1961.[134] Describing the affinity he felt between his own work and that of the director of the film Alain Resnais, Robbe-Grillet indicates as central to that feeling of affinity their common attempt to *'construire un espace et un temps purement mentaux'*. (*L'Année dernière à Marienbad*, pp. 9–10). In an interview published in the same month in which the introduction appeared in *Réalités* Robbe-Grillet declared that 'La subjectivité est je crois—et contrairement à ce qu'on pense d'habitude—la caractéristique *essentielle* de ce qu'on a appelé le nouveau roman',[135] and in an extended theoretical essay published that same year Robbe-Grillet insisted categorically on the total subjectivity at the heart of the nouveau roman; '*Le Nouveau Roman ne vise qu'à une subjectivité totale*' (*Pour un Nouveau Roman*, p. 117). The supposed objectivity of his novels ('une intention que me prête la critique'[136]) is characterized as a complete misapprehension :

'Le mot de *littérature objective* que Roland Barthes appliquait alors à mes romans, s'entendait dans un sens très particulier et qu'il définissait lui-même dès les premières lignes de son étude : il s'agissait d'une littérature tournée vers l'objet, ce qui ne l'empêchait nullement d'être tout à fait subjective, comme on l'a remarqué par la suite.'[137]

There is no question that Barthes did indeed thus define *objective* and that Robbe-Grillet himself used the term on occasion in stipulating this sense after Barthes,[138] but there is equally no question that

[133] The general terms of the discussion of *La Jalousie* (1957) are also important here, and Robbe-Grillet's cover-note for that novel is, as it were, one 'opening' to the 'new' Robbe-Grillet.

[134] The *ciné-roman* appeared in the latter half of that year but the introduction had already been published under the title 'Alain Robbe-Grillet vous parle de l'*Année dernière à Marienbad*' in May in the magazine *Réalités*, No. 184, pp. 95–8, 111–5.

[135] *Le Monde*, 13 May 1961, p. 9 (my italics).

[136] (Interview) *L'Express*, 8 October 1959, p. 32.

[137] 'La littérature aujourd'hui VI', *Tel Quel*, No. 14, Spring 1963, p. 41. (Robbe-Grillet is referring to the first of Barthes's articles, 'Littérature objective'; cf. *Essais critiques*, p. 29.)

[138] Cf. e.g. 'Révolution dans le roman', *Le Figaro Littéraire*, 29 March 1958, p. 9. 'Relation objective, précisez-le, ne signifiant pas impartiale, mais tournée vers l'objet.' It seems that Robbe-Grillet now has to dissociate himself from his original *chosiste* emphasis by dissociating himself from Barthes's essays : in 1970 he comments, 'Barthes a abouti à une véritable distorsion de mon oeuvre'; (interview) *Les Nouvelles Littéraires*, 5 February 1970, p. 2. This is to repudiate his own confusion by transferring it to Barthes, but it was never the latter who was confused, as his distinction in 1959 between the notion of the presentation of things and the accomplishment of an 'être-là du langage littéraire' and his connection of Robbe-Grillet's novels with the latter makes clear; *Essais critiques*, p. 106.

there *is* a real shift in emphasis on Robbe-Grillet's part, a shift that is a part of the confusion of his theoretical writings and not a simple misunderstanding on the part of his critics, however much they may have misunderstood his novels. If the idea of 'un regard tourné vers l'objet' is central to 'Nature, humanisme, tragédie' it is in terms of the emphasis brought out above in Section II on its 'pouvoir laveur', its capacity to register the distances of the objects themselves and thus, through its visual objectivity, to establish the separation between man and the world of things on which the new 'humanism' is to be based. This emphasis had, to say the least, been radically modified by the time of such formulations as the following :

'Non seulement c'est un homme qui, dans mes romans par exemple, décrit toute chose, mais c'est le moins neutre, le moins impartial des hommes; engagé au contraire *toujours* dans une aventure passionnelle des plus obsédantes, au point de déformer souvent sa vision.'
Pour un Nouveau Roman, pp. 117–8

The mode of this deforming vision in *La Jalousie*, following Robbe-Grillet's own account of the reality of that novel is the very geometrical description of objects and their distances which in 'Nature, humanisme, tragédie' had been proposed as the authentic non-anthropomorphical, non-deforming mode of the report of 'le pouvoir laveur du regard'. Thus, the mode of complicity being exactly the mode previously distinguished as that of non-complicity, it is hardly possible to take the novels, as some critics have done, as 'cautionary tales', demonstrations after the early theories of the fate that awaits those who enter into complicity with objects. Paradoxically, the emphasis on description as against sense, the desire to provide a presentation of non-significant objects for contemplation, opens the way to the abundance of sense. *Everything* remains to be interpreted and sense becomes obsession, the function of the repetition of the insignificant.[139] In the recurrence of the figure-of-eight in *Le Voyeur* or the counting of the banana tree in *La Jalousie* we must (the realist imperative) attend to the discourse of paranoia. Robbe-Grillet *chosiste* is really Robbe-Grillet novelist of the subjective world of the pathologically disturbed, a change and a recuperation which the shift of emphasis in his own theories supports.

The new *realism* that was the aim of 'Nature, humanisme, tragédie' is equally the watchword of the novelist of subjectivity.

139 Cf. Bernard Pingaud, *Inventaire* (Paris, 1965), p. 151.

There is no call for surprise at this application of *realism* now to the one, now to the other, for the theoretical justification of the realism of the subjective emphasis is based on exactly the same set of premisses as that of the justification of the objective emphasis of 'Nature, humanisme, tragédie', and the new theoretical basis, contrary to popular belief, is, in fact, equally alien to the thinking of existential phenomenology. The theory, then, is fully expounded in the introduction to *L'Année dernière à Marienbad*. The images of novel or film are the images of the mental world of the characters, the succession of such images being, indeed, a person's life :

'Les souvenirs que l'on "revoit", les régions lointaines, les rencontres à venir, ou même les épisodes passés que chacun arrange dans sa tête en en modifiant le cours tout à loisir, il y a là comme un film intérieur qui se déroule continuellement en nous-mêmes dès que nous cessons de prêter attention à ce qui se passe autour de nous. Mais, à d'autres moments, nous enregistrons, au contraire, par tous nos sens, ce monde extérieur qui se trouve bel et bien sous nos yeux. *Ainsi le film total de notre esprit admet à la fois tour à tour et au même titre les fragments réels proposés à l'instant par la vue et l'ouïe, et des fragments passés, ou lointains, ou futurs, ou totalement fantasmagoriques.*'
  p. 16 (my italics)

This is the so-called *magic-lantern* view of consciousness of classic materialism,[140] which once again reveals itself as an underlying presence in Robbe-Grillet's theoretical work and which, as was emphasized above, was a crucial point of critique for existential phenomenology. The idea of the 'film total de notre esprit' depends on the very refusal of the phenomenological insight of the intentionality of consciousness that characterized the development of the idea of the 'pouvoir laveur du regard'. Consciousness, conceived as passive, can be regarded as *filled with* images (of equal status, admitted *au même titre*, whether perceptions of the present, memories of the past, anticipations of the future, fantasies, hallucinations, or whatever) that flicker across the screen of the mind like the frames of a film. The mind is thus, in Taine's expression (Taine, indeed, is a crucial reference for the tradition in which Robbe-Grillet places himself with this kind of theory), 'un polypier d'images'.[141] Whence

---

140 '. . . our Ideas do while we are awake, succeed one another in our Minds at certain Distances, not much unlike the Images in the inside of a Lanthorn, turned round by the Heat of a Candle.' Locke, *An Essay Concerning Human Understanding*, II. XIV. 9. (London, 1710), I, p. 143.
141 H. Taine, *De l'Intelligence* (Paris, 1870), Vol. I, p. 139.

117

arises the problem central to classical thinking about perception, namely the problem of distinguishing different types of images all of which, in principle, have exactly the same status as images in the mind. Robbe-Grillet, giving a Berkleyan precision to the mental images in his theory, collapses the problem in the simple equation of reality and imagination in the perpetual present of the image : 'ce qui caractérise l'homme c'est que sa vie réelle est imaginaire . . . Notre réalité, c'est notre imagination.'[142] *La Jalousie* can thus claim a faithful realism in its rendering without discrimination of the *presence* of the images that are the mental life of the husband 'point-of-view'. The opposition of all this to existential phenomenological thinking about consciousness is clear. If the mind contains a set of images then there can be no place for the concept of intentionality which breaks against their presence *in* consciousness, but, as Sartre pointed out in his early critique of this kind of theory, 'Il n'y a pas, il ne saurait y avoir d'images *dans* la conscience . . . *l'image est un certain type de conscience*. L'image est un acte et non une chose. L'image est conscience *de* quelque chose.'[143] In a famous passage, to which Sartre refers in his work, Alain demonstrated the fallacy of assuming the same status equally for present perception of a thing and the attempt to image that thing in the mind in its absence :

'Beaucoup ont, comme ils disent, dans leur mémoire, l'image du Panthéon et la font aisément paraître, à ce qu'il leur semble. Je leur demande, alors, de bien vouloir compter les colonnes qui portent le fronton; or non seulement ils ne peuvent pas les compter, mais ils ne peuvent même pas l'essayer. Or cette opération est la plus simple du monde, dès qu'ils ont le Panthéon réel devant les yeux.'[144]

Sartre insists on the fact that there is no confusion between thing perceived and image in everyday experience.[145] The image is a certain manner of posing experience (an act) and is present to consciousness, intended, as such. This is a revaluation of traditional

142 (Interview) *Le Figaro Littéraire*, 7–13 October 1965, p. 3.
143 *L'Imagination* (Paris, 1936), p. 162.
144 Alain, *Système des beaux-arts* (Paris, 1964), p. 338.
145 *L'Imagination*, p. 3. Merleau-Ponty points out in *Phénoménologie de la perception* that the hallucinations of pathological subjects are not lived as though of the same status as real perceptions; a point worth bearing in mind in considering the claims for the realism of Robbe-Grillet's novels made by critics in terms of their representation of pathological states of mind. It may be remembered here that Taine finally reduces all perception to hallucination in a way close to Robbe-Grillet's emphasis in this 'subjective period': 'la perception extérieure, même véridique, est une hallucination'. *De l'Intelligence*, Vol. II, p. 6.

theories that owes its impetus to the work of Husserl : [after Husserl] 'l'image cesse d'être un *contenu* psychique : elle n'est pas *dans* la conscience à titre d'élément constituant; mais dans la conscience d'une chose *en image*.'[146] If this upsets not only the claims made for a phenomenological basis to these theories of Robbe-Grillet's, but also the claim to realism of the subjective emphasis in the novels, this latter claim is in any case refuted by the novels themselves in the terms of the realistic explanation that is proposed for them in which they are described not as offering a realistic fidelity to the film of ordinary human perception, but, symptomatically, a realistic fidelity to (a representation of) *pathological* states of mind.

It is, in fact, evident that Robbe-Grillet has never completely accepted realist interpretations of his novels as representing obsessional states of mind, nor, indeed, the similar interpretations of his films. *Marienbad*, explicable for many critics as representation of hallucination and dream, *retrievable* as such, is seen by Robbe-Grillet as a failure precisely in so far as it lends itself to this possibility of *explanation* : 'J'avais été gêné moi-même par ce côté "onirique" que j'avais donné à Marienbad,' he commented in the course of a colloquium some years later, and he went on to stress that 'Le récit moderne, qu'il soit dans le roman ou dans le cinéma, affirme l'invention. Les personnages sont des fictions; ils ne sont que des fictions, et c'est leur caractère fictif qui est justement le sujet même de l'oeuvre.'[147] In a lecture given in 1960 he was able to treat the composition of *La Jalousie* as a matter of greater importance than the situation of the jealous husband which is now seen as no more than a prop for the accomplishment of the writing,[148] and in his cover note for Morrissette's *Les Romans de Robbe-Grillet*, a study which defined Robbe-Grillet's achievement in terms of representation of the obsessional, Robbe-Grillet writes, with evident irony : 'Ce livre . . . nous permet de découvrir, autant et peut-être mieux encore que "l'objet" du débat, le "sujet" qui le dirige.'

Morrissette's book played a fundamental part in the critical revaluation of the initial notion of Robbe-Grillet *chosiste*, it marked

[146] Ibid., p. 146.
[147] 'Table ronde'. *Cahiers internationaux de symbolisme*, Nos 9–10, 1965–1966, pp. 99–100.
[148] Cf. Jean Ricardou, 'Description et infraconscience chez Alain Robbe-Grillet', *Nouvelle Nouvelle Revue Française*, November 1960, p. 898: 'Lors d'une récente conférence présentée à la Maison des Lettres, Robbe-Grillet expliquait à propos de ce roman qu'il avait appliqué, *par exemple* à un jaloux, un postulat technique . . .'

the moment of the appearance, as Barthes noted in the preface he provided for the book, of the second Robbe-Grillet, and, as Barthes also noted, though a brilliant piece of constitution of sense, Morrissette's analysis reduced the radical experience of Robbe-Grillet's texts.[149] Morrissette's reading of Robbe-Grillet is a quest for meaning, an activity of *fixation* that operates against what might be called the *textuality* of his work. It reduces the plurality of the work in the name of a representational readability :

'le *premier* effort du critique doit être *avant d'aborder les problèmes de structure, de dégager la ligne rationnelle qui relie les éléments de l'action.*'[150]

The action is grasped outside and before the complexity of the textual structuration which is thus reduced to the locus of a *precedent*, of a line of rationality that the critic will reinstate in its original unity, assimilate into the world of the already read, in order to read the novels. A priori the text is explicable and explicated, 'le premier effort' : the writing is no more than a posterior function of the explication and Morrissette has no hesitation in abandoning it in order to get back to the more comfortable area of the rational. He thus spends a large number of pages in his book literally telling the story which Robbe-Grillet's novels 'hide', disengaging that rational line of action which they distort, and the result is necessarily the fixation of the texts in a final sense, a final explanation :

'Dans *Les Gommes*, le complexe d'Oedipe relie et explique toute l'intrigue; dans *La Jalousie* les liaisons entre scènes procèdent d'une obsession paranoïaque qui transforme le soupçon en folie délirante; le soldat de *Dans le labyrinthe* est atteint d'une sorte d'amnésie, etc.'[151]

This is basically the same mode of reading that the 'Balzacian novel' commands : a reading as realist writing that proceeds by the recovery from the text of a narrative truth. But Robbe-Grillet's novels offer precisely an attempt to *recover the text itself*, in the same way that Robbe-Grillet insists on the recovery in reading of the text in Kafka. In Morrissette's account the text is nowhere, the problems of structure are left aside until the explication is complete. The implications of this are brought out clearly in a startling passage in Morrissette's account of *La Jalousie* :

149 Cf. Roland Barthes, *Essais critiques*, p. 202.

150 *Les Romans de Robbe-Grillet*, p. 84 (my italics). It may be that Morrissette is now modifying his approach to Robbe-Grillet's texts: cf. 'Games and games structures in Robbe-Grillet', *Yale French Studies*, 1968, No. 41, pp. 159–67.

151 Ibid., p. 102.

'Que fait le mari, après ces visions angoissantes? Passe-t-il la nuit dans le lit même de A. sur lequel il imagine la jeune femme étendue dans une posture érotique? Se livre-t-il à des pratiques solitaires? *Un texte allusif permet de tout supposer*.'[152]

It is, however, exactly the non-allusiveness of the Robbe-Grillet text in this sense (which is not the same as saying that the Robbe-Grillet text is not founded on a plurality) that is so striking. In any *reading* there is nothing to suppose because everything is given in the *composition* of the text, the play of its writing. Morrissette achieves not a *reading*, but a *recovery* of the text into a *vraisemblable* the quality of which is sufficiently demonstrated in the passage just cited. The insistence here must be that the divorce between Robbe-Grillet and Balzac *is* radical and it is to be understood at this level of the *textuality* of their work. It is the *practice* of writing that is the crucial project of the research of the Robbe-Grillet text.

VI

'L'importance de Robbe-Grillet, on la mesure à la question que son oeuvre pose à toute oeuvre qui lui est contemporaine. Question profondément *critique*, touchant des possibilités du langage . . .'
MICHEL FOUCAULT

It is at the level of the experience of reading Robbe-Grillet's texts that the essential nature of his project of research may be understood, a project that is fundamentally *critical*. The difficulty of the separate critical theories expounded by Robbe-Grillet (in all their various forms) is their transference of the criticism operated in the actual practice of writing to a generalized description that is non-contemporaneous with the achieved texts. The reality of the novel-texts is transformed in a process of reduction into the theory of 'Nature, humanisme, tragédie' or into that of the introduction to *L'Année dernière à Marienbad*; a transformation that hides (and

---

[152] Ibid., p. 120 (my italics). One is reminded somewhat of the excesses L. C. Knights tried to counter in his *How many children had Lady Macbeth?*, (Cambridge, 1933). Excesses have indeed followed Morrissette's book in the discussion of Robbe-Grillet's work. A fine example, to which reference will be made later, is provided by Ben F. Stoltzfus in his *Alain Robbe-Grillet and the New French Novel* (Carbondale 1964).

121

apparently to Robbe-Grillet himself at these times) the fact that at the centre of his work lies the exploration of the activities of writing and reading, of their intelligibility—the central emphasis noted by Roland Barthes (as also, parenthetically, the danger of its transformation), in a passage qualifying the demystification by Robbe-Grillet of 'les qualités prétendues naturelles de la littérature d'introspection (le *profond* étant de droit préférable au *superficiel*) au profit d'un *être-là* du texte (qu'il ne faut surtout pas confondre avec *l'être-là* de la chose même).[153] It is this process of transformation and the subsequent to-and-fro between 'objective' and 'subjective' poles of *explanation* ('une dialectique de l'erreur qui fonctionne mécaniquement', as Sollers put it in his review of *Pour un Nouveau Roman*[154]) that Robbe-Grillet is able to acknowledge in 1963 as his having fallen prey to *'l'illusion réaliste'* :

'Mais je sais bien que mon propos est ailleurs. Je ne transcris pas, je construis. C'était déjà la vieille ambition de Flaubert : bâtir quelque chose à partir de rien, qui tienne debout tout seul sans avoir à s'appuyer sur quoi que ce soit d'extérieur à l'oeuvre; c'est aujourd'hui l'ambition de tout le roman.'
Pour un Nouveau Roman, p. 139[155]

Thus Robbe-Grillet can recognize the 'subjective' explanations of his novels as inadequate simplifications even if he himself has appeared to encourage them, as, for instance, in his cover note to *La Jalousie* : 'c'est peut-être pour simplifier les choses que j'ai écrit moi-même au dos du livre que le personnage principal était le mari qui surveillait sa femme.'[156]

This new critical awareness is not by any means absent from Robbe-Grillet's earliest theoretical writings. It can be traced clearly enough in the rejection, centred on the notions of *personnage* and *histoire*, of the narrative organization of the traditional 'Balzacian' novel which is regarded by Robbe-Grillet as a fundamental mode of the intelligibility of a particular social order in the process of the *naturalization* of which the novel form has been complicit. The stable order of the narrative resting on a rationality assured by a

---

153 *Essais critiques*, p. 200.
154 *Tel Quel* No. 18, Summer 1964, p. 93.
155 Robbe-Grillet is referring to a passage in a letter by Flaubert to Louise Colet: 'Ce qui me semble beau, ce que je voudrais faire, c'est un livre sur rien, un livre sans attache extérieure, qui se tiendrait de lui-même par la force interne de son style.' 16 January 1852, *Correspondance* (Conard edition, Deuxième série, Paris, 1926), p. 345.
156 'Table ronde', p. 106.

whole generalized social code, the text ending in the definite truth of a conclusion, the fixed stability implied in the notion of a 'character' (defined precisely in the achievement of an *atextuality*, a reading out of the text) together with the whole series of underlying values supporting these 'natural' elements of narrative, are called into question in the Robbe-Grillet text. These conventions are challenged as such: 'Bien raconter, c'est faire ressembler ce que l'on écrit aux schémas préfabriqués dont les gens ont l'habitude, c'est-à-dire à l'idée toute faite qu'ils ont de la réalité.' (*Pour un Nouveau Roman*, p. 30.) It is here that Robbe-Grillet is close to Sartre, for the statement of the inauthenticity of living the forms of coherence provided by traditional modes of narration is central to *La Nausée* with its recognition, in Roquentin's phrase, that 'il faut choisir: vivre ou raconter'.[157] 'Raconter', says Robbe-Grillet, 'est devenu proprement impossible.' (*Pour un Nouveau Roman*, p. 31.) The Autodidacte in Sartre's novel yearns for a life of *aventures*,[158] while Anny has tried to live her life in the creation of a series of *moments parfaits* or *situations privilégiées*;[159] both are ways of not living the present, of falsifying and fleeing from man's existential situation by their provision of the illusion of a fixed essence in which he can take refuge from the responsibility of his freedom.[160] The rejection of narrative is the rejection of 'mauvaise foi': symptomatically, Roquentin ceases to write the life of the Marquis de Rollebon.

It is the 'natural' modes of narrative organization that Robbe-Grillet is contesting at the level of the limits of writing, of the opposition readable/unreadable, and this attempt, from the traditional standpoint of the absention of writing, places him outside the terms

157 *La Nausée*, p. 57.
158 Ibid., p. 53.
159 Ibid., pp. 180f.
160 There is a critique of Proust at work in the presentation of Anny. In the light of moments of happiness experienced in childhood (and the volume of Michelet's *Histoire de France* with its engravings plays something of the same role for her as *François le Champi* for the Proustian narrator), Anny attempts to transform life into a succession of such moments ('En somme, c'était une sorte d'oeuvre d'art', comments Roquentin: p. 187). This involves, however, a continual existence in the past and of the present and future as if they were past, already the series of *moments parfaits* which are to be salvaged in the life of the memory—a position fully recognized by Proust: 'j'allais être enrichi de cette pure substance de nous-mêmes qu'est une impression passée, de la vie pure conservée, car en ce moment où nous la vivons elle ne se présente pas à notre mémoire, mais au milieu des sensations qui la suppriment.' *Contre Sainte-Beuve* (Paris, 1954), p. 55. For the Proustian narrator, however, these moments represent not an end, but the beginning of a textual work, a *reading* of his reality, 'la seule vie par conséquent réellement vécue.' This is perhaps not clearly grasped in Sartre's various critiques of Proust.

of any *realism*. His work depends on the denaturalization of modes of writing:

> 'Désormais . . . c'est le roman lui-même qui se pense, se met en cause et se juge; non pas par l'intermédiaire de personnages se livrant à d'oiseux commentaires; mais par une réflexion constante, au niveau du récit et de l'écriture, de chaque élément sur soi-même; gestes, objets, ou situations.'[161]

This passage is of cardinal importance (it is to be noted that it dates from 1955): as Robbe-Grillet insists, it is not a question of clever tricks with novelists inside novels, after the manner of Gide or Huxley, (though in his work as a cinéaste he has not been altogether averse to such tricks himself), but of *'le roman lui-même qui se pense'* : thus, *'L'aventure dans mes romans peut être l'aventure d'une écriture'*.[162] The emphasis on writing signifies the retrieval of the text from its absence as a kind of figurative analogue of the 'Real', in fact as a repetition of a naturalized text. It is against this absence that Robbe-Grillet's novels work, whence their specificity, the *être-là* of the text noted by Barthes ('L'oeuvre d'art est une forme vivante : elle *est*'. *Pour un Nouveau Roman*, p. 41), together with the stress on its irrecuperability into the terms of traditional reading, a stress that Robbe-Grillet formulates with reference to Flaubert's ambition to accomplish 'un livre sur rien'; 'l'oeuvre doit s'imposer comme nécessaire, mais nécessaire *pour rien*; son architecture est sans emploi; sa force est une force inutile'. (Ibid., p. 43.) Such a formulation may itself be misleading : Robbe-Grillet's work is always a work *from*, and this is the point of its *critical* project, it is not 'sur rien', but an exploration of conventions, of modes of discourse. His work operates at the level of the *suspension of sense*, refusing to take for granted accepted forms of writing but questioning and demonstrating them in a construction the aim of which is the hesitation of their received sense. Robbe-Grillet expresses this operation in speaking of the literary text as being *anterior* to sense : 'L'important n'est pas qu'un roman *veuille dire* quelque chose : c'est qu'il *soit* quelque chose, sans s'occuper de rien signifier';[163] 'dès qu'apparaît le souci de signifier quelque chose . . . la littérature

---

[161] 'Pourquoi la mort du roman?' p. 8.
[162] 'De *Marienbad* à *L'Immortelle*', (interview) *Le Figaro Littéraire*, 1 September 1962, p. 9. In 1957, discussing *Les Gommes* and *Le Voyeur*, Robbe-Grillet writes, 'le mouvement de l'écriture y est plus important que celui des passions et des crimes.' *Pour un Nouveau Roman*, p. 32.
[163] *L'Express*, 8 October 1959, p. 32.

commence à reculer, à disparaître.' (*Pour un Nouveau Roman*, p. 39.) The novel is a construction which, in its activity on conventional received forms, accomplishes an equilibrium, a plurality of interacting elements all the purpose of which is in the 'tension' of their relations, lacking any fixed final sense. 'Il crée lui-même son propre équilibre et pour lui-même son propre sens.' (Ibid., p. 42.) The terms connected with notions of game and play that Robbe-Grillet today uses almost exclusively to describe his work are expressions of this activity of questioning, contesting, revealing, exploring, demonstrating the limits of, the possibilities of, *playing* with conventional forms.

In this activity of hovering conventional forms (of writing them as such), description is crucial, and finds its function in Robbe-Grillet's writing in terms of its *textual work* and not at all in terms of its non-anthropomorphic presentation of the world of things. Parallel to the theory of cleansing geometrical description, Robbe-Grillet develops a radical theory of the nature and effect of literary description which is a complete revaluation and critique of his former position. The extent of the revaluation can be seen, dramatically enough, in the reassessment of the benefit to be derived by the writer from photography :

'La photographie m'est-elle utile en tant qu'écrivain? Je vous répondrai qu'il n'y a aucun rapport entre une description et une image. L'image montre, la description détruit.'[164]

Photography which had been the key for modern literature in its attempts at description ('maintenant on *voit* la chaise') is now regarded as directly opposed to those attempts ('il n'y a aucun rapport . . .'). Moreover, description which in 'Nature, humanisme, tragédie' had been seen as having the function of recording distances and, in so doing, placing the object 'out there' before the reader, free from contamination, is now defined as destructive and the idea of description as representing image is set aside as inadequate by virtue of the very fact of its representation, the fact that it *shows* things. 'L'image, prise isolément, ne peut que faire voir, à l'instar de la description balzacienne et semblerait donc faite au contraire pour remplacer celle-ci, ce dont le cinéma naturaliste ne se prive pas, du reste.' (Ibid., p. 128.) A further indication of the extent of the revaluation emerges here, for Balzac, one-time destroyer of the *être-là*

[164] 'Des écrivains chasseurs d'images', (interview) *Arts* No. 890, 14–20 November 1962, p. 3.

of things by shrouding them in significance in his descriptions, is now regarded as having precisely *shown* things in these descriptions. The passage just cited repeats the assessment of Balzac in these terms made a little earlier by Robbe-Grillet in the same article:

'Reconnaissons d'abord que la description n'est pas une invention moderne. Le grand roman français du XIXe siècle en particulier, Balzac en tête, regorge de maisons, de mobiliers, de costumes, longuement, minutieusement décrits, sans compter les visages, les corps, etc. *Et il est certain que ces descriptions-là ont pour but de faire voir et qu'elles y réussissent.*'
Ibid., p 125 (my italics)

Though Robbe-Grillet does indeed go on to point out the *significant relation* of these descriptions to the characters of the classic nineteenth-century novels, the fact that he now connects Balzacian description with the power successfully to *faire voir les choses*, the power of the photograph as it had been central to the programme of 'Nature, humanisme, tragédie', is still sufficiently startling. The culmination of this theoretical dissociation from the idea of description to be found in that programme comes in the course of an article by Robbe-Grillet published in the *Revue d'Esthétique* in 1967:

'J'ai déjà eu l'occasion de dire à quel point toute description littéraire —d'un objet, d'une scène, d'un geste, d'un décor—était pour moi radicalement différente non seulement des choses réelles (c'est-à-dire celles que l'on peut toucher, saisir, utiliser, traverser, etc.), mais aussi, et même tout autant sinon davantage, des diverses images à deux dimensions qui en reproduisent pour l'oeil le contour apparent : dessin, photographie, plan du cinéma.'[165]

This revaluation is the corollary of the elaboration of a theory of description in terms of its textual function linked to the idea of the discourse of literature as a suspension of sense. (Important formulations of such a theory are to be found in the work of Roland Barthes and Jean Ricardou, with which it is clear Robbe-Grillet is acquainted.) Description is seen as a mode of destruction (of sense) or, more exactly, as a process of simultaneous creation-destruction. Here lies the importance for Robbe-Grillet of the work of Raymond Roussel in which he finds a '*recherche* qui détruit elle-même, par l'écriture, son propre objet' (*Pour un Nouveau Roman*, p. 74):

165 'Brèves réflexions sur le fait de décrire une scène de cinéma', *Revue d'Esthétique*, 1967, Nos. 2-3, p. 131.

'La description littéraire est créatrice-destructrice, elle n'est pas descriptive. La phrase n'est pas un compte-rendu sur un objet qui existerait avant et en dehors d'elle. Si au XIXe siècle, la description balzacienne prétend parler du monde, la description moderne sait qu'elle ne décrit rien que soi-même.'[166]

The importance of the 'object' becomes clear in this context. Barthes, describing the character of the object as a discursive point in Robbe-Grillet's novels, spoke of its function as a *résistance optique*,[167] but it has to be understood that this resistance is operative *literally* at the level of the progress of the writing as grasped in the experience of reading. It might be better perhaps to speak of its function in terms of a *résistance scripturale*. The acknowledgement by Robbe-Grillet of Flaubert as precursor in this connection is just:[168] the description of Charles Bovary's cap, or that of the hideous toy he offers the Homais children ('l'incroyable cadeau de M. Bovary'[169]), evidently stress the character of Monsieur Bovary,[170] but they seem to overstep the limits of this function and in a certain manner to congeal the free flow of the narrative into a surface the hard presence of which, in its literality, stops short the reading of the novel.[171] Flaubert also obtains this effect with his placing of single words, as, for example, as has often been pointed out, in the final sentence of *Hérodias* describing the carrying of John the Baptist's head—'Comme elle était très lourde, ils la portaient alternativement',[172]—where the position of the adverb 'alternativement', a kind of hyperbaton, *fixes* the reading at an unexpected level of textual presence, in some sort 'unbalancing' the sense. It would be worth looking in this respect at Robbe-Grillet's use of the adverb 'imperceptiblement' at the close of the description of the tomato slice in *Les Gommes*.

It is at this textual level that Robbe-Grillet's description is so *decep-*

166 (Interview) *L'Express*, 1–7 April 1968, p. 46.
167 *Essais critiques*, p. 30.
168 'Il y a chez Flaubert une amorce de ce qu'on pourrait appeler la présence de l'objet dans la littérature moderne.' 'Révolution dans le roman?', p. 7.
169 This description figures only in the original version of *Madame Bovary*: cf. *Madame Bovary: Nouvelle version, précédée des scénarios inédits*, ed. J. Pommier and G. Leleu (Paris, 1949), p. 458.
170 Cf. Flaubert's insistence in a letter to Sainte-Beuve on the direct integration of his descriptions with characters and action: 'Il n'y a point dans mon livre une description isolée, gratuite; toutes *servent* à mes personnages et ont une influence lointaine ou immédiate sur l'action.' 23–24 December 1862, *Correspondance*, Cinquième série (Paris, 1929), pp. 60–1.
171 Cf. George Steiner, *Tolstoy or Dostoevsky* (London, 1960), pp. 50–1.
172 *Oeuvres* (Pléiade edition), II, p. 634.

tive in contrast to the effect of stability produced in the process of naming in the passage from the Goncourts' *Journal*. The writing of the tomato slice is decisively and derisively literal. The description reveals itself and thus, in a central image of Robbe-Grillet's writing, it is a 'rubbing out' of sense : 'lorsque la description prend fin, on s'aperçoit qu'elle n'a rien laissé debout derrière elle : elle s'est accomplie dans un double mouvement de création et de gommage, que l'on retrouve d'ailleurs dans le livre à tous les niveaux et en particulier dans sa structure globale—d'où vient la *déception* inhérente aux oeuvres d'aujourd'hui.' (*Pour un Nouveau Roman*, p. 127.) That the vestiges of anecdotal organization in Robbe-Grillet's novels should run into images of murder and rape does not surprise, for the deception worked through the destructive figure of description offers a violence imaged by the tear that appears in the flesh of the tomato in the trace of the writing, a violent disruption of the expectations of convention.[173] What is in question is not the presence of the object in the sense in which this was proposed in 'Nature, humanisme, tragédie', but the presence of the writing which 'comes to the surface' in the activity of description : 'les objets sont le support d'une parole s'enroulant autour d'eux; on ne voit pas plus mes objets qu'on n'entend la sonate de Vinteuil.'[174] The surface is not the 'out there' of some thing described, but the presence of the adventure of the writing, taken in a self-reflection ('un roman lui-même qui se pense') that gives the fundamental work on the possibilities of language :

'La phrase littéraire est aussi abstraite que l'équation mathématique, aussi vide et aussi pure. Je peux écrire : "Il y a un verre sur la table", alors qu'il n'y a pas de verre, pas de table, rien . . .'[175]

The acknowledgement is that of Sterne's Dr Shandy when he demonstrates to the awed Trim that he can talk meaningfully of a white bear even though he may never have seen one. It is the acknowledgement that language offers a semantic *system* and it is important to Robbe-Grillet for its emphasis of the possibilities of *fiction* that are to be explored through the research on those accepted

173 Cf. Roland Barthes: 'le *non* au sens, qui est le contraire même du non-sens, ne peut avoir qu'un effet de violence, tant les signes, quels qu'ils soient, sont en définitive rassurants pour l'homme.' 'Préface', *Catalogue de l'Exposition Emmanuel Pereire* (Paris 1965) (non-paginated).

174 *Les Nouvelles Littéraires*, 5 February 1970, p. 2.

175 *L'Express*, 1–7 April 1968, p. 46. Cf. 'Brèves réflexions sur le fait de décrire une scène de cinéma', p. 135.

modes of fiction through which we have learned to define our lives.

Robbe-Grillet's remark directly echoes a similar remark by Jean Ricardou, itself in turn an echo of a remark by William James ('il faut sans cesse répéter que le mot couteau ne coupe pas ou qu'on ne dort pas dans le mot lit, que le couteau ou le lit d'une fiction ne sont pas les *choses mêmes*.'[176]), and in a series of brilliant articles collected in a section of his *Problèmes du Nouveau Roman* entitled 'Problèmes de la description' Ricardou explores the nature of literary description in terms of a process of creation-destruction very close to that proposed as its prime reality by Robbe-Grillet. It was Ricardou who provided an accompanying commentary for the fragment of Robbe-Grillet's first novel *Le Régicide*, written between 1948 and 1950 and so far unpublished in its entirety, that appeared in 1962 in the short-lived review *Médiations*.[177] Ricardou noted the confusion in Robbe-Grillet's work between what according to the conventional expectations of anecdotal realism would be the real and the imaginary or imagined : the murderer awaiting the arrival of his victim remembers a previous scene on the beach with his girlfriend and recreates that scene imaginatively, but the text offers both scenes at the same status of presence without any explanatory indications such as would conventionally be found in realist writing. It has been seen that the emphasis of the 'second Robbe-Grillet' provides a way of recuperating this confusion (of real and imaginary) for a realist reading in terms of a particular theory of perception, but that this recuperation and its premisses are false to the reality of the experience of reading Robbe-Grillet and recognized as such by Robbe-Grillet himself. The very terms employed by Ricardou, the idea of a confusion between the real and the imagined, are perhaps (potentially) misleading in the possibility they give of conceiving the text as a story to be reassembled in the redemarcation of the elements it confounds. The Robbe-Grillet text proposes not the representation of a confused experience, but the construction of a fiction. (It might be noted that for *L'Année dernière à Marienbad*, the work most deeply implicated in the explanation of his works as representations of the mental life of a central character, Robbe-Grillet planned a series of false *fondus* in order to destroy completely the possibility of this kind of explanation, but Resnais apparently suppressed

[176] Jean Ricardou, *Problèmes du Nouveau Roman*, p. 13.
[177] *Médiations*, Summer 1962: Alain Robbe-Grillet, 'Un régicide', pp. 5–16; Jean Ricardou, 'Par-delà le réel et l'irréel', pp. 17–25.

them.[178]) Anecdotal time is abandoned, and this is not to be understood simply as the jumbling of the sequences of a basic story. A novel such as Conrad's *Lord Jim* has an intricate and complex narrative organization but within the complexity of that organization, and while recognizing the effect of that complexity for the meaning of the book, the reader can read a basic narrative sequence which he is able to reassemble in his reading. Robbe-Grillet's novels, despite the attempts of Bruce Morrissette and his less responsible successors, are not available to this kind of reading.[179] This is what Robbe-Grillet insists on when he talks of the atemporality of the nouveau roman : 'dans le récit moderne, on dirait que le temps se trouve coupé de sa temporalité. Il ne coule plus.' (*Pour un Nouveau Roman*, p. 133.) His emphasis is on the *présent perpétuel* of the work and the literal equation of time of writing and time of reading :

'Ainsi la durée de l'oeuvre moderne n'est-elle en aucune manière un résumé, un condensé, d'une durée plus étendue et plus "réelle" qui serait celle de l'anecdote, de l'histoire racontée. Il y a au contraire identité absolue entre les deux durées . . . [*La Jalousie*] n'était pas une narration emmêlée d'une anecdote simple extérieure à lui, mais ici encore le déroulement même d'une histoire qui n'avait d'autre réalité que celle du récit, déroulement qui ne s'opérait nulle part ailleurs que dans la tête du narrateur invisible, c'est-à-dire de l'écrivain, et du lecteur.'
Ibid., pp. 131–3

Time rests on the surface in the presence of the text, grasped as 'l'aventure d'une écriture'.

That adventure is the point of the *critical* effort of Robbe-Grillet's work, to take up Foucault's characterization cited at the head of this present section. It is a work on the *language of fiction*, an expression of the conventions of that language. Language is grasped as fiction in the moment of a particular work on the forms of fiction as such, a work on that which in so large a part contributes to the naturalization of a social reality, the novel. 'Je ne suis pas de ceux justement qui veulent supprimer du roman tous ces éléments du passé, je suis de ceux qui veulent les contester, et pour les contester

---

178 Cf. 'Table ronde', p. 123 ('pour *Marienbad*, il y a certaines simplifications qui ont été introduites par Resnais pour rendre justement une certaine tranquillité aux spectateurs').
179 In an excellent essay M. Mouillaud has demonstrated the impossibility of rearranging *La Jalousie* into this kind of narrative coherence: 'Tentative de roman et roman de tentative', *Revue d'Esthétique*, August-December 1964, pp. 228–63.

il faut qu'ils soient présents. Ce qui m'intéresse, *c'est de les inter-roger.*[180]

VII

'Suite d'un patient travail sur le langage, la littérature entend former les plus complexes ensembles de signes entrecroisés. Ainsi ne suppose-t-elle guère cette lecture courante en laquelle une transparente prose offre aussitôt son intelligibilité. Elle exige plutôt un acte de déchiffrement qui considère le texte, en son tissu, comme le lieu du permanent problème. Dès lors, pas d'illusionnisme; point d'accès direct au sens à travers un discours invisible. Le sens déchiffré se définit toujours, irrécusablement, comme un effet du texte. En somme, *déchiffrer*, c'est avoir franchi deux analphabétismes : le premier, visible (on ne sait pas lire), perçoit un texte et pas de sens; le second, caché (on croit savoir lire), un sens et pas de texte. C'est percevoir sens et texte, savoir se rendre sensible à toutes procédures de production.'

JEAN RICARDOU

'Loin de négliger le lecteur, l'auteur aujourd'hui proclame l'absolu besoin qu'il a de son concours, un concours actif, conscient, *créateur.* Ce qu'il lui demande, ce n'est plus de recevoir tout fait un monde achevé, plein, clos sur lui-même, c'est au contraire de participer à une création, d'inventer à son tour l'oeuvre et le monde—et d'apprendre ainsi à inventer sa propre vie.'

ALAIN ROBBE-GRILLET

Centrally situated in each of Robbe-Grillet's novels there are images of a fundamental unreadability. Franck and A. in *La Jalousie* discuss the novel they are both reading in terms of plot and character, as a mirror reflecting in image a solid presence outside itself :

'Les discussions, entre eux, se sont toujours gardées de mettre en cause la vraisemblance, la cohérence, ni aucune qualité du récit.'
La Jalousie, p. 82

Towards the end of *La Jalousie* this reading of the novel is undermined, posed as problem :

'Le personnage principal du livre est un fonctionnaire des douanes. Le personnage principal n'est pas un fonctionnaire mais un employé

---

[180] (Interview) ORTF, 'Cinéastes de notre temps,' 29 September 1969.

supérieur d'une vieille compagnie commerciale. Les affaires de cette compagnie sont mauvaises, elles évoluent rapidement vers l'escroquerie. Les affaires de la compagnie sont très bonnes. Le personnage principal—apprend-on—est malhonnête. Il est honnête, il essaie de rétablir une situation compromise par son prédécesseur, mort dans un accident de voiture. Mais il n'a pas eu de prédécesseur, car la compagnie est de fondation toute récente; et ce n'était pas un accident. Il est d'ailleurs question d'un navire (un grand navire blanc) et non de voiture.'

Ibid., p. 216

The novel is unreadable according to traditional expectations, the sense wavers constantly in a kind of textual to-and-fro, rests 'en suspens', like the last sentence of the manuscript in *La Maison de rendez-vous* (p. 72), or the letter that Wallas and Laurent in *Les Gommes* are unable to decipher :

'notons qu'un mot est illisible dans une des phrases considérées par vous comme significatives—un mot de sept ou huit jambages, qui ressemble à "ellipse" ou "éclipse" et qui peut aussi bien être "aligne", "échope", "idem" ou encore beaucoup d'autres choses.'

Les Gommes, p. 160

There is, in fact, a short history of the presence of the text in Robbe-Grillet in the unreadability of that little word, undecipherable to the hunters after sense and truth, that in the trajectory of its variants almost sketches an itinerary of Robbe-Grillet's writing. The writing aligns (*aligne*) in the line of its progression, but is elliptical (*ellipse*) in its play of repetition (*idem*) and difference (*ou encore beaucoup d'autres choses*); an elliptical alignment that is the instrument of the cutting away of sense (*échoppe*), so ending in an eclipse (*éclipse*), a moment of dark unreadability, as here in the resistance of the little word to the attempts at reading of Wallas and Laurent. This resistance finds many commentaries in Robbe-Grillet's novels :

'Au milieu des mots habituels se dresse çà et là comme un fanal quelque terme suspect, et la phrase qu'il éclaire de façon si louche semble un instant cacher beaucoup de choses, ou rien du tout.'

Ibid., p. 43

'Son interlocuteur avait une façon curieuse de répondre, commençant toujours par abonder dans son sens, répétant au besoin les propres termes de sa phrase d'un ton convaincu, pour introduire le doute une seconde plus tard et tout détruire par une proposition contraire, plus ou moins catégorique.'

Le Voyeur, p. 49

'Sans doute est-ce toujours le même poème qui se continue. Si parfois les thèmes s'estompent, c'est pour revenir un peu plus tard, affermis, à peu de chose près identiques. Cependant ces répétitions, ces infimes variantes, ces coupures, ces retours en arrière, peuvent donner lieu à des modifications—bien qu'à peine sensibles—entraînant à la longue fort loin du point de départ.'
La Jalousie, p. 101

Thus a problem of reading poses itself thematically, and the posing textually of the readability of the text is the project of the work as an adventure of writing. Voyeur and labyrinth, reader and text;[181] the writing offers itself as construction, series of forms, labyrinth to be explored, not decoded into some fixed sense; the reader is called upon to respond to the experience of his reading, to the construction of the text ('une construction permanente'), to concern himself not with the reception of a message but to assist in a reflection on the structuration of a message, *'un roman lui-même qui se pense'*.

The Robbe-Grillet text is a saturation of propositions and relations that operate in a tension of continuous interdependence, a tension which is the play of variations accomplished in the alignment of the progress of the writing. The difference between a Robbe-Grillet text and a novel by Balzac might be compared to that between dodecaphony and the traditional principles of tonality. Robbe-Grillet himself indeed suggested this image in 1959 : 'Mon style est plus proche de la musique dodécaphonique, basée sur une série de douze sons, que de la musique tonale.'[182] The development of a narrative harmonized and sustained in a process of relations across a series of codes to which the writing refers for its readability,[183] gives way in Robbe-Grillet's texts to a play of difference and repetition the readability of which is structural, in terms of the

---

181 Critical discussion of *Le Voyeur* has raged round the problem supposedly posed by the title (who is *le voyeur*?), and the voyeur has been variously identified with one after another of the characters critics have found in the novel, with everyone, in fact, from Mathias to the sea-gulls. But the problem is created only in so far as *Le Voyeur* is subjected to a realist reading, is read, that is, as a nineteenth-century novel. Far from intending his title as descriptive in the way in which a title such as *Les Derniers Chouans, ou la Bretagne en 1799* was intended as descriptive by Balzac, Robbe-Grillet offered in his title 'un point de vue sur l'oeuvre . . . le titre donne *un mode de lecture* du livre et indique que le personnage principal en est le lecteur. Le 'voyeur', ce n'est pas Mathias, c'est vous.' 'Table Ronde', p. 119.
182 (Interview) *Revue de Paris*, January 1959, p. 134.
183 Cf. Barthes's discussion of the readability of the classic text in his *S/Z*. See below pp. 210–15.

internal interdependence of its elements (hence the difficulty and perverseness of speaking about a Robbe-Grillet novel in the way in which Franck and A. talk about the novel they are reading in *La Jalousie*) and of which Philippe Sollers has defined the principle :

'Tout se passe comme si la matière de ses livres se composait d'éléments bruts de réalité, agencés rythmiquement dans une durée qui surgit de leur juxtaposition. Or cette association n'est pas irrationnelle, s'il évite le plus souvent la chronologie. Il semble que certains éléments "s'appellent" l'un l'autre par une nécessité de structure (visible à la charnière qui les réunit) ou parce que brusquement, "il est temps" de retrouver cette chambre, ce tableau.'[184]

This fitting together of elements in a rhythm that structures the tissue of the text is crucial and it might well be called *bricolage* somewhat after the fashion in which Claude Lévi-Strauss in *La Pensée sauvage* has described mythical thought as 'une sorte de bricolage intellectuel'.[185] *Bricolage* is not an activity of free creation but an activity of reassembling, of constructing from, existing elements.[186] It is an activity of reassembling that is the adventure of the writing in a Robbe-Grillet novel (adventure precisely in the reflection this process of reassembling sustains), reassembling not so much of what Sollers, somewhat misleadingly perhaps, calls elements of brute reality, but of syntagmatic elements of traditional narrative. It is hardly necessary to collect all Robbe-Grillet's statements of a fundamental lack of concern with the kind of 'subject-matter' or 'content' approach of traditional critical expectation[187] (a 'matter', that is, which can be disengaged from the text and recounted, as Morrissette disengages and recounts the matter of *La Jalousie*), to indicate what the texts themselves indicate with sufficient clarity; namely that

[184] 'Sept propositions sur Alain Robbe-Grillet'. *Tel Quel*, No. 2, Summer 1960, p. 49.
[185] *La Pensée sauvage*, p. 26.
[186] 'Tous ces objets hétéroclites qui constituent (le trésor du bricoleur), il les interroge pour comprendre ce que chacun d'eux pourrait "signifier" contribuant ainsi à définir un ensemble à réaliser, mais qui ne différera finalement de l'ensemble instrumental que par la disposition interne des parties.' *La Pensée sauvage*, p. 28. Claude Simon talks of the creation of his *Orion aveugle* in terms of a *bricolage* ('les pages que voici, nées du seul désir de "bricoler" quelque chose à partir de certaines peintures que j'aime', p. 12).
[187] Cf. e.g. 'Ne vaut-il pas mieux choisir les événements les plus anodins, des personnages aussi peu "personnages" que possible et pas d' "histoire" du tout? ... Il y avait dans mon premier livre, *les Gommes*, une intrigue de convention, calquée d'ailleurs sur Oedipe-Roi, et qui n'avait pour moi aucune importance.' 'Réponse à une enquête autour de l'autobiographie et de la fiction', *Prétexte*, January-February 1958, pp. 99–100.

what is central for Robbe-Grillet is the *fiction*, the forms of narrative organization, the elements that the *bricolage* takes as its material. The most obvious example of this *bricolage* is perhaps *La Maison de rendez-vous*, where the Hong-Kong that everybody knows ('Tout le monde connaît Hong-Kong, sa rade, ses jonques, ses sampans, les buildings de Kowloon, et l'étroite robe à jupe entravée, fendue sur le côté jusqu'à la cuisse, dont sont vêtues les eurasiennes, longues filles flexibles, moulées dans leur fourreau de soie noire à petit col droit et sans manches, coupé net au ras des aisselles et au cou', p. 13), conventional locus of popular oriental mystico-erotic adventure, of drugs, prostitutes, spies, and so on, is taken as the material for the assembly that is the writing of *La Maison de rendez-vous*. This writing puts into suspense the conventional narrative sense of the material, revealing its constituent elements, as it were, as pure forms the significance of which is found at the level of the text, precisely, that is, at the level of the wavering of their sense. The conventional narrative, a mise-en-scène of the real ('l'anecdote elle-même n'était-elle pas déjà une sorte de *mise en scène* du réel?' *L'Année dernière à Marienbad*, p. 12) is itself dramatized : we are present at the representation of writing in all its activity, a representation that is the principle of the theatrical imagery which permeates Robbe-Grillet's work and *La Maison de rendez-vous* in particular,[188] and that would seem to be equally the principle of the 'scenic' organization of Robbe-Grillet's novels, the disposition of the elements gleaned by the *bricoleur*. *Les Gommes* uses the conventions of the detective story together with the possibilities of the Oedipus plot and its set of post-Freudian expectations; *La Jalousie* the conventional husband-wife-lover triangle novel stereotype, as in the novel being read by Franck and A.

The construction which is the Robbe-Grillet text is, then, a kind of activity of literary *bricolage* the sense of which is in the experience of the construction, the presence of the text—there is no sense to be made of the changing number of rooms in the descriptions of the house in *La Jalousie* in terms of realist expectations. This activity has, as Sollers' comment suggests, certain recurring principles and these must be characterized briefly here in a discussion of one of the novels. Before moving on to this discussion, it might perhaps be useful to cite here a seminal passage from an essay by Gérard Genette in which he describes Robbe-Grillet's texts in the light of

---

[188] Cf. the excellent study of *La Maison de rendez-vous* by Jean Alter; *La Vision du monde d'Alain Robbe-Grillet* (Geneva, 1966).

some of the ideas of the linguist Roman Jakobson. Jakobson distinguishes two fundamental modes of arrangement in linguistic activity, *selection* and *combination* : the former operates on the basis of equivalence, the substitution of elements through similarity or dissimilarity; the latter on the basis of contiguity in the relation of elements in a sequence. Jakobson refers to these two modes as the metaphorical and the metonymical respectively since they may be said to find their most condensed expression in those two figures. In literature, poetry depends heavily on emphasis of the former, while narrative, and especially the realist novel, depends on emphasis of the latter.[189] Referring to this distinction Genette describes the organization of a Robbe-Grillet novel as follows :

'Si l'on adopte cette classification commode, on observe que l'art de Robbe-Grillet consiste à disposer dans l'ordre métonymique de la narration et de la description romanesques un matériel de nature métaphorique, puisque résultant d'analogies entre éléments différents ou de transformations d'éléments identiques. Après une scène d'un roman de Robbe-Grillet, le lecteur attend légitimement, selon l'ordre classique du récit, une autre scène contiguë dans le temps ou dans l'espace; ce que lui offre Robbe-Grillet, c'est la même scène légèrement modifiée ou une autre scène analogue. Autrement dit, il étale horizontalement, dans la continuité spatio-temporelle, la relation verticale qui unit les diverses variantes d'un thème, il dispose en série les termes d'un choix, il transpose une *concurrence* en *concaténation* . . .'[190]

This is indeed an exact description of the composition of a Robbe-Grillet text. The development of the writing (the 'narrative') is the repetition and variation of a paradigmatic series of elements, (as in *La Maison de rendez-vous* the breaking of the glass, the erotic entertainment, the murder of Manneret, the statues in the garden, the Eurasian girl Kim with the dog, the ferry, etc.). The alignment of these elements horizontally, in the play of repetition and variation, produces a kind of 'declension' of the elements of fiction, giving what was called at the beginning of this chapter a *scriptural* of narrative (as Leibniz talked of the *geometral* of an object) that invites the reader to read the writing of the text.

189 See R. Jakobson, 'Two aspects of language and two types of aphasic disturbances'.
190 G. Genette, *Figures* (Paris, 1966), p. 85. Genette's essay 'Vertige fixé' from which this passage is taken is one of the few really vital pieces of writing devoted to Robbe-Grillet's work. It should be mentioned here how important it has been in the development of the present discussion of Robbe-Grillet, as a catalyst in learning to read his work.

VIII

'Je suis parti de cette idée : une forme d'itinéraire qui pouvait être également une forme d'écriture, un labyrinthe, c'est-à-dire un chemin qui a toujours l'air guidé par des parois strictes, mais qui, néanmoins, à chaque instant conduit à des impasses et oblige à revenir en arrière, à repasser plusieurs fois aux mêmes endroits sur des parcours plus ou moins longs, à explorer une nouvelle direction et à retomber sur une nouvelle impossibilité.'

ALAIN ROBBE-GRILLET

'Labyrinthe : Lieu coupé de plusieurs chemins, embarrassé de beaucoup de détours, et duquel il est presque impossible de trouver l'issue.'
Dictionnaire de l'Académie Française, 1694

The boundaries of the labyrinth, the discursive points of the writing, are firmly defined in the construction of the text : soldier, child, woman, 'invalid', doctor, room, street, building, corridor, military barracks-cum-hospital, café, painting, box, lamp-post, greatcoat, and so on—those elements the repetition of which in the adventure of the writing tissues the text that confronts us in *Dans le labyrinthe*.[191] This repetition may be read as the production of a 'story'. Such a reading is that attempted by Bruce Morrissette who approaches the text with the following questions : 'Qu'*arrive*-t-il donc dans *le Labyrinthe*? Qui agit, qui parle, que voit-on? Que nous livre le texte?'[192] A story is to be *extracted from* the text which, as it were, instrumentally assures its passage. This is the product that the text offers to the reader (*Que nous livre le texte?*); the point of the text's fulfilment of its contract, the contract assumed by the reader-consumer in order to read the text. The text is the moment of an act of exchange and what is exchanged (the merchandise) is the story. Faith in the contract, which is, in fact, not known as such but as a set of 'natural' expectations, is sacrosanct; the reader must be able to assume the validity of the question 'Qu'*arrive*-t-il donc . . . ?', of the demand for the story.

There is, however, need for pause here with regard to this so

---

[191] Reference must be made here in connection with this image of the *labyrinth* to the magnificent issue of the *Situationist Times* (International Edition) entitled 'Le Labyrinthe': No. 4, 1963. Though only very brief mention is there made of the significance of that image for the nouveau roman in general (cf. p. 23), the whole issue, even in its very organization, bears the closest study in this respect.

[192] *Les Romans de Robbe-Grillet*, p. 151.

natural phenomenon of the story. A story might be defined (loosely, but sufficiently for present purposes) as a sequence of elements held in a body of relations. The problem (the problem of manufacture) lies in the relations. In fact, the manufacture of the story in a text achieves its goal-effect of coherence (to relate is to render coherent) in the assumption of a set of conventions exterior and prior to itself that may be called, to take up and extend a term from classical literary theory, a *vraisemblable*, both in the sense of the general and diffused representation of reality of a given society or social group and in the sense of the conventional expectations of an artistic genre (and it is perhaps not strictly necessary to add that the two kinds of convention are mutually dependent). To read a novel as Morrissette reads a novel is not some immediate natural response, though it may be felt to be such, but a heavily conventional and conventionalized activity dependent on a shared *vraisemblable* between novel and reader sited in the text, in the context of a code, or set of codes, that offers the prospect of extracting the fixed and anticipated message of the story. Crucial here in so far as the novel is concerned are those codes described elsewhere in the present essay after Barthes as the proairetic and hermeneutic codes.[193] Within this prospect Morrissette tells his readers what *Dans le labyrinthe* is 'about' : not 'que lisons-nous?', but 'que nous livre le texte?' This extraction of the story is, in fact, a mode of a more general aim of extraction; the extraction of *sense*. The sign or series of signs must be opened and the sense, supposedly enclosed by the sign, delivered; the *signifiant* discarded in the assumption of the full original *signifié*. The possibility of this 'opening' is the contract of the sign received as moment of exchange between language and reality of which it is no more than the instrument of delivery, the transparent envelope. *Dans le labyrinthe* provides a central image for this process in the box carried by the soldier which cannot but occasion the contractual expectation, the demand for the meaning it must contain : 'Qu'est-ce qu'il y a dans ton paquet?' (*Dans le labyrinthe*, p. 44.) In fact, the box contains nothing, or at least simply the papers and effects of a dead soldier, *the box itself being included* in these effects. There is no spectacular ('que voit-on?', demands Morrissette) full final Sense, no resolution, just as in the sign there is no final sense, no opening onto a fixed point of rest 'outside', but simply an opening into the circulation of the system of signs. In the natural attitude signs are consumed, the

193 Cf. pp. 210–15.

circulation continually arrested, the sign discarded for its natural sense, fixed and stable, and the text is similarly consumed, the story extracted, the production ignored. Such consumption is in Robbe-Grillet's terms an operation of recuperation and it is precisely this consumption that *Dans le labyrinthe* aims to distort. Robbe-Grillet projects the accomplishment of an irrecuperable text. Let us try, then, to read the terms of this project. But first, the story that the conventional expectation insists on extracting.[194]

We have, then, a soldier wandering through a town after the defeat of his regiment at Reichenfels. We follow in the course of the novel his desperate attempts to return a box containing some letters and a few other trivial objects to the next of kin of its owner, a comrade who died after the battle in a military hospital and who in his dying moments entrusted the box to the soldier for delivery. Weak and feverish, the soldier strays through the town guided now and then by a child into whose home he is taken for care after being wounded by enemy soldiers arriving to occupy the town, and where he finally dies. The story is narrated by the doctor who attends the soldier on his deathbed. The labyrinth of the title is an image of the soldier's labyrinthine wanderings in the strange town, the streets and other features of which are reduced to a bleak uniformity by the exigencies of war.

There is the outline of the story that is the object of the reading of many critics ('*Dans le labyrinthe* n'est pas l'histoire d'un livre qui se fait, mais l'histoire d'un soldat perdu dans un labyrinthe.'[195]), the reading that extracts what is to be read according to the conventions of expectation. This reading involves not simply an extraction, but also an *explanation*. If the text is the envelope of a story that has a full presence beyond or outside the text, then the area of that presence, which is, we have seen, conventional but which is felt as natural, as, finally, Reality, can furnish in its turn, and indefinitely, details to *explain* the text. Thus Bruce Morrissette introduces the concept of amnesia to help explain both the soldier's state

---

[194] The procedure followed here need not surprise. Any system of intelligibility may assume any object into the terms of its coherence, even if that assumption is cast in the form of the definition of the object as unintelligible, as, to give a few examples from within our own system, *mad, fantastic, imaginary, poetic* even. Thus, in the terms that concern us in the present context, there is always a story, always a point of explanation available. What is in question, then, for Robbe-Grillet is the disruption of the conventional coherence in writing a fiction as fiction, creating a plurality, a play of conventional forms. To extract the story here is to place oneself within the convention and copy the story it insists on writing, to reassume its expectations.

[195] Jean Miesch, *Robbe-Grillet* (Paris, 1965), p. 26.

of mind (since it is necessary to find for him the coherence of a *character*) and the mode of narration with its winding progress, its skein of reality and delirious fantasy (it is, indeed, to the opposition Reality/Fantasy as the supreme tool for the making sense of the text that we have quickly come), its doubts and hesitations, its 'retours en avant', and all its other 'difficulties'.[196] The labyrinthine narration of the book *mirrors* the wanderings of the soldier's mind. The breaking open of the text in the name of the representation of psychological reality offers, it is true, a different focus to that of the representation of social reality assumed for the nineteenth-century novel, but the premiss of the reading is exactly the same in the two cases, the premiss, that is, of the text as reflection. The text is absented as the condition for the presence of the story, the story dominating as the condition for the text which thus becomes its function.

It is, in fact, the opposite of this process of occultation that is proposed in *Dans le labyrinthe*, where it is the story (those elements related conventionally above) that is the function of the presence of the text or, better, of the *construction of a textuality*. The story of the realist reading itself offers a hint of the prime importance of the presentation of this construction in what Morrissette, in one of his articles on Robbe-Grillet, calls 'the interior duplication of an author composing a novel'.[197] The text begins, 'Je suis seul ici, maintenant, bien à l'abri' (p. 9), but the first person 'Je' as assumption of the process of the text is then 'lost', though the room ('bien à l'abri') is a constant point of return for the writing. A presence is felt in the room in the attention of an eye gazing at the circle of light the lamp throws on the ceiling, 'L'oeil qui a fixé trop longtemps celui-ci [le rond éclatant de clarté découpé sur le plafond blanc] n'aperçoit plus, lorsqu'il s'en détourne, aucun détail sur les autres parois de la pièce.' (p. 79); further, an observer is obliquely suggested, 'Cette imperfection dans la surface blanche n'est du reste pas également visible de tous les points. Elle est surtout remarquable pour un observateur placé contre la cloison de droite, mais en bas de celle-ci et à l'autre bout de la pièce, regardant en l'air obliquement, suivant à peu près la diagonale de cette cloison, comme il est normal pour une personne alongée sur le lit, la tête posée sur

---

196 *Les Romans de Robbe-Grillet*, p. 102. (It ought to be stressed that if it is Morrissette's reading that has been taken here as an example for discussion, it is because of the quality of that reading, a quality that contrasts strongly with the general run of the readings of Robbe-Grillet's texts.)

197 'The Evolution of Narrative Viewpoint in Robbe-Grillet', *Novel* Vol. I, No. I, Fall 1967, p. 29.

le traversin'. (p. 126.) It is not until the final section of the book, however, that the first person reappears ('A *ma* dernière visite le soldat était mort', p. 211, my italics) and (in the realist reading) a narrator is revealed in the doctor who meets the soldier in the street at a late stage in the story, who treats him after he has been wounded and who finally clarifies one or two points of uncertainty for the reader, revealing, for instance, the nature of the contents of the box which the soldier guards with such jealous obsession. The book ends with the first person, that has been identified at this point with the doctor, leaving the room in the phrase 'et toute la ville derrière moi' (p. 221), the final 'moi' linking symmetrically to the initial 'Je'.

So, for Morrissette, the key is 'the inner author whose struggles in the labyrinth of novelistic creation form the real subject of the book'.[198] (There is a lot to be said about that concept of *the real subject* which is so centrally ingrained in the whole of our critical discourse, and which is perhaps the exact point of our alexia.) The image of the labyrinth slips here from the feverish tortuous wanderings of the soldier's mind (his amnesia) to the process of the writing (a position which, precisely in the dual terms of the slip, is certainly more relevant), and what is in question in that slip is not the abandonment of the realist reading but the saving of that reading by shifting the terms of the extraction, of the real subject, what the book is about. The book is now seen as being about an author writing a book about a soldier, the author apparently to be identified with the doctor as narrator. (It might be worth bearing in mind at this point Robbe-Grillet's own comment on the ending of *Dans le labyrinthe* : 'Rien n'est résolu à la fin du *Labyrinthe*, on ne révèle dans les dernières pages que des choses sans importance, des petits faits adjacents et dérisoires.'[199]) Significantly, Morrissette while clearly wanting to acknowledge the importance of the inner author —'What has Robbe-Grillet gained by this narrative stucture, involving the interior duplication of an author composing a novel? One could easily imagine another version of the novel in which the wanderings of the soldier, described more or less in the third person style used here, would alone form the text. Even brief reflection should show that such a simplification would not only impoverish the novel; it would in fact negate its meaning.'[200]—has nothing finally to say about its importance nor about the meaning that its

[198] Ibid., p. 30.
[199] *Cinéma* 64, cit. Jean Miesch, op. cit., p. 26.
[200] 'The Evolution of Narrative Viewpoint in Robbe-Grillet', pp. 30–1.

absence would negate. Morrissette's insight is not sufficiently radical for all the brilliance of his reconstitution of the novel which, indeed, is the point of its insufficiency : to declare that it is easy to imagine *another version* of the novel is to refuse to read the play of the *text*, to recuperate the text totally into the conventions of a general reading in which the text is no more than the repetition of the achieved and natural story, of the natural expectations of a general intelligibility.

The very formulation of 'the interior duplication of an author composing a novel' is an indication of the insufficiency of the response to the experience of reading the text to the degree to which it suggests a resemblance between Robbe-Grillet's text and, say, Gide's *Les Faux-Monnayeurs*. In Gide's novel the clash of real/ fictive (false, counterfeit) is always finally assessable in straight realist terms : the counterfeit coin produced by Bernard is real, the real genuine coins in the novel written by Edouard are not. In other words, despite the dazzling display of paradox, there are remountable stages, different levels which are carefully distinguished, the whole novel depending, indeed, on this careful distinction in order to produce its series of dazzling paradoxes. There is no such clear distinction in *Dans le labyrinthe* and its absence is indicated in the 'circle' that disrupts the inner author explanation and that depends on the terms of the equation of narrator and inner author. The 'je' in the room composing the story of the soldier is simultaneously the narrator narrating the story of the soldier, a story in which he (the narrator) plays a part : the 'je' is at once the creator of the soldier and the doctor who cares for the soldier and then narrates his experience. The logic is that of the unreadability of the novel discussed in *La Jalousie* : 'son prédécesseur, mort dans un accident de voiture. Mais il n'a pas eu de prédécesseur . . . et ce n'était pas un accident. Il est d'ailleurs question d'un navire . . . et non de voiture.' There is no possibility of a final explanatory division between real and fictive. It is as construction, as fiction and consciousness of fiction that *Dans le labyrinthe* presents itself, and the images of composition follow inevitably from this presence : 'les feuilles éparses' (p. 219) left behind at the end of the novel as the 'je' passes out of the room and away, 'et toute la ville derrière moi' (p. 221). The stress on fiction was made clear by Robbe-Grillet, in the course of a discussion of the nouveau roman, in the following terms :

'Le récit moderne, qu'il soit dans le roman ou dans le cinéma, affirme . . . l'invention. Les personnages sont des fictions; ils ne sont que des fictions et ne vivent que comme des fictions, et c'est leur caractère fictif qui est justement le sujet même de l'oeuvre.'[201]

The resonances of the fiction as which *Dans le labyrinthe* presents itself should be fully attended to. Morrissette writes that 'one could easily imagine another version of the novel in which the wanderings of the soldier, described more or less in the third person style used here, would alone form the text', but he does not comment on the banality and extreme conventionality of such a text. Just how banal and conventional it would be is demonstrated by some of the readings which have been proposed of this text (the text extracted from *Dans le labyrinthe*), readings which may be loosely called 'symbolical' but which are generally more or less allegorical (and there is nothing more directly conventional, of course, than allegory); the very readings against which Robbe-Grillet warns in his *prière d'insérer* : 'Il s'agit ici d'une réalité strictement matérielle, c'est-à-dire qu'elle ne prétend à aucune valeur allégorique.' Thus the anguished wanderings of the soldier through the anonymity of the town are those of Angst-ridden modern man in search of his soul which the mysterious box (a type of grail?) may or may not contain.[202] There is a possible pattern of redemption : the guidance of the innocent child who brings the sick soldier to the love and care of the woman and the grace offered in the forms of the cross strewn in the text,[203] a hope of salvation from the bleak nothingness revealed in the Beckettian conversations.[204] The book has to be an allegory of man's condition, it is only as such that it can be read. It is as such that it has to be read by Ben F. Stoltzfus in his study of Robbe-Grillet's novels and a few points of his reading should be

[201] 'Table ronde', p. 100.

[202] Several critics have drawn a parallel between the soldier's box and Karl's trunk in Kafka's *Amerika*. The parallel is eminently valid, but only in terms of what has been called above Robbe-Grillet's recuperation of the Kafka text. Most of the critics who have drawn this parallel have immediately proceeded to the metaphysico-symbolic abandonment of the Kafka text against which Robbe-Grillet is so keen to protest. Cf. e.g. Ben F. Stoltzfus, *Alain Robbe-Grillet and the New French Novel*, pp. 97–8.

[203] E.g. 'C'est une sorte de croix . . .' (p.13); 'C'est la même croix à quatre branches . . .' (p.19); 'Il a, sous son bras droit, un paquet enveloppé de papier brun, quelque chose comme une boîte à chaussures, avec une ficelle blanche nouée sans doute en croix.' (p. 22). There is a whole irony in this assemblage of crosses (similar to that of the assemblage of references to the Oedipus myth in *Les Gommes*) and the *sans doute* in the last example cited is one moment of its appearance.

[204] E.g. 'Qu'est-ce que vous allez faire . . . puisque vous avez perdu le nom de cette rue?—Je ne sais pas, dit le soldat.—C'était pour une chose importante?—Oui . . . Non . . . Probablement.' (p. 62).

cited here in order to bring out the very terms of the recuperation against which Robbe-Grillet is writing in *Dans le labyrinthe*. 'If the sick soldier stands for a sick humanity, if the box's contents symbolize man's racial, social, individual, and political inheritance, and if a young boy whose legs form the image of a prominent V is a symbol of youth, that is, of a future humanity, then the image of a young Theseus clutching the box to his chest, while not saying so overtly, does nevertheless state covertly that there is a way out of the labyrinth if youth, the future's collective Theseus, will only kill the Minotaur';[205] 'the red curtains of the room . . . this colour red (blood? life?);[206] 'the uselessness of the third injection is, therefore, not an insignificant detail for, if the soldier is an analogue for a sick humanity, then indeed it will take more than an injection to cure him';[207] 'These "trifling" objects have a far greater significance than their cursory treatment in the novel would seem to imply. They apparently stand for all the activities of man (past and present) as an individual, biological, social, religious and political animal';[208] 'the V theme (Victoire?) is repeated several times . . . There is evolution in time from a cross-legged boy holding a box on his chest, to a V-legged boy also holding, not the same shoe-box, but a newer different one of tin. This constant emphasis of the V suggests a solution.'[209] Evidently Stoltzfus already knows the text to which *Dans le labyrinthe* has to conform and its banal comfort is indicated adequately enough in the passages just cited.

It is precisely this text and the naturalness of its reading that is the material of *Dans le labyrinthe*, providing the elements of its activity of *bricolage*, of construction. It is this text, this story, with all its received significance, on which Robbe-Grillet's text works and which, in this sense, is taken as its precedent. Discussing his film *L'Immortelle*, Robbe-Grillet linked it to *Dans le labyrinthe* and commented, 'Comme dans *Le labyrinthe*, l'histoire de *L'Immortelle* est déjà presque achevée au moment où commence le film . . .'[210] If there is evaluation and judgement in *Dans le labyrinthe* it is not in the story as it is read by Stoltzfus and other critics but in the construction or composition, in the work—work on conventional fictions—that is the activity of the text, 'une construction perma-

205 *Alain Robbe-Grillet and the New French Novel*, pp. 99–100.
206 Ibid., p. 82.
207 Ibid., p. 85.
208 Ibid., pp. 86–7.   209 Ibid., p. 98.
210 Cit. Miesch, op. cit., p. 26

nente qui jamais n'aboutira à quelque chose de définitif',[211] a suspension of sense in the exploration of the forms of the text's production which may well evoke in its disruption of reading a certain anguish, an anguish that in *Dans le labyrinthe* has taken on revealing resonances from the forms of the chosen material itself. 'De la première page jusqu'à la dernière page, le sentiment d'angoisse domine l'ouvrage,' writes Lucien Goldmann.[212] The concept of *vraisemblable* mentioned earlier in this chapter may profitably be reintroduced at this point. One reference of the vraisemblable is to literary convention and in the case of the novel this convention, which crystallizes round the organization of the narrative, the production of a story, is interdependent with the vraisemblable of general opinion, the general social representation of reality. In realist writing and reading of the novel the vraisemblable does not exist, or rather its existence is unknown, the novel supposedly mirroring the immediately known Real : the novel repeats the generalized social text that realizes that 'Real' in the accomplishment of a realism which thus sustains and confirms that text, an accomplishment that entails the novel in its own convention of narrative organization (a 'realistic' or 'natural' organization), its own vraisemblable that is, dialectically, a mode of the creation of that reality taken and naturalized as the Real. The vraisemblable is known as such only at the distance of reflection, whether historical, phenomenological or semiological : as Tzvetan Todorov has re-

---

211 'Table ronde', p. 109.
212 *Pour une Sociologie du Roman*, p. 205. Goldmann, in fact, while avoiding, of course, the allegorical euphoria of a Stoltzfus, locates the anguish simply at the level of the story which is taken as a direct expression of the alienation and reification of a particular stage in the development of Western capitalism. The fault of Goldmann's general thesis with regard to Robbe-Grillet in *Pour une Sociologie du Roman* and elsewhere is to take the novels as critical *representations* of contemporary society, as in their *content* a kind of social realism. Goldmann writes: 'si on donne au mot réalisme le sens de création imaginaire d'un monde dont la structure est homologue à la structure essentielle de la réalité sociale au sein de laquelle l'oeuvre a été écrite . . . Robbe-Grillet est un des écrivains les plus profondément réalistes de la littérature française d'aujourd'hui.' ('Les deux avant-gardes', *Médiations* No. 4, Winter 1961– 1962, p. 78). It is difficult to know in what sense the word *structure* is here being used, but the scope of Goldmann's definition depends, it is clear from his analyses of the novels, on a representative structure in the content of the novels. It is significant that he has nothing to say about what must be evidently central in any *reading* of Robbe-Grillet, the work of the construction of the text. It is at this level of construction that Robbe-Grillet's work is *critical* in the sense given that term by Michel Foucault in the passage cited as heading to Section VI above. Robbe-Grillet has indicated this in his refusal of the notion of the *engagement* of the writer other than in terms of 'la pleine conscience des problèmes actuels de son propre langage' (*Pour un Nouveau Roman*, p. 39).

marked, 'Les lois de notre propre discours sont à la fois vraisembl-ables (par le fait même d'être des lois) et inconnaissables, car ce n'est qu'un autre discours qui peut les décrire'.[213] It is just such a reflective action that is accomplished in Robbe-Grillet's novels as a *scriptural* of narrative. The vraisemblable of traditional narrative is 'brought to the surface', the expectations of the novel, so much a part of our Real, are demonstrated in the forms on which they depend; the 'subject' of the novels is their composition, the structuration of the *text* itself which is present(ed) as such, strictly 'un roman qui se pense lui-même'. The project of the Robbe-Grillet text finds a fore-echo in a famous passage by Valéry :

'Peut-être serait-il intéressant de faire *une fois* une oeuvre qui mon-trerait à chacun de ses *noeuds* la diversité qui peut s'y présenter à l'esprit, et parmi laquelle il *choisit* la suite unique qui sera donnée dans le texte. *Ce serait là substituer à l'illusion d'une détermination unique et imitatrice du réel, celle du possible-à-chaque-instant, qui me semble plus véritable.*'[214]

The first paragraph of *Dans le labyrinthe* at once poses its presence as textual construction :

'Je suis seul ici, maintenant, bien à l'abri. Dehors il pleut, dehors on marche sous la pluie en courbant la tête, s'abritant les yeux d'une main tout en regardant quand même devant soi, à quelques mètres devant soi, quelques mètres d'asphalte mouillé; dehors il fait froid, le vent souffle entre les branches noires dénudées; le vent souffle dans les feuilles, entraînant les rameaux entiers dans un balancement, dans un balancement, balancement, qui projette son ombre sur le crépi blanc des murs. Dehors il y a du soleil, il n'y a pas un arbre, ni un arbuste, pour donner de l'ombre, et l'on marche en plein soleil, s'abritant les yeux d'une main tout en regardant devant soi, à quelques mètres seule-ment devant soi, quelques mètres d'asphalte poussiéreux où le vent dessine des parallèles, des fourches, des spirales.' (p. 9)

The first sentence announces a project, that of making progress a narration, which is resolved symmetrically at the end of the text in the exit from the 'now' of the room (the accomplishment of the text). In the space of this passage, the project is held in the phrase 'bien à l'abri' against which the rest of the paragraph is balanced in the initial progress of the writing. (It is not by chance that the term

---

213 'Du vraisemblable que l'on ne saurait éviter', *Communications* No. 11, p. 147.
214 *Oeuvres* I, p. 1467 (my italics in second sentence).

'balancement' appears in this paragraph.[215]) 'Abri' calls directly for its opposite 'dehors' : 'bien à l'*abri. Dehors* il pleut . . .' The opposition is central to the development of the course of the writing which moves constantly from room to street, and is one example of a basic structural principle of the text, progression by the substitution of elements in a relation of antonymy the one with the other along the narrative line of the novel. This use of oppositions as a structural principle presents an immediate rhythm of composition and this rhythm is stressed in the development of the individual paragraphs and sentences of the text. Read, for example, the second sentence of this first paragraph :

'*Dehors* il pleut, *dehors* on marche sous la pluie en courbant la tête, s'abritant les yeux d'une main tout en regardant quand même *devant soi*, à *quelques mètres devant soi, quelques mètres* d'asphalte mouillé.'

The rhythm is that of the construction of the sentence through the fitting together of various segments according to a process of extension via repetition and resumption. Here the element of the rain (*il pleut, pluie, mouillé*) is extended through the points of progression italicized above, the writing recovering a word or phrase previously used and extending itself in the movement of its repetition : '*devant soi/à quelques mètres/devant soi/quelques mètres* d'asphalte mouillé.' The play of repetition and difference, rhyme and dissonance, is the tissue of the paragraph, as it is of the novel. This play might be described in its structuration of the text as *metaplasmic*, adapting from rhetoric the term *metaplasm* meaning, in the definition given by the *Oxford English Dictionary*, 'change or transmutation in a word by adding, transposing or retrenching a syllable or a letter'. The transmutation accomplished in the two main sentences of the first paragraph of *Dans le labyrinthe* offers a good example of this metaplasmic movement of the Robbe-Grillet text. The sentences might be transcribed as follows in order to demonstrate this movement :

A. 1 Dehors il pleut
    2 dehors on marche sous la pluie/en courbant la tête

215 Robbe-Grillet has always emphasized his activity as a writer as being that of a *work* of composition, refusing conventional ideas of inspiration: 'J'écris lentement et avec soin. Le mode matériel d'écriture qui est le mien ne va pas très bien avec ce qu'il est convenu d'appeler l'inspiration, qui serait une sorte d'élan de la plume qui me ferait couvrir des pages rapidement . . . j'écris avec lenteur, mot par mot, ne terminant jamais plus d'une page par jour. Le choix de chaque mot, de chacune des formes grammaticales, de l'arrangement des phrases est accompagné d'un travail précis et vigilant.' (Interview) *VH 101* No. 2, Summer 1970, p. 94.

    3 s'abritant les yeux d'une main
    4 tout en regardant quand même devant soi
    5 à quelques mètres devant soi
    6 quelques mètres d'asphalte mouillé

B. 1 Dehors il y a du soleil
    2 et l'on marche en plein soleil
    3 s'abritant les yeux d'une main
    4 tout en regardant devant soi
    5 à quelques mètres seulement devant soi
    6 quelques mètres d'asphalte poussiéreux

This metaplasmic movement is operative as a basic structural principle at the level of the discursive points of the text, its elements or 'words', so to speak, taken in a continual process of repetition-variation-modification, as, for instance, the scene of the soldier waiting under the lamp-post, always the same and always different. It is perhaps *La Jalousie* that provides the clearest example of this movement in the series of versions of the killing of the centipede and the various descriptions of the stain left on the wall of the bungalow.[216]

The close of the first paragraph of *Dans le labyrinthe* offers an image of this movement, 'le vent dessine des parallèles, des fourches, des spirales', and that image refers us to the *labyrinth*, the text *in* which (*DANS le labyrinthe*) the reader is forced to find himself. The image of the wind is taken up in the book as the point of definition of that *resistance* of the text commented on in Section VII above (p. 11):

'Le vent chasse sur l'asphalte sombre du trottoir les fins cristaux secs, qui se déposent après chaque rafale en lignes blanches, parallèles, fourches, spirales, disloquées aussitôt, reprises aussitôt dans les tourbillons chassés au ras du sol, puis figées de nouveau, recomposant de nouvelles spirales, volutes, ondulations fourchues, arabesques mouvantes aussitôt disloquées.'

Hence the doubt continually traced in the writing of the book (p. 179, 202):

---

[216] The metaplasmic movement can in fact be found in Robbe-Grillet at the level of single words, metaplasmic thus in the strict sense. An example is the movement in *La Maison de rendez-vous* from *Johnson* to *Jonestone*. It is particularly significant that it operates there on the name of a character: in realist writing it is precisely the name that is the supreme point of fixity.

'C'est sans doute à cet endroit que se place la scène de l'assemblée muette . . . Mais cette scène ne mène à rien.'

'Viennent ensuite des scènes encore moins claires—encore plus fausses, aussi, probablement.'

A doubt that operates the closure of the text on itself, as the 'confusion' of the following passage (p. 143) indicates :

'Ce gamin-ci est celui du café, semble-t-il, qui n'est pas le même que l'autre qui a conduit le soldat (ou qui le conduira, par la suite) jusqu'à la caserne—d'où, justement, il a rapporté la bille.'

The action of *Dans le labyrinthe* is, then fundamentally the action of the narrative taking possession of itself. This self-possession is manifested in the refusal of the smooth passage of metonymic movement into the absence of representation and the dramatization of narration as action. This dramatization demands not a work carried out at the level of individual words (Robbe-Grillet is quite different from Joyce in this respect) but at the level of conventional narrative forms. *Dans le labyrinthe* is not a novel in the conventional sense which defines an area of expectation (story, character, in short, Sense), but a handful of novelistic fragments (the material for the *bricolage*) which intersect, contradict one another, are varied, repeated, modified, cancelled in their interaction, and the 'subject' of the book is not in the conventional sense of these fragments, but in their *articulation*, their exploration as *forms* in the text. Robbe-Grillet gives, as has been said, a kind of scriptural of narrative, a demonstration of possibilities and limits from the basis of the handful of received elements, a mise-en-scène of the production of narrative. This is to offer an experience of reading : to *read* a Robbe-Grillet text is not to pass through the text to some product (story, representation, Sense), but to respond to the activity of the text, to its construction. Hence the difficulty here : it is necessary to guard against covering that activity of the text with a discourse without relevance to that experience of reading. All that may here pertinently be done in conclusion is to follow the book's construction a little further by describing briefly the central opposition of its structure, the opposition between the picture 'La Défaite de Reichenfels' and the 'action'.

The picture is mentioned straight away in the book (p. 22) and described carefully at the opening of the second section (the text dividing into fourteen sections). It is defined at once in terms of

149

presence : the first section ends 'Et toute la scène demeure vide : sans un homme, ni une femme, ni même un enfant', (p. 24), with, that is, an emptiness (stressed throughout the last paragraph, 'la même blancheur sans éclat', 'la rue est déserte', 'la même couleur blanche terne et neutre', 'la même teinte jaunâtre', 'les fenêtres sont vacantes de toute silhouette', 'il n'y a rien', 'vide', p. 23–4) which is filled immediately by the picture that offers a full scene, 'le tableau, dans son cadre de bois verni, représente une scène de cabaret' (p. 24). The scene is described in an act of *reading* the picture, an act that is difficult and uncertain ('leurs mouvements . . . sont figés par le dessin . . . ce qui en rend la signification également très incertaine' p. 25) and that is mimicked in the centre of the representation of the picture itself ('se pressant les uns contre les autres pour apercevoir quelque affiche ou image placardée contre le mur' p. 25); an act that runs inevitably into that inscription, 'calligraphiée en écriture anglaise', at the bottom of the picture, *La défaite de Reichenfels* (p. 26).

It is from and to that inscription, a point of semantic fixity that opens a range of possibilities in its reading, that the adventure of the writing runs, ceaselessly working and reworking the basic set of narrative elements. Thus, for example, in the opening of the fifth section of the text where, the soldier alone in front of the door of the barracks, the writing goes through a series of analogous scenes in a process of repetition and rejection, e.g. (pp. 95–6) :

'Il remarque à cet instant que la porte est entrouverte : porte, couloir, porte, vestibule, porte, puis enfin une pièce éclairée et une table avec un verre vide dont le fond contient encore un cercle de liquide rouge sombre, et un infirme qui s'appuie sur sa béquille, penché en avant dans un équilibre précaire. Non. Porte entrebâillée. Couloir. Escalier. Femme qui monte en courant d'étage en étage, tout au long de l'étroit colimaçon où son tablier gris tournoie en spirale. Porte. Et enfin une pièce éclairée : lit, commode, cheminée, bureau avec une lampe posée dans son coin gauche, et l'abat-jour qui dessine au plafond un cercle blanc. Non. Au-dessus de la commode une gravure encadrée de bois noir est fixée . . . Non. Non. Non. La porte n'est pas entrebâillée . . .'

Passing through these variations the writing arrives, in a kind of para-rhyme or paromoion (*la porte est entrouverte/la porte n'est pas entrebâillée*), at a point from which, after further variations, it will move to one of the scenic descriptive blocks of the text. In the course of these variations the picture reappears, 'une gravure encadrée de bois noir', to be rejected in its turn in the passage of

150

the writing, 'Non. Non. Non.' Picture and space of the 'action' of the narrative elements of the text are confounded : the picture is at once *source*—from the scene it represents the writing departs in a process of animation (e.g. pp. 28–9) and deanimation (e.g. pp. 46–7) —and *derivation*—the engraving in the room of the doctor who cares for the soldier. The confusion (in a non-pejorative sense) is in the writing (as in the case of the inner author/participant in the 'story' confusion discussed earlier), in the fiction explored from the opening of the phrase '*La défaite de Reichenfels*', signalled as writing ('*calligraphiée en écriture anglaise*'), that demands an activity of reading and that offers the point of the articulation of the text, the experience of reading given here in *le labyrinthe*.

It is on that experience that it has been the purpose of the present chapter to lay the emphasis in the consideration and discussion of Robbe-Grillet's work. By way of conclusion to a chapter that, for reasons that will by now be evident, can have no conclusion in the sense of a rounded final assessment of the 'meaning' of Robbe-Grillet's novels, one last brief remark may be appended.

The Russian formalist critic Shklovskij defined the process of art in terms of a 'device for making strange', *priëm ostranenija*, a process of defamiliarization : art makes us aware of forms, those forms that habitually are simply received passively in vacant recognition. One of his examples of habitual passiveness was drawn from the material presence of writing : reading the proofs of a book written in a language we know well it is only with difficulty that we can make ourselves *read* the words, and so pick out the misprints, instead of simply taking the text for granted in an unthinking and immediate recognition of the words expected.[217] Is it not a strangeness (*ostranenije*) that is felt in the presence of a Robbe-Grillet text? That text is troubling (of the number of critics it has troubled something has been seen in the course of this chapter) : what we expect to read is missing or else is strangely present with an insistence that disturbs, deriding the sense it ought to have. We are confronted with a *text*, something material, a construction that in its formality, its use of various elements which we recognize as elements of comforting sense and which we would like to relate as usual to achieve the satisfaction of meaning, and yet which here, in their variation and repetition, their exploration as forms, resist our recuperation, disrupts our ex-

217 Cf. T. Todorov, *Théorie de la littérature* (Paris, 1965), pp. 43–4; V. Erlich, *Russian Formalism* (The Hague, 1955), pp. 150–1.

pectations, forces us to *read* and not to recognize. Perhaps the anguish felt in *Dans le labyrinthe* finds its reality here : soldier and reader are locked in a quest, for delivery of the box, for reception of the meaning, all the possibility of which—whence the anguish, the trouble—is in its process alone. That process for us is the text and the experience of its reading.

4

Claude Simon

'Le travail de l'écrivain reste travail de langage, plutôt que de "penser" : il s'agit de produire un système de signes qui restitue par son agencement interne le paysage d'une expérience, il faut que les reliefs, les lignes de force de ce paysage induisent une syntaxe profonde, un mode de composition et de récit, qui défont et refont le monde et le langage usuels.'

MAURICE MERLEAU-PONTY

'Il faut se mettre à l'écoute de la réalité, il faut saisir le moment où la réalité commence à parler . . .'

MICHEL BUTOR

'Le roman se fait, je le fais, et il me fait.'

CLAUDE SIMON

Claude Simon has published no extended theoretical writing on the novel equivalent to *L'Ere du soupçon* or *Pour un Nouveau Roman*. His major work has been the achievement of a series of novels that contain in themselves a whole criticism of, or better, a continual work on, the novel form. More precisely these novels may be said to constitute a work on what Philippe Sollers describes as the *romanesque* ('cette parole insidieuse, incessante, et qui semble toujours être là avant que nous y pensions'[1]), on, that is, modes of the experience of identity, of the narration of ourselves. This questioning of the realization of identity gives the series of novels its coher-

[1] *Logiques*, p. 228.

ence, and its foundation, inevitably, is the biography of the author: 'la seule chose dont je puisse écrire sans malhonnêteté . . . c'est-à-dire de moi, et de moi seul.'[2] The same names, the same incidents, the same situations, recur from text to text, now obliquely mentioned in passing, now a central point of the writing. The Spanish Civil War, of which Simon had first-hand experience, continues, varying in importance, from *Le Sacre du printemps* (1954) to *Le Palace* (1962) to *Histoire* (1967) to *La Bataille de Pharsale* (1969). The memories of cavalry service—Simon having done his military service in the dragoons and having been mobilized in the same regiment during the war—that appear in *La Corde raide* (1947), a kind of 'fictitious' mixture of autobiographical fragments (what is in question in Simon is exactly the fiction of identity), become central in the later novel *La Route des Flandres* (1960). It would be appropriate to recall here the work of Proust, as indeed Simon often does himself, even finding in his *La Bataille de Pharsale* the necessity for extensive quotation from *A la recherche du temps perdu*. Explorations of identity through time and memory are crucial to both writers, and it will be seen that metaphorical relation plays as important a role in the development of Simon's writing as it does in that of Proust. It would be appropriate too to think of the descriptive work of phenomenology (Merleau-Ponty was, in fact, a great admirer of Simon's novels and used them as points of discussion and reference in his lectures at the Collège de France). Simon's work could well be seen as a work on the description of the activity of consciousness, of its constitution. There is, however, a proviso to be made in this connection (and the same proviso would have to be made in a consideration of Proust), which is that what has to be centrally attended to and thought in reading Simon is the reality of the *text*, the reality of the *work* of the text. What is the space, or scene, of the realization of identity? The answer for Simon is clear; that of *language*, the milieu of our trans-formation. To define an identity, the reality of that identity, becomes, as for Proust, a task of writing, the production of that text ('le seul livre vrai'[3]) that gives the possibility of the discovery of the constitution of one's self through the reading operated by its writing ('cette lecture—un acte de création où nul ne peut nous suppléer'[4]), the text thus grasped as reality ('la vraie vie, la vie enfin découverte et éclaircie, la seule vie

---

[2] 'Je ne peux parler que de moi', (interview) *Les Nouvelles Littéraires*, 3 May 1962, p. 2.
[3] *A la recherche du temps perdu*, III, p. 890.
[4] Ibid., III, p. 879.

par conséquent réellement vécue'[5]). It is in these terms that Simon's work becomes a project of bio-*graphy* : as Sollers puts it in the course of an essay on Artaud, 'Il s'agit, en somme, non pas de produire et d'écrire, mais de *s'écrire* et de se produire, d'entrer dans la seule réalité des signes où l'on est soi-même un signe'.[6] Simon expresses his conception of the novel, in terms that evoke the entrance into this textual reality, as 'l'aventure singulière du narrateur qui ne cesse de chercher, découvrant à tâtons le monde dans et par l'écriture' (*Orion aveugle*, p. 15).

It is here, then, that Simon's work is to be understood in the context of the practice of writing, and it is no surprise to find that such a work, directing its attention there 'où la réalité commence à parler', disturbs a certain expectation of literature that has already been mentioned in these pages in connection with Robbe-Grillet. The criticism that is the custodian of this expectation finds Simon's novels '*imbuvable*'.[7] The word is indicative : the novel is desired as object for consumption, as nourishing sustenance through repetition of all one's expectations, and the refusal of Simon's work to be consumed, its insistence on its presence as textual production, as writing, that must be *read*, and hence its unpalatability, demands its rejection as 'imbuvable'. It is this reality of the work that must be respected here in the avoidance of any kind of 'consumption' of the novels. As is the case in the discussion of all these novelists situated in the practice of writing, there can be no question of attempting to draw out from Simon's novels some story or final meaning, to arrange the elements of their composition according to some conventional narrative expectation : it is indeed exactly on and against such conventional modes that Simon's writing works. What is attempted in the following pages is simply a general presentation of some of the main elements of Simon's novels which leads to a more detailed account of his writing in terms of a discussion of *La Route des Flandres*.

The world of Simon's novels is a world in perpetual movement. 'Tout bouge. Rien n'est sûr, rien n'est fixe.'[8] That remark was made by Simon with reference to *La Route des Flandres*, but it will serve

[5] Ibid., III, p. 895.
[6] *Logiques*, p. 137.
[7] René Georgin, *L'Inflation du style* (Paris, 1963), p. 140.
[8] (Interview) Madeleine Chapsal, *Quinze écrivains* (Paris, 1963), p. 170.

as a description of the whole general vision of which that particular novel is a representation, a representation in the sense in which Merleau-Ponty talks of the literary work as the production in a work of and in language of the landscape of an experience. All the novels are moments in that production which is carried through ceaselessly from text to text. In this perpetual movement, nothing is sure, including the self. In *La Corde raide* Simon records his sense of astonishment at the assumptions of continuity basic to the traditional novel, at 'the old stable *ego* of character', to take up Lawrence's phrase again, and concludes in contrast, 'moi qui ne suis pas le même pendant la durée d'un millième de seconde puisque *je ne suis pas moi.*' (*La Corde raide*, p. 175.) Time is 'immobile à grands pas' (Simon borrows the image in *La Bataille de Pharsale* from Valéry's poem 'Le cimetière marin'): everything is taken in a constant flux that is motionless or without significance. 'Si le monde signifie quelque chose, c'est qu'il ne signifie rien.'[9] Nothing or anything; it is insignificant and any word may be applied, just as *Le Sacre du printemps* will speak of 'le hasard, ou si tu préfères le vent, ou si tu préfères les engrenages bien réglés' (*Le Sacre du printemps*, p. 247). The key recognition here is that of the void, of the absence of a centre, of a point of fixity in which to anchor the process of signification; the recognition that is expressed, for example, at the end of *Gulliver* where the images of pain, cold, night, labyrinth, lonely wandering through the city, come together as images of absence :

'il continuait, insensible au froid, insensible à la douleur qui lui brûlait l'orbite, à suivre au hasard rue après rue l'interminable dédale de tranchées noires, dans la nuit tombante envahissant le ciel tragiquement vaste, tragiquement vide.'
Gulliver, p. 373

At the centre of *La Bataille de Pharsale* is placed the cipher 0, mark of absence, marking now man now woman, assuming the function of the writing ('0 écrit'), and that may be read here, after Lacan, as 'l'atome 0 du signe, du signe en tant d'abord qu'il connote la présence *ou* l'absence, en apportant essentiellement l'*et* qui les lie, puisqu'à connoter la présence ou l'absence, il institue la présence sur fonds d'absence, comme il constitue l'absence dans la présence'.[10]

The wandering imaged in that passage from *Gulliver* is that of

[9] Cit. Madeleine Chapsal, 'Le jeune roman', *L'Express*, 12 January 1961, p. 32.
[10] *Ecrits*, p. 594.

the memory which is precisely the endeavour to live the present as significant, to shape a coherent identity. As a mode of existing the Simon world, memory is thus a means of fighting the endless insignificant flux, but where for Proust it is possible to conceive of a space of victory the *achieved* text in the organization of the relations of which the identity of the self may be read, for Simon there is no such space; the notion of text is supreme but the text is never achieved, never finished, instead there is a ceaseless process of textualization from novel to novel, of continuation, repetition, modification —'une permanente remise en question'.[11] Sartre, comparing Faulkner (a major factor in Simon's consciousness of his writing) with Proust, once commented that 'la technique romanesque de Proust *aurait dû* être celle de Faulkner. Seulement Faulkner est un homme perdu . . .'[12] Thus too Claude Simon, 'un homme perdu'. Always, 'cette connaissance fragmentaire, incomplète, faite d'une addition de brèves images, elles-mêmes incomplètement appréhendées par la vision, de paroles, elles-mêmes mal saisies, de sensations, elles-mêmes mal définies, et tout cela vague, plein de trous, de vides, auxquels l'imagination et une approximative logique s'efforçaient de remédier par une suite de hasardeuses déductions . . .' (*Le Vent*, p. 9). To exist the world as significant in the scope of the memory is to exist an act of *reconstitution* (as one speaks in detective novels of the reconstitution of the crime, except that in Simon there is no final reconstitution, no passage to a fixed truth), to attempt to order the scattered pieces, themselves continually fragmenting, newly combining, shifting, changing, of an ever-expanding and altering mosaic, or mirror, to take up another of Simon's images : 'tenter de rapporter, de reconstituer, ce qui s'est passé, c'est un peu comme si on essayait de recoller les débris dispersés, incomplets, d'un miroir . . . n'obtenant qu'un résultat incohérent . . .' (*Le Vent*, p. 10). As Stendhal's description of Fabrice at Waterloo in the opening pages of *La Chartreuse de Parme* (itself already an experience of fragmentation) has become the confusion of the experience of *La Route des Flandres*, so his novel as 'miroir qui se promène sur une grande route'[13] has become a 'miroir brisé'[14] or, better, a 'miroir fixe', the space of memory or, as will be seen, of writing, composing itself in a

---

11 'Qu'est-ce que l'avant-garde en 1958?', *Les Lettres Françaises*, 24–30 April 1958, p. 1.
12 *Situations I*, p. 77.
13 Stendhal, *Romans et nouvelles* (Pléiade) I, p. 557.
14 'Techniciens du roman: Claude Simon', (interview) *Les Nouvelles Littéraires*, 29 December 1960, p. 4.

ceaseless spiral round a handful of elements: 'comme un mobile se déformant sans cesse autour de quelques rares points fixes' (*La Bataille de Pharsale*, p. 186), where even the fixed points are completely taken up in the movement, each always deferring to the others in a chain without break or point of rest. 'Tout bouge. Rien n'est sûr, rien n'est fixe.'

Significantly *Le Vent* is subtitled *Tentative de restitution d'un retable baroque*: the baroque with its whirling spirals is the very style of the movement of the memory in Simon, a movement to coordinate time in space,[15] and the *retable*, the triptych worked on three adjacent panels, is the very organization of a Simon novel (as in *Le Vent, La Route des Flandres, La Bataille de Pharsale*), the organization stressing constant interaction and movement and refusing some privileged moment of fixity, as, for instance, in *La Bataille de Pharsale* where the last section or 'panel', which carries the (in terms of traditional expectations) promising heading 'Chronologie des événements', in no way finally fixes and explains a story or meaning, but offers a process of resumption, extension and variation that interacts with the other two sections. The activity of restitution is always to be recommenced. As motto to *Histoire* Simon places some lines by Rilke that epitomize the general vision of the novels: 'Cela nous submerge. Nous l'organisons. Cela tombe en morceaux. Nous l'organisons de nouveau et tombons nous-mêmes en morceaux.'[16] The 'end' of a Simon novel is not the achievement of a stable conclusion, but a temporary rest in the process of an incessant work: 'Aussi ne peut-il avoir d'autre terme que l'épuisement du voyageur explorant ce paysage inépuisable. A ce moment se sera fait ce que j'appelle un roman . . .' (*Orion aveugle*, pp. 14–5). Always that 'énigme insoluble, vertigineuse', to take up a phrase from *Histoire* (p. 283).

The title of that novel, *Histoire*, is a word that re-echoes throughout Simon's writing, giving a theme to which it returns time and time again, and which is a corollary of the idea of memory. 'Histoire', as both story and history, is a full mode of fixity, of identity and significance, which is to say, for Simon, that it is a mode of falsity, in fact part of the *romanesque*. There is a revealing passage in *Le Vent* in this connection: 'Le récit qu'il m'en fit fut sans doute

---

[15] Cf. *La Bataille de Pharsale*, p. 160: 'Critique anglais qui définit le baroque *movement into space* malheureusement intraduisible . . .'

[16] The lines are from the eighth of the *Duino Elegies*: 'Uns überfüllts. Wir ordnens. Es zerfällt./Wir ordnens wieder und zerfallen selbst.'

lui-même faux, artificiel, comme est condamné à l'être tout récit des événements fait après coup, de par le fait même qu'à être racontés les événements, les détails, les menus faits, prennent un aspect solennel, que rien ne leur confère sur le moment.' (p. 49.) Sartre's critique of the distortion of existence offered by the *aventure* to which the Autodidacte dreams of making his life conform may be remembered here. To narrate is a mode of bad faith, a refusal to live the contingent and a taking refuge in the false consciousness of the idea of a rounded, finished self. This false consciousness similarly characterizes history, the conventionally stabilized social ordering of the past (remember Roquentin's abandonment of his historical biography of the Marquis de Rollebon): 'L'Histoire n'est pas, comme voudraient le faire croire les manuels scolaires, une série discontinue de dates mais au contraire sans limite.' (*L'Herbe*, p. 35). History is nowhere (as motto to *L'Herbe* Simon quotes Pasternak, 'Personne ne fait l'histoire, on ne la voit pas, pas plus qu'on ne voit l'herbe pousser') and everywhere, the very weft of existence ('la terne existence d'une vieille dame, c'est l'Histoire elle-même', *L'Herbe*, p. 36). In fact, what Simon understands by *histoire* is, finally, any process of signification; any ordering of the in-significant world is a fiction, 'les menus faits prennent un aspect solennel, que rien ne leur confère sur le moment'. Yet this conception is itself to be questioned. At what point does the fiction that deforms an original presence of object or event begin? In terms of individual identity, for example, may one think of a full transcendental self always there before, 'sur le moment'? Simon himself answers this question with a categoric denial in his '*moi qui ne suis pas le même pendant la durée d'un millième de seconde puisque je ne suis pas moi*'. There is no full original presence: man finds himself always already an absence, the point of return of a discourse, of a process of signification in which he is included. The image of the void and Lacan's comment on the zero element of the sign that institutes presence on the ground of absence may be recalled at this point. It may also be noted how the importance of memory is defined here: consciousness *is* memory in that it is never fully 'sur le moment', but always already elsewhere in the tissue of relations that realize its structure. Held in a network of fictions, the individual is himself a fiction and to pursue an identity is not to mine some deep-buried stable source (the 'buried life' of the Victorian poets), but to decentre oneself, to put oneself where one is not ('où la réalité commence à parler'), to lose oneself in order to find oneself there in one's absence, in that *circula-*

tion of signs that gives one's reality. As in Proust, such a work is an act of writing, of producing oneself as text to read the text of oneself. It is language that is the space of consciousness : 'Je ne vois pas de conscience en dehors du langage. Dans la mesure où j'écris, j'accède à la conscience.'[17] Whence the problem and the response that is the work carried through in Simon's practice of writing. The problem is the intense distrust of language as fiction, the feeling of language as unreal that Simon expresses, as has been seen, as a gap between linguistic signification and reality 'sur le moment', speaking of 'des paroles que prononçaient nos lèvres pour nous abuser nous-mêmes vivre une vie de sons sans plus de réalité sans plus de consistance que ce rideau sur lequel nous croyions voir le paon brodé remuer palpiter respirer imaginant rêvant à ce qu'il y avait derrière . . .' (*La Route des Flandres*, pp. 274–5.) But precisely, as has also been seen, that attempt to *see behind*, to arrest the movement of signification, blinds itself to the reality without depth of the movement of language as system. 'Clair pour qui ne cherche pas à l'approfondir', concludes *La Bataille de Pharsale* (p. 91), and Simon defines the reality or, better, the realism of his work exactly in its presentation of a text and not in an 'elsewhere' or a 'behind' : 'il ne faut rien chercher *derrière* ce qui est écrit. Il n'y a que ce qui est écrit.'[18] The subject must accede to the creativity of language of which he himself, supreme fiction, is a creation, must accede to that 'dynamique du langage', as Simon puts it.[19] It is in the space of language that the drama of identity is played : to know oneself is to lose oneself in language, to decentre oneself in the system (formal play of differences) in which one finds oneself. One must listen where reality begins to speak, dispersing oneself as subject in the acknowledgement of the reality of language. (Remember Foucault's account in *Les Mots et les Choses* of the growth of man as fixed original subject in the absention of language.) Merleau-Ponty recognized clearly in Simon's writing the process of this endeavour : in October 1960 he jotted down in a note-book the following comment on that writing :

'Il naît des personnes intermédiaires . . . des modes intermédiaires (participe présent à valeur de "simultanéité") ceci ne se comprend absolument pas soit dans conception classique du Je pense soit dans conception de l'ipséité comme néantisation : car alors le cercle de

17 'Claude Simon, franc-tireur de la révolution romanesque', (interview) *Le Figaro Littéraire*, 6 April 1967, p. 7.
18 (interview) *Les Lettres Françaises*, 13–19 April 1967, p. 3.
19 'Je ne peux parler que de moi', p. 2.

l'ipséité je le tiens, je le trace—Ces usages du langage ne se com-
prennent que si le langage est un être, un monde, que si c'est la Parole
qui est le cercle.'[20]

Man is placed in the circulation of language grasped as milieu of
(his) production : to achieve this situation (in the active sense of
the word) is to accede to that kind of intermediary stage described
by Merleau-Ponty—a stage which is the novel, *Le roman se fait,
je le fais, et il me fait*.[21] In that difficult formulation Simon wishes
to express his position in a text which he writes as it writes him. To
realize this text is to accept the circulation of that discourse in which
one finds oneself ('Au lieu de repousser les ouvertures insoupçonnées
que recèle le langage, les mots, la phrase, je les accepte'[22]) and in
its writing read it as text, as a tissue of relations ('Il me semble que
l'art est, au même titre que la science, un instrument de connaissance,
en ce sens qu'il consiste en l'établissement de "rapports" '[23]). It is in
this realization, understanding that word in all its senses, conceived
as work of research, that Simon's work is to be defined in the context of the practice of writing. As he himself puts it, 'il me semble
que le livre se fait au niveau de l'écriture';[24] 'mot après mot par le
cheminement même de l'écriture' (*Orion aveugle*, p. 6).

La Bataille de Pharsale is thus the 'bataille de la phrase' : that
book, indeed, is entirely held in the moment of the writing of a
sentence ('Jaune et puis noir *temps d'un battement de paupières* et
puis jaune de nouveau.' pp. 9, 271, my italics) in which a whole
discourse makes itself heard. The battle is never over : in the constant flow of time everything—memories, images, incidents, words,
sounds—is to be ceaselessly reworked in the project of writing.
'Pourquoi écrivez-vous? Pour essayer de me rappeler ce qui s'est
passé pendant le moment où j'écrivais.' (*La Corde raide*, p. 178).

In an interview given at the time of the publication of *La Route
des Flandres* in 1960, Simon remarked that he had been thinking

[20] Maurice Merleau-Ponty, 'Cinq notes sur Claude Simon', *Médiations*, No. 4,
Winter 1961/1962, p. 6.
[21] *Les Lettres Françaises*, 13–19 April 1967, p. 4.
[22] 'Claude Simon, franc-tireur de la révolution romanesque', p. 7. ('L'un après
l'autre les mots éclatent comme autant de chandelles romaines, déployant leurs
gerbes dans toutes les directions.' *Orion aveugle*. p. 10).
[23] 'Qu'est-ce que l'avant-garde en 1958', p. 1.
[24] 'Débat sur le roman', *Les Nouvelles Littéraires*, 22 June 1961, p. 7.

of the book for some twenty years.[25] Something of this thinking can be seen in *La Corde raide* with its description of the four cavalrymen in retreat after an engagement with the enemy (p. 79–91), and will indeed be seen again, after *La Route des Flandres*, in the similar description taken up at the close of *La Bataille de Pharsale* (pp. 259–65). The same names recur in *La Route des Flandres* as had previously appeared in *L'Herbe* and as will appear in subsequent novels. This is that process of continuous retextualization that has been stressed above. To put the thinking about *La Route des Flandres* back twenty years is exact: from 1960 Simon sends us back to 1940, the date at which, having been mobilized in the 31ᵉ Dragons in 1939, he is taken prisoner after the battle of the Meuse. The material of the book, thought and rethought over the years, is here in this experience: 'Je suis incapable d'inventer quoi que ce soit. Pendant la guerre un type que je connaissais, un capitaine, est mort sous mes yeux. Dans de telles conditions que j'ai eu nettement l'impression d'assister à un suicide. Voilà le thème.'[26]

As title for the book Simon hesitated for a time over the alternative *Description fragmentaire d'un désastre*, and that alternative title plunges us into the vision of the novel. *Disaster* because here we have the *description* of the four cavalrymen lost in the confusion of the aftermath of defeat in battle; *disaster* also in what may be called the instability of the *description*, ('Rien n'est sûr, rien n'est fixe'), nothing is achieved that is not in that very achievement *fragmentary*, that is not to be immediately questioned and remade; *disaster* again because in that consciousness of the *fragmentary* the subject, here assumed as 'Georges', is lost, the book hovering between the first and third person of the verb, thus creating, as Merleau-Ponty saw, a kind of intermediary reality that is precisely this act of writing. Simon has said that the book is 'la mort de Georges'.[27]

The book composes itself round several central discursive points. There is the (?) suicide of Captain de Reixach, Georges' cousin and his commanding officer in the dragoons, which is taken up time and time again in the course of the novel (as it is in other Simon texts, *Histoire*, for example). There is Corinne, de Reixach's wife and essence of femininity ('la femme la plus femme qu'il eût encore jamais vue, même en imagination', p. 140), who is described and

[25] 'Les secrets d'un romancier', (interview) *Les Lettres Françaises* 6–12 October 1960, p. 5.

[26] (Interview) *Le Monde*, 8 October 1960, p. 9.

[27] 'Les secrets d'un romancier', p. 5.

162

redescribed in her real or imagined relations with her husband, with Inglésia, jockey and later valet to de Reixach, with Georges one night after the war. There are horses, race-horses and cavalry mounts, giving a whole vocabulary and set of references and images. There is the portrait of one of de Reixach's ancestors, who is said to have himself committed suicide in circumstances that are endlessly turned over and discussed in the book. What is crucial is the landscape (*paysage*, referring always to that characterization of the work of the writer given by Merleau-Ponty in the passage placed at the head of this chapter and, indeed, to Simon's own description of the working of this 'paysage inépuisable' quoted earlier from *Orion aveugle*) charted in the relation of these elements in the composition of the text.

Aiming for himself as subject, Georges undertakes a pursuit of identity; pursuit *against* language ('obstacle majeur', p. 60) which is grasped as a pursuit against his father—*normalien, agrégé*, teacher, writer, in short, representative and guardian of the word.[28] In a central and oft-repeated conversation with his father, Georges pours scorn on any work in language which is seen as 'empty', devoid of that reality 'sur le moment' : 'Je n'ai surtout pas envie d'aligner encore des mots et des mots et encore des mots.' (p. 36.) The pursuit of identity is the pursuit of a fixed point of surety, of the truth concerning the death of the de Reixach in the portrait, of the truth concerning the death of his descendant the cavalry officer, of the truth, of *his* experience, a pursuit carried finally to the body of Corinne that night after the war : 'qu'avais-je cherché en elle espéré poursuivi jusque sur son corps dans son corps . . .' (p. 274). At this point the pursuit is seen as being as hopeless as the father's belief in language : 'ce ne serait pas de cette façon c'est-à-dire avec elle ou plutôt à travers elle que j'y arriverai (mais comment savoir?) peut-être était-ce aussi vain, aussi dépourvu de sens de réalité que d'aligner des pattes de mouche sur des feuilles de papier et de le chercher dans des mots . . .' (p. 295.)

It is the writing of this pursuit, the relation of its cardinal points, that gives the reality, and it is this landscape that must now be explored a little. Its overall thematic constituent, in which all the other

---

[28] Cf. the role played by the father (*non* and *nom*) as fundamental *signifiant* in the dialectic of the desire of the child, as support of the symbolic network in which he is taken, in the thinking of Lacan: 'C'est dans le *nom du père* qu'il nous faut reconnaître le support de la fonction symbolique qui, depuis l'orée des temps historiques, identifie sa personne à la figure de la Loi.' *Ecrits*, p. 278.

images of the text are grasped, is time. Time is that flowing immobility already commented on above, the major images for which in *La Route des Flandres* are the rain and the horses. The rain, 'tombant toujours et peut-être depuis toujours' (p. 64), invisible, no more to be seen than 'le multiple et secret grignotement d'invisibles insectes en train de dévorer insensiblement les maisons, les arbres, la terre entière' (p. 65) or than history or time, except when focused 'devant un objet foncé' (p. 64), as history may be seen in a sudden moment of dramatic emphasis ('un autre Reixach . . . se tirant volontairement une balle dans la tête (à moins que cela ne lui soit tout bêtement arrivé en nettoyant son pistolet, ce qui se produit couramment, *mais dans ce cas il n'y aurait pas d'histoire* . . .)' p. 84, my italics), or as time may be seen in the war that seems to accelerate and emphasize its movement ('as-tu remarqué comme tout cela va vite, cette espèce d'accélération du temps, d'extraordinaire rapidité avec laquelle la guerre produit des phénomènes . . .?' p. 205). The horses with the rhythmic feel of their movement, 'une sorte de va-et-vient immobile' (p. 26),[29] the feel and the thematic connections of which Simon explores in the text in the word *chevauchement* (and the verb *chevaucher*), as in the following passage where the relations with time are made in conjunction with the image of the rain : 'nous n'étions nulle part mille ans ou deux mille ans plus tôt ou plus tard en plein dans la folie le meurtre les Atrides, chevauchant à travers le temps la nuit ruisselante de pluie sur nos bêtes fourbues . . .' (p. 122.) In history the *chevauchement* is a ceaseless composition-decomposition-recomposition, a process of repetition, events, as it were, straddling time in time, in the way of the two Reixach suicides, for example. Whence the fascinating surface presence of history in Simon's writing, as here in *La Route des Flandres* the continual questioning of the portrait of de Reixach[30] or the copying of a translation from the Italian in a sixteenth-century commonplace book discovered amidst a collection of de Reixach papers (pp. 55–6).[31] The *chevauchement* invokes too the sexual act : Iglésia, the jockey,

<hr/>

[29] Cf. the image of the horse in *La Bataille de Pharsale*, 'galopant sur place oscillant d'avant en arrière sans avancer', p. 116.

[30] It might perhaps be noted here to emphasize the degree to which Simon's writing is placed as a bio-graphy that a long interview with the novelist which appeared in *Les Lettres Françaises* in 1960 actually included a photograph of the portrait that is so important a discursive point in *La Route des Flandres*. Cf. 'Les secrets d'un romancier' p. 12.

[31] Cf. *La Bataille de Pharsale* where Caesar's description in *De Bello Civilo* of the battle with Pompey at Pharsalia is read simultaneously with the description of the cavalry engagement.

mounts both de Reixach's horse and his wife ('l'alezane-femme, la blonde femelle', p. 185); Georges *straddles* Corinne in that night after the war. This chain of relations could be extended a little at this point in its significance, in citing, for example, the following moment of the text in which the writing takes up precisely this straddling by Georges of Corinne : 'comme si toute cette interminable chevauchée nocturne n'avait eu d'autre raison, d'autre but que la découverte à la fin de cette chair diaphane modelée dans l'épaisseur de la nuit : non pas une femme mais l'idée même, le symbole de toute femme, c'est-à-dire . . .' (p. 41), the discovery, that is, as the sudden break emphasizes, of an absence; 'l'orifice de cette matrice le creuset originel' (p. 42). The discovery is that of an absence, *orifice* ('cette éternelle blessure', p. 191), as centre and origin, *le creuset originel* : it is pertinent to note in a text the activity of which is as great as that of Simon's the possibility of the passage from *orifice* to *creuset* via the homonymous *creuser*, with its repetition of *orifice* in *creux*, that gives the intended relation *absence-origin*, or, as it may be put more directly in terms of language, *difference-origin*.[32]

The discovery as centre of an absence is the moment of the dispersion of the subject, 'couché entre les lèvres du fossé comme si je pouvais m'y fondre y disparaître m'y engloutir' (p. 257). In the chain of relations composed in the writing, that phrase reads in two directions : at once the man buried in the woman and the man huddled in the ditch of war. The phrase returns us to war and time, just as *l'amour* 'calls' *la mort*, ('se cherchant à l'aveuglette cherchant trouvant l'amour la mort', p. 78), and this return is crucial in the general imaging of dispersion. The disaster of war with its acceleration of time provides the images for that unceasing process of decomposition (already briefly glimpsed in that image of the devouring insects cited above) central to Simon's vision, 'un sentiment de permanente impuissance et de permanente décomposition' (p. 216) : 'en pleine retraite ou plutôt débâcle ou plutôt désastre au milieu de cette espèce de décomposition de tout comme si non pas une armée mais le monde lui-même tout entier et non pas seulement dans sa réalité physique mais encore dans la représentation que peut s'en faire l'esprit . . . était en train de se dépiauter se désagréger s'en

---

[32] Cf. the following passage from an essay by Julia Kristeva : 'le creuset même de la signifiance résorbant le corps du sujet, où se produit la distribution et la refonte des différences...' *Semeiotiké*, p. 311. Coincidence doubtless, but coincidence is to be understood here not in its weaker sense of a casual or chance encounter, but in the strong sense of the occupation of the same space of discourse.

aller en morceaux en eau en rien . . . (pp. 16–7). In the chain of relations this war serves as the point for the relation of men and horses, until man finally assumes the reality of horse, the reality, that is, of decomposition : 'je me jetai par terre mourant de faim pensant Les chevaux en mangent bien pourquoi pas moi j'essayai de m'imaginer me persuader que j'étais un cheval je gisais mort au fond du fossé dévoré par les fourmis mon corps tout entier se changeant lentement par l'effet d'une myriade de minuscules mutations en une matière insensible . . .' (p. 258).

Following this chain of relations (to read a Simon text is to accomplish just this operation) we have arrived at the centre of *La Route des Flandres*. Recurrent in the text, as one of the main discursive points of the writing, is the image of a dead horse decomposing by the roadside. Slowly, from occurrence to occurrence, the process of decomposition progresses, and at the centre of the book, at the beginning of the second of the three parts, is placed this image of the horse. As on the woman at the end of the pursuit there is read an absence, so too in this image of the rotting horse is read an emptiness at the centre of the text, the horse 'faisant penser à ces jouets d'enfants amputés ou crevés laissant voir l'intérieur béant, caverneux, de ce qui n'avait été qu'*une simple forme entourant du vide*' (p. 106, my italics). Like, in fact, a sign.

It is possible here to begin to read the writing of the book. That writing is, indeed, commented on in the book in the description of Sabine, Georges's mother, with her 'trois ou quatre thèmes autour desquels sa pensée semblait graviter avec le monotone, opiniâtre et furieux acharnement de ces insectes suspendus dans le crépuscule, voletant, tournoyant sans trève autour d'un invisible—et inexistant, sauf pour eux seuls—épicentre' (p. 53). Like a *mobile* the text offers just this activity of a circling through its three or four main discursive points round a 'point zéro' (p. 313), an epicentre where only an absence is to be read, a centre defined only in the process of the circulation. In organization *La Route des Flandres* has that kind of triptych structure common to Simon's novels. Simon has likened this structure to a clover in this respect : 'J'avais songé à construire mon livre comme est construit un trèfle. Il y a un centre, et trois boucles d'inégale importance. Le cheval mort est au centre du trèfle.'[33] Dispersion, he said in the same interview, was to be the geometrical centre of the book's organization.

[33] 'Les secrets d'un romancier', p. 5.

Within this three-part organization is contained a movement that may be understood as *baroque* in the sense Simon assigns to that difficult term : 'Le mouvement du baroque, c'est la spirale. C'est-à-dire le retour de la même ligne, sur la même génératrice, mais avec à chaque fois un décalage de niveau. L'imperceptible différence . . .'[34] Thus the opening pages of *La Route des Flandres* give, as it were, a résumé of the whole book, bringing in all the elements that will be taken up again and again in the composition of the text. Simon has again been quite explicit about this : 'j'ai essayé . . . de donner un aperçu, une sorte de résumé, de première vision de l'ensemble du livre dans les quinze premières pages. Le reste n'étant ensuite qu'un approfondissement de ces quinze premières pages.'[35] The idea of an *approfondissement* needs to be clearly understood. Simon has already been quoted to the effect that there is no 'depth' or 'behind' to his texts, and what is to be understood by the process of *approfondissement* carried through in the writing of *La Route des Flandres* is not a movement towards some final, ultimate truth, after some hermeneutic code such as was basic to the writing of the traditional novel (Simon's text, as has been seen, offers an absence as centre), but a continual movement of rereading, a succession of relations. It is a question of representing in the activity of the text a landscape, charting all its strata (as Simon will talk of a kind of archaeological excavation of memory[36]), but a landscape that has no presence other than spread out in the movement of the text, discovered in that establishment of relations realized in the text and which defines art for Simon as an 'instrument de connaissance'. It is this reality of the text that Merleau-Ponty is trying to describe in that passage cited at the head of this chapter. It is this too that is described and understood, within the terms of its interest, by contemporary psychoanalytical theory. Serge Leclaire, for instance, discussing the structure of desire in the unconscious, comments, 'il n'y a point de vérité au-delà ni en deçà du désir inconscient; *la formule qui le constitue, le représente en même temps qu'elle le trahit*',[37] and his study of 'Le désir inconscient' ends, indeed, with an emphasis that recalls Simon's stress on the *superficial reality* of his texts, an emphasis that will be seen as crucial : 'il n'y a pas d'au-delà du texte, ou mieux encore de la lettre'.[38]

[34] Ibid.   [35] Madeleine Chapsal, *Quinze écrivains*, p. 169.
[36] Cf. e.g. *Le Monde*, 8 October 1960, p. 9.
[37] Serge Leclaire, *Psychanalyser* (Paris, 1968), p. 53.
[38] Ibid., p. 54.

consc always trace of an 'other' always already inscribed
on way slab in a tissue of relations

In 1924 Freud, fascinated by a toy that had recently appeared on the market, took up once again the descriptions he had previously attempted of the functioning of the mental apparatus and reformulated them in terms suggested by analogy with that toy. The result was the short paper 'Notiz über den "Wunderblock" '. This 'Wunderblock' or 'Mystic Writing-Pad', as the English translation of the paper puts it, is a writing tablet consisting of a slab of wax covered by a thin sheet of waxed paper and, over that sheet, a further sheet, this time of celluloid. To make use of the pad one writes with a pointed stylus on the celluloid cover, thus depressing the underlying waxed sheet onto the wax slab and revealing the tracings of the stylus as legible writing. To erase the writing it is only necessary to lift the covering sheets off the slab. The interest of this 'Wunderblock' for Freud lay in the fact that when the writing was erased, the traces made by the stylus were left intact on the wax slab : 'its construction shows a remarkable agreement with my hypothetical structure of our perceptual apparatus . . . it can in fact provide both an ever-ready receptive surface and permanent traces of the notes that have been made upon it.'[39]

Freud's use of the analogy of the 'Wunderblock' describes the process of the inscription of the mnemic-traces on the palimpsest of the wax slab, every trace inscribed in relations with other traces. In an extended commentary on Freud's paper, Jacques Derrida has demonstrated that such a conception involves the recognition that 'L'écriture supplée la perception avant même que celle-ci ne s'apparaisse à elle-même. La "mémoire" ou l'écriture sont l'ouverture de cet apparaître lui-même. Le "perçu" ne se donne à lire qu'au passé, au-dessous de la perception et après elle.'[40] Thus Freud stresses that 'The layer which receives the stimuli—the system *Pcpt.-Cs.* [i.e. perceptual-consciousness]—forms no permanent traces; the foundations of memory come about in other, adjoining systems'.[41] The effect of this is to make of consciousness always the trace of an elsewhere, of an 'other', always already inscribed on the wax slab in a tissue of relations, and it may be further noted here that it is in the discontinuity, grasped through the working of the 'Wunderblock', between the perceptual-consciousness system and the system inscribing the mnemic-traces of perceptions that Freud discerns,

---

[39] 'A Note upon the Mystic Writing-Pad', *Standard Edition of the Complete Psychological Works of Sigmund Freud*, Vol. XIX (London, 1961), p. 228.
[40] *L'Ecriture et la Différence*, p. 332.
[41] 'A Note upon the Mystic Writing-Pad', p. 230.

though he does not elaborate the point, the origin of the experience of *time*.[42]

In this context, it may be worth recalling Simon's notation in *La Corde raide* of the 'reason' of his writing : 'Pourquoi écrivez-vous? Pour essayer de me rappeler ce qui s'est passé pendant le moment où j'écrivais.' Writing is pursued as a process of the composition of relations in which the 'instituting' subject, who is always taken in a vertical continuity-discontinuity and grasped in time (that of the insistence of these relations), may be read in his perpetual displacement from himself. In a famous letter written to Fleiss in 1896, Freud wrote of the process of the rearrangement of the mnemic-traces in accordance with new circumstances as of a process of re-transcription,[43] and the concept of a work of retranscription might be used in a description of Simon's writing. Writing for Simon is exactly a work in this process of retranscription; an attempt to re-mount the chain of relations it imposes in order to pinpoint oneself in that movement.

I should like to refer for a moment at this point to the writing of Philippe Sollers' *Nombres*, which is a powerful activity of fissuration (more appropriately, it needs to be described as an 'écriture de la brisure' in so far as the various resonances of the term 'brisure' indicate the full extent of its procedure). One crucial area of this activity is the specular image of the body which is caught up in a constant fracturation ('il fallait prendre pied, être désarticulé, laminé, cassé, découpé'[44]) and the mouth, where air becomes sound and the subject defines his mastery of himself (of his sense), is a key focus in this context. There is a point in the text in which this decisive passage of the subject to himself and his sense is put in question by the articulation of a name which burns in the throat :

'Je pensais que si j'arrivais au tissu qui nous composait, je saurais en même temps ce qui le maintient, le nourrit, l'anime—quelque chose devant malgré tout disparaître au moment de la réponse juste, se jeter dans ce qui autrefois avait été appelé "mer" en criant . . . Cette réponse était liée à la prononciation d'un seul mot qui me désignerait à la fois de façon ramassée et multiple, une syllabe n'existant dans aucune autre

[42] Ibid., p. 231. Freud had already mentioned this conjecture in *Beyond the Pleasure Principle*: *Standard Edition*, Vol. XVIII (London, 1955), p. 28.
[43] S. Freud, *Aus den Anfängen der Psychanalyse (Briefe an Wilhelm Fleiss)* (London, 1950), p. 185 (letter of 6.12.1896).
[44] *Nombres*, p. 18.

langue connue, un nom pour toujours acide me brûlant la gorge, les dents?'[45]

This 'primitive' name, which is felt as a material object and the function of which is to unify an unmasterable multiplicity ('me désignerait de façon à la fois ramassée et multiple'), recalls the name ('Poord'jeli') uncovered by Serge Leclaire in the course of a psychoanalytic treatment and representing the secret name given himself by the analysand as an infant. Such a name is operative in the development of the subject in the setting into position of the phallic stage, in which the phallus assures the unity of the surface of body hitherto experienced as series of marks or 'letters' defining the erotogenic zones. The 'letter' for Leclaire is thus a pure phonemic difference in relation to the differentiation of the erotogenic zone. The secret name, which is rarely uncovered in analysis so great a resistance does it offer to the violation of avowal, forms a sequence of these letters and, in its convergence with the phallus, marks the unity that allows the passage to the unfolding of the Oedipus and the drama of castration. It is a point of movement between two scenes; the point, that is, of the mise-en-scène. Leclaire has finely summarized the meaning of this in a key passage of his *Psychanalyser* :

L'ensemble des lettres peut alors être décrit comme un corps (ou livre) où s'inscrivent et sont inscrits les traits qui limitent la jouissance. C'est ce corps, dans son altérité première et le manque constituif du terme qui le nomme, qui se trouve impliqué par la mise en jeu de toute lettre; ce corps, ou mieux, cette suite de corps engendrés constitue cet *autre* champ, à la fois complet et incomplet auquel se réfèrent nécessairement toute littéralité, objectalité et subjectivité possibles.'[46]

This other scene (one may remember Freud's characterization of the unconscious as precisely an *other* scene, *andere Schauplatz*) that is, as it were, the underside of the subject's 'Reality', forming its point of reference but never separable as such, is constituted as text in the chain of *signifiants* (of 'letters'). It is in this context that the analogy of the 'Wunderblock' with its wax slab as guardian of series of traces might take its full force. For the analyst, evidently, that text is the point of the real, of which it is organized as a function. In an attention to the discourse of the analysand, the analyst has constantly to uncover the real in the moments when it is signified—in the dream-

[45] Ibid., p. 19.
[46] *Psychanalyser*, p. 145.

work, negation, slips of the tongue and so on; it is a question of the decipherment of the text of the unconscious. It is thus that in his long analysis of 'Philippe' Leclaire can uncover the formula 'Poord'-jeli' in its relation to the setting into position of the subject and the text of the unconscious in which the subject is to be comprehended.

This brief indication of some factors in contemporary psycho-analytical theory has not been given with the intention of trying to effect some kind of straight equivalence between Simon's work and that of, say, Leclaire. It is evident that Simon is not attempting the extended and complex theoretical discourse that is Leclaire's achievement in *Psychanalyser*. The intention has been rather to open a certain perspective, of which Simon's 'Le roman se fait, je le fais, et il me fait' reads as a recognition, not in terms of the acknowledge-ment of some 'influence' but in those of a situation in the area of a contemporary thinking of the subject in his realization in the activity of processes of signification—a thinking in which the work of Leclaire and that of Simon play, in their different ways, a part.

The passage from *Nombres* spoke of reaching, of trying to reach, the tissue of our composition, which would give at the same time its underside, the point of its maintenance. Simon's work, and within that work *La Route des Flandres*, reads exactly as a perpetual attempt to read the tissue of himself, to situate himself in his posi-tion within the multifarious orders of his sense. It is a question of deciphering himself within the circulation of signs, of reading him-self in the text of his construction. This practice of writing moves in its attempt to reconstitute this text very much as Leclaire moves in his analysis of Philippe's dream of the unicorn ('licorne'), pin-pointing little by little through the relation of elements-'letters' (*Lili* —soif—plage—trace—peau—pied—*corne*) the text of the uncon-scious; very much as Georges and Blum in *La Route des Flandres* attempt to make Iglésia speak, 'peu à peu, bribe par bribe, ou pour mieux dire onomatopée par onomatopée arrachées une à une par ruse et traîtrise (la tactique consistant à lui forcer en quelque sorte la langue . . .)' (p. 137.)

We come then to the central question the formulation of and the response to which make up the *reading* of a Simon text : How is the text woven?[47] The answer might best begin from another

[47] Cf. in connection with this discussion of the realization of the text, the two fundamental essays on Simon by Jean Ricardou: 'Un ordre dans la débâcle', *Critique* No. 163, December 1960, pp. 1011–24 (*Problèmes du nouveau roman.* pp. 44–55); 'La bataille de la phrase', *Critique* No. 274, March 1970, pp. 226–56.

question the drift of which will be clear in the light of the discussion of that passage from Merleau-Ponty on the intermediary zone achieved by Simon's writing: Who speaks? In fact, no one speaks. It has always been easy in the terms of the realist writing of the novel to assimilate the text, according to a realist alibi, to the terms of the speaking voice that founds an origin and source, and there is a whole range of studies of the 'problem' of the 'teller in the tale' written in response to this. At one extreme this alibi literally becomes the recording of speech and its transcription as 'Fact-Fiction', as, for example, in the work of Oscar Lewis which is offered as 'a new kind of literature of social realism'[48] while at the other extreme where 'Reality speaks', it is founded in that movement from observation to expression in which the source is external Reality and language is without trace, no more than a clear mirror. In the writing of *Finnegans Wake* Joyce demonstrated clearly that the question of Who speaks?, of the origin of expression, avoids the recognition of the real problematic. No one speaks in *Finnegans Wake*: the drama is played *between* Joyce as subject and language (personal, cultural, historical, social, etc.), and in its attention to that drama Joyce's book realizes its scene, reads itself as '*polyhedron of scripture*'. For all that it conceals the scene of its production, a semiotic analysis could, in fact, reconstitute this scriptural scene of a realist text.[49] To pose the question: Who speaks? with regard to Simon's text (a text that is post-Joyce) is to pose exactly that problematic the consciousness of which is at the heart of Simon's *practice* of writing, as is recognized in that brief note by Merleau-Ponty.

The text of *La Route des Flandres* is composed in an oscillation between the first and third person of the verb in which 'Georges' is inscribed as subject; inscribed and lost, 'et Blum (ou Georges): "C'est fini?", et Georges (ou Blum): "Je pourrais continuer", et Blum (ou Georges): "Alors continue . . ."' (p. 188). and in an oscillation between past and present. It is in this kind of oscillation which gives the effect of an intermediary reality that the specific quality of the Simon text is to be felt. The opening of the novel plunges into the transcription of memory ('Il tenait une lettre à la main, il leva les yeux me regarda puis de nouveau la lettre puis de nouveau moi . . .' p. 9), but the basic mode of Simon's writing is the *present participle*, and as he himself has remarked with regard to his

---

[48] Oscar Lewis, *The Children of Sanchez* (London, 1962), p. xii.

[49] Cf. my *Structuration of the Novel-text: Method and Analysis*: in *Signs of the Times* (Cambridge, 1971), pp. 52–78.

use of this mode, 'L'emploi du participe présent me permet de me placer hors du temps conventionnel . . . il n'y a ni commencement ni fin dans le souvenir'.[50] The present participle gives, as it were, a kind of neutral time or, to be more exact, a specific time of the text; a perpetual present but ever deferring to the chain of relations, grasped through the movement of the participles, in which the present element is defined. This movement is accomplished additionally in the absence of punctuation, in the battle against the sentence (Simon's sentences are often pages long, coming to a perfunctory halt), and in the flow of the writing into 'digression', into parentheses that move into parentheses within parentheses and that are often never finally closed. This seamless flow of writing has (it realizes), however, its own coherence, even if it is not that of a straightforward progression to a fixed point of truth. All the significance of the text is precisely in the organization of this coherence achieved in a *practice* of writing.

This organization may be understood in terms of a play of metonymy and metaphor. The following passage gives a very simple example of metonymy where, the father as writer and guardian of the word being defined in terms of the facts of his writing, the word *encre* found in the course of the writing (where it functions already, in fact, as metaphor) calls metonymically for the father :

'il croyait entendre tous les chevaux, les hommes, les wagons en train de piétiner ou de rouler en aveugles dans cette même nuit, cette même *encre*, sans savoir vers où ni vers quoi, le vieux et inusable monde tout entier frémissant, grouillant et résonnant dans les ténèbres comme une creuse boule de bronze avec un catastrophique bruit de métal entrechoqué, pensant à son *père* assis dans le kiosque aux vitres multicolores au fond de l'allée de chênes où il passait ses après-midi à travailler, couvrir de sa fine écriture raturée et surchargée les éternelles feuilles de papier . . .'
La Route des Flandres, p. 33 (my italics)

A more complex example, and typically so, of metaphor may be seen in the movement in the following passage from sword to woman via a form of antanaclasis (the sword is already, in fact, a metaphor for the penis, as other points of the text make explicit) :

'un instant l'éblouissant reflet de soleil accroché ou plutôt condensé, comme s'il avait capté attiré à lui pour une fraction de seconde toute la

[50] *Le Monde*, 8 October 1960, p. 9.

lumière et la gloire, sur l'acier *virginal* . . . Seulement, *vierge*, il y avait belle lurette qu'elle ne l'était plus, mais je suppose que ce n'était pas cela qu'il lui demandait espérait d'elle le jour où il avait décidé de l'épouser . . .'
p. 13 (my italics)

The transition accomplished here under *virginal-vierge* is from de Reixach's (?) suicide to Corinne, from, that is, one to another of those key points round which the writing turns. These key points or elements are the relation of the text : that is, the material on which the process of retextualization works (returning nine or more times, for instance, to the (?) suicide of de Reixach), and what it relates, connecting and tying together. The relation of these elements in the writing is *metaphorical*, working on the basis of substitution and selection, as Jakobson has defined the metaphorical aspect of linguistic activity : 'A selection between alternatives implies the possibility of substituting one for the other, equivalent to the former in one respect and different from it in another . . . selection and substitution are two faces of the same operation.'[51] Simon's text composes a kind of multiple condensation (in the sense in which Freud uses the term in his discussion of the *Traumarbeit*) where every element covers and is covered by all the others. To select from the paradigm of elements the (?) suicide of de Reixach, for example, is irresistably, in its fact of substitution (the other face of the operation of selection in metaphorical relation), to present, in its sameness and difference, Corinne or the portrait of the de Reixach ancestor or the image of the horse or any other of the elements. What has to be stressed, in order to grasp the activity of Simon's text, is that this paradigmatic relation is established *in* the practice of writing : it is this work of relation that is, indeed, its *practice*. The writing progresses through a process of selection and substitution, changing direction under the metaphorical relation, very often in that *virginal-vierge* kind of movement in the example given above, and it is in this progression that the elements are grasped in their relationship, they are related as such.

This movement of the writing can only be demonstrated and defined more precisely in reading a fairly extended section of the text. The following passage that is cited here for this purpose is taken from the beginning of the third part of the novel :

51 R. Jakobson, 'Two aspects of language and two types of aphasic disturbances', p. 60.

174

'tout à coup tout fut complètement noir, peut-être étais-je mort peut-être cette sentinelle avait-elle tiré la première et plus vite, peut-être *étais-je toujours couché là-bas dans* l'herbe odorante du *fossé dans ce sillon* de la terre *respirant humant sa noire et âcre senteur d'humus* lappant son chose rose mais non pas rose rien que le noir dans les ténèbres touffues me léchant le visage mais en tout cas mes mains ma langue pouvant la toucher la connaître m'assurer, mes mains aveugles rassurées la touchant partout courant sur elle son dos son ventre avec un bruit de soie rencontrant cette touffe broussailleuse poussant comme étrangère parasite sur sa nudité lisse, je n'en finissais pas de la parcourir rampant sous elle explorant dans la nuit découvrant son corps immense et ténébreux, comme sous une chèvre nourricière, la chèvre-pied (il disait qu'ils faisaient ça aussi bien avec leurs chèvres qu'avec leurs femmes ou leurs soeurs) suçant le parfum de ses mamelles de bronze atteignant enfin cette touffeur lappant m'enivrant blotti au creux soyeux de ses cuisses je pouvais voir ses fesses au-dessus de moi luisant faiblement phosphorescentes bleuâtres dans la nuit tandis que je buvais sans fin sentant cette tige sortie de moi cet arbre poussant ramifiant ses racines à l'intérieur de mon ventre mes reins m'enserrant lierre griffu se glissant le long de mon dos enveloppant ma nuque comme une main, il me semblait rapetisser à mesure qu'il grandissait se nourrissant de moi devenant moi ou plutôt moi devenant lui et il ne restait plus alors de mon corps qu'un foetus ratatiné rapetissé couché entre les lèvres du fossé comme si je pouvais m'y fondre y disparaître m'y engloutir accroché comme ces petits singes sous le ventre de leur mère à son ventre à ses seins multiples m'enfouissant dans cette moiteur fauve je dis N'allume pas, j'attrapai son bras au vol elle avait un goût de coquillage salé je ne voulais connaître, savoir rien d'autre, rien que lapper sa

et elle : Mais tu ne m'aimes pas vraiment
et moi : Oh bon Dieu
et elle : Pas moi ce n'est pas moi que tu
et moi : Oh bon Dieu pendant cinq ans depuis cinq ans
et elle : Mais pas moi Je le sais pas moi M'aimes-tu pour ce que je suis m'aurais-tu aimé sans je veux dire si
et moi : Oh non écoute qu'est-ce que ça peut faire laisse-moi te Qu'est-ce que ça peut faire à quoi ça rime laisse-moi je veux te
moule humide d'où sortaient où j'avais appris à estamper en pressant l'argile du pouce les soldats fantassins cavaliers et cuirassiers se répandant de le boîte de Pandore (engeance toute armée bottée et casquée) à travers le monde la gent d'armes ils avaient une plaque de métal en forme de croissant suspendue au cou par une chaîne étincelante comme de l'argent des galons des torsades d'argent ça avait quelque chose de funèbre de mortel; je me rappelle ce pré où ils nous avaient mis ou plutôt parqués ou plutôt stockés : nous gisions couchés par rangées

successives les têtes touchant les pieds comme ces soldats de plomb rangés dans un carton, mais en arrivant elle était encore vierge impolluée alors je me jetais par terre mourant de faim pensant Les chevaux en mangent bien pourquoi pas moi j'essayai de m'imaginer me persuader que j'étais en cheval, je gisais mort au fond du fossé dévoré par les fourmis mon corps tout entier se changeant lentement par l'effet d'une myriade de minuscules mutations en une matière insensible et alors ce serait l'herbe qui se nourrirait de moi ma chair engraissant la terre et après tout il n'y aurait pas grand-chose de changé, sinon que je serais simplement de l'autre côté de sa surface comme on passe de l'autre côté d'un miroir où (de cet autre côté) les choses continuaient peut-être à se dérouler symétriquement c'est-à-dire que là-haut elle continuerait à croître toujours indifférente et verte comme dit-on les cheveux continuent à pousser sur les crânes des morts le seule différence étant que je boufferais les *pissenlits* par la racine bouffant là où elle *pisse* suant nos corps emperlés exhalant *cette âcre et forte odeur de racine*, de mandragore, j'avais lu que les naufragés les ermites se nourrissaient de racines de *glands* et à un moment elle le prit d'abord entre ses lèvres puis tout entier dans sa bouche comme un enfant goulu c'était comme si nous nous buvions l'un l'autre nous désaltérant nous gorgeant nous rassasiant *affamés, espérant apaiser calmer un peu ma faim* j'essayai de la mâcher, pensant C'est pareil à de la salade . . .'
La Route des Flandres, pp. 256–9 (my italics)

The words and phrases italicized are the moments at which the writing changes direction in a kind of passage through an extended sylleptic point. Thus : 1) in the series of phrases connected with the idea of being buried in a ditch or hollow the writing moves from the experience of war to the experience of the night with Corinne after the war; 2) in the word *moule*, which the text has already defined in a chain—'moule poulpe pulpe vulve' (p. 42)—as metaphor for the female genital organs, the writing passes from the night with Corinne to a memory of childhood which then gives way, through an obvious resemblance (toy soldiers to real soldiers) that will provide the straight analogy of simile ('comme ces soldats de plomb rangés dans un carton'), to the experience of war, now after having been taken prisoner; 3) in the transition *pissenlits-pisse* the writing moves from the imagination of death to Corinne, returning quickly to the war through the phrase *cette âcre et forte odeur de racine*; 4) in the word *glands* (acorn and sex) the writing moves from war to Corinne and then back again and through the phrase *affamés, espérant apaiser calmer un peu ma faim*. This account of the principal points of movement leaves aside the host of relations of support and emphasis also to be found in the writing. Thus, for example (any real analysis would have to be scrupulously worked through over the whole text): the series connected with the experience of lying in the ditch is taken up again directly twice in the passage, once on each side of its two directions, confirming the original metaphorical point ('couché entre les lèvres du fossé comme si je pouvais m'y fondre y disparaître m'y engloutir', 'je gisais mort au fond du fossé dévoré par les fourmis'); the initial change of direction does not in its change lose the original point of departure even in its moment of change, as the subdued sylleptic recall of such phrases as 'mes mains ma langue pouvant la toucher la connaître m'assurer, mes mains aveugles rassurées la touchant partout courant sur elle', where *la* may be read not simply *Corinne* but also *terre* suggests, and which results finally in the change back at *moule*; the movement under *glands* seems to be prepared in the simple metaphorical relation of penis and *arbre* with its *racines* recalled in the subsequent proximity of *racine* and *glands*; and so on, for the complexity of the weave of the text could be demonstrated a good deal more fully and at a level of detail that could relevantly include even, finally, the anagrammatic.

In the light of this brief demonstration of the movement of writing in a chosen section of *La Route des Flandres* it may perhaps be possible to grasp more clearly the play of metaphor-metonymy as foundation. It has been seen how the text offers a certain number of basic elements or discursive points and that these elements are in a metaphorical relation with each other and that *it is this relation that the text relates*. The main area of the metonymy of the text lies here, although, like metaphor, it also operates in simple classic terms, as in the example given above of *encre-père*. The writing is composed in the combination in a horizontal chain of the metaphorical or paradigmatic elements, a composition that may be understood as *poetic* after Jakobson's definition of the poetic function :

'The selection is produced on the base of equivalence, similarity and dissimilarity, synonymity and antonymity, while the combination, the building of the sequence, is based on contiguity. *The poetic function projects the principle of equivalence from the axis of selection into the axis of combination.*'[52]

The writing spirals round a set of elements, each of which is continually repeated, and in its movement progresses through them in

[52] R. Jakobson, 'Linguistics and Poetics', p. 358.

their metaphorical relation which is discovered as such by that movement. What has to be grasped in the fact of writing-reading the text is the simultaneous relation in both senses : combining these paradigmatically related elements the text relates, reads and discovers, as such, their relation. That relation, named here after Jakobson *poetic*, is what makes of *La Route des Flandres* a *text*, situating it within the, and defining its, *practice of writing*.

Perhaps the brief and sketchy account given here will have indicated something of the richness of Simon's writing, but that richness is only fully available, of course, in the experience of reading his texts. Proust, it may be remembered, offered *A la recherche du temps perdu* as a demonstration in reading, the work on the text of oneself ('l'oeuvre de soi'[53]), as, in the work of *reading* it demands (and be it remembered too in this connection that Joyce could propose his work as a lifetime's study for his readers), a potential instrument for the realization of that text in which the reader is constituted : 'L'ouvrage de l'écrivain n'est qu'une espèce d'instrument optique qu'il offre au lecteur afin de lui permettre de discerner ce que, sans ce livre, il n'eût peut-être pas vu en soi-même.'[54] Simon's work likewise is a demonstration of reading in just this sense, but where Proust came to rest in the achievement of the 'seul livre vrai', written obliquely through the narration of the necessity for its writing, for Simon there is no rest, only a continual work of extension and rerelation under the exigences of, as the closing phrase of *La Route des Flandres* expresses it, 'l'incohérent, nonchalant, impersonnel et destructeur travail du temps' (p. 314).

[53] *Contre Sainte-Beuve*, p. 141.
[54] *A la recherche du temps perdu*, III, p. 911.

5

Philippe Sollers

'Nous avons le *droit* d'exiger des écrivains une attitude critique et pratiquement scientifique vis à vis d'eux-mêmes, en rupture définitive avec l'individualisme du prétendu créateur des formes.'

PHILIPPE SOLLERS

The practice of writing has been described in the preceding chapters in terms of an exploration of the processes of signification, of the production of meanings. That exploration is worked through by the various novelists in various areas of reality, a reality which is grasped as by definition significant, as a process of articulation. It is on the recognition of reality as process that this literature grounds its practice: 'La littérature? C'est pouvoir dire par quels signes notre réalité vient vers nous.' The development of such a practice has run parallel with a general development of semiotics or semiology as a crucial area of contemporary theory and within this area there has been, and is being, elaborated a textual semiotics the theoretical reflection of which has made a key contribution towards the possibilities of reading the texts of the practice of writing. This 'parallel' should, in fact, finally be conceived of rather as a direct interaction, so that, for example, the texts of Mallarmé and Joyce are thought of not as 'literature' (now, almost inevitably, irredeemably a term of recuperation that serves to situate texts in a carefully defined marginal position as 'fiction', 'imaginative fantasy', or whatever) but as a *work*, an *activity* of *writing* breaking through the categories into which we 'naturally' divide our discourse; in the same way that semiotics or semiology, the general science of signs, working on modes of signification and thus itself calling in question these 'natural' divisions by thinking their *systematic* reality in a particular social practice, cannot but reflect on itself in *its* form of discourse as a process of signification, in, that is, its reality as *writing*. There is no call for surprise if the work of a semiologist like Roland Barthes leads to a text such as *L'Empire des signes* in which the author, through the personal experience of Japan, places himself 'en situation d'écriture',[1] tracing in the writing of that other culture the limits of his own writing. The same reflexive presence of writing could be demonstrated in different ways in the *Ecrits* of Jacques Lacan or the *Mythologiques* of Claude Lévi-Strauss. So too the work of Philippe Sollers, whose first books were written from within the traditional limitations of 'literature', can today be understood as a practice of writing carried through simultaneously, and without break, both in his development of a textual science and in his production of texts still headed *'roman'* : a practice that is aimed precisely at the disruption of those traditional categories in the naturalization of which there operates the refusal to grasp the significance of reality. As Sollers himself put it at an early stage of the formulation of his work in these terms : 'Aujourd'hui je suis presque libre d'écrire un livre, le livre par excellence, inclassable, ne correspondant à aucune forme précise, qui soit à la fois un roman, un poème et une critique.'[2]

It is with an introduction to the work of Sollers that this present essay will conclude, with the aim thereby of drawing together some of its own main themes by stressing the context of this semiotic activity that comprehends the practice of writing and by indicating the terms of the extension and critique of the nouveau roman by a body of contemporary French writing, the theoretical-critical-creative achievement of which is already considerable. This chapter moves, therefore, from a brief insistence on some main points in semiological thinking (thinking of the sign, of sign-ification) to the more particular consideration of Sollers' work.

I

In the course of *Die Frage nach dem Ursprung der Geometrie als intentional-historisches Problem*,[3] the remarkable study in which he

---

[1] Roland Barthes, *L'Empire des signes* (Geneva, 1970), p. 11.

[2] (Interview) *Le Figaro Littéraire*, 22 September 1962, p. 3.

[3] The title was given to the piece by E. Fink on the occasion of his publication of the transcript made from the manuscript, *Revue Internationale de Philosophie* No. 2, January 1939, pp. 202–25. My references are to the text established by W. Biemal in *Gesammelte Werke*, Vol. VI (The Hague, 1954), pp. 365–86.

discusses the exemplary case of geometry in the perspective of a phenomenological 'history', the description of the sense of the objective idealities of which geometry provides an example, Husserl introduces the concept of *reactivation (Reaktivierung)*. The development of this concept in Husserl is bound up with the notion of *crisis* which, as is well known, increasingly crystallized his analysis of the predicament of Western thought and society. The crisis is the methodological ignorance of man's various modes of knowledge (philosophy included), of their origin, or, properly speaking, of their *sense* : they are, to put it another way, taken for granted, their sense is no longer consciously questioned, they are accepted al(l-)ready in the thesis of the natural attitude (*natürliche Einstellung*).

Let us consider again at this point Husserl's characterization of the natural attitude in the *Ideen* to which reference was made above in the course of the discussion of Robbe-Grillet :

'I find ever present and standing facing me a single spatio-temporal reality of which I myself am a part, as do all other men found in it and relating to it in the same way. This "reality", as the word already indicates, I find *existing out there and I receive it just as it presents itself to me, as something existing out there.* "The" world as reality is always there : at the most it is here and there "other" than I supposed it, and should it be necessary to exclude this or that under the title "figment of the imagination", "hallucination", etc., I exclude it from this world which in the attitude of the general thesis is always the world existing out there. It is the aim of the *sciences issuing from the natural attitude* to attain a knowledge of this world more comprehensive, more reliable, and in every respect more perfect than that offered by the simple information received from experience, and to resolve all the problems of scientific knowledge that offer themselves upon its ground.'[4]

It is this attitude, of course, that it will be the task of phenomenology to suspend in the practice of the phenomenological reduction (*epoché*), the putting into brackets of the general thesis; its aim being the description of the objects of consciousness as they present themselves, the investigation of phenomena as the correlates of the acts which intend them, the exploration, finally, of the construction of the natural attitude. It is not necessary in the context of the present work to enter into detailed discussion of the difficult problem of the status of a 'phenomenological residuum' ('phänomenologisches

4 *Gesammelte Werke*, Vol. III, p. 63.

Residuum', 'züruck als eine prinzipiell eigenartige Seinsregion'[5]) in the development of Husserl's philosophy (though it will be seen later how semiotic reflection must call into question and reject the concept of an original presence or idea), nor into discussion of the radical extension and recasting of that philosophy in what has come to be called existential phenomenology (something of which was indicated in the chapter on Robbe-Grillet). What must concern us here is the recognition of a natural attitude in which a particular reality, *'sinnlich menschliche Tätigkeit, Praxis'* in Marx's words,[6] is taken for granted, regarded as in some sense immediate and absolute, and, above all, the recognition of a social status with regard to this natural attitude, of its social construction.

Marx has described the position of society as area of production between man and nature, an area which is the very possibility of their realization :

'Just as society itself produces *man as man*, so is society *produced* by him. Activity and mind, both in their content and in their mode of existence, are *social* : *social* activity and *social* mind. The *human* essence of nature first exists only for *social* man; for only here does nature exist as a *bond* for him with *man*—as his existence for the other and the other's existence for him—as the life element of human reality. Only here does nature exist as the *foundation* of his own *human* existence, and nature become man for him. Thus society is the unity of being of man with nature, the naturalism of man and the humanism of nature both brought to fulfilment.'[7]

Man is born into a society, into a particular social construction of reality, a particular real-ization, which he learns in the process of his growth as an individual and which, as part of that growth, is necessarily projected in its normality as natural : it is as real as himself. This is the learning of the natural attitude and, as Husserl's description of it suggests, the reality of the natural attitude has as its principle a system of *intelligibility* that can contain (as 'hallucination', 'imagination', 'nonsense', 'madness', or whatever) even those elements which are 'other'.[8] Reality is a formal process generated in a social production that transforms in its generation. The ground of this intelligibility of reality is, of course, language as articulation of reality :

5 Ibid., p. 72.   6 *Marx-Engels Werke*, Vol. 3, p. 5.
7 *Marx-Engels Gesamtausgabe*, I. 3., p. 116.
8 Michel Foucault's *Histoire de la folie à l'âge classique* (Paris, 1961), 'histoire de l'autre', traces clearly the fact of madness as a form (not as a sickness), a differential function in the system of a given society's knowledge.

'Le langage *re-produit* la réalité. Cela est à entendre de la manière la plus littérale : la réalité est produite à nouveau par le truchement du langage . . . Le langage reproduit le monde, mais en le soumettant à son organisation propre.'[9]

Language operates a *découpage*, articulates a reality out of the plenitude of existence in and through which man realizes himself and his world, and in this productive role is crucial to the processes of perception and thought. The world of things is realized in language. Reality is always intelligible or significant and, as Husserl stressed, thingness (*Dinglichkeit*) is more than the materiality of an object :

'men, necessarily existing in community, cannot be thought of as simple bodies [*als blosse Körper*] and whatever the cultural object relating to them structurally, it is not exhausted in its material being [*sich ja nicht im körperlichen Sein erschöpfen*].'[10]

Language is not, of course, however, the only mode of semiotic activity of society in its production of social reality which can, in fact, be grasped in terms of the interaction of a series of languages or systems of articulation and communication of meanings. It is from this standpoint that Lévi-Strauss defines a culture as a body of symbolic systems :

'Toute culture peut être considérée comme un ensemble de systèmes symboliques au premier rang desquels se placent le langage, les règles matrimoniales, les rapports économiques, l'art, la science, la religion. Tous ces systèmes visent à exprimer certains aspects de la réalité physique et de la réalité sociale, et encore plus, les relations que ces deux types de réalité entretiennent entre eux et que les systèmes symboliques entretiennent les uns avec les autres.'[11]

Lévi-Strauss studies kinship systems as 'une sorte de langage, c'est-à-dire un ensemble d'opérations destinées à assurer un certain type de communication'.[12] It is here that we can begin to locate the field of semiotics or semiology, the science of signs, that it is necessary to follow through in the path of its development from the key source of Ferdinand de Saussure's posthumous *Cours de linguistique générale*.

In the *Cours de linguistique générale* Saussure insisted on the need to operate within the general faculty of *langage*, the distinction, with-

[9] Emile Benveniste, *Problèmes de linguistique générale*, p. 25.
[10] *Gesammelte Werke*, Vol. VI, pp. 383–4.
[11] 'Introduction à l'oeuvre de Marcel Mauss': in M. Mauss, *Sociologie et anthropologie* (Paris, 1950), p. xix.   [12] *Anthropologie structurale* (Paris, 1958), p. 69.

in which is found the object of linguistics, between *langue* and *parole*. Thus the tripartite articulation of *langage—langue—parole* : where the first is the general phenomenon and the third the individual moments of language use, particular utterances, the second is the transindividual system or code (*'le code de la langue'*) of elements and rules underlying and assuring individual messages. *Langue* and *parole* are thus in a complex relationship of, as it were, inter-realization : *langue* is realized in *parole*, but there is no parole without *langue*. It is impossible to think *parole* as in some sense *before langue*. The problem of origin loses its sense : it is not a question of tracing an 'evolutionary' development of language from early crudity to ever greater complexity and perfection, but of describing structural transformation. *Parole* is always already the realization of a complex structural reality ('every language so far studied, no matter how "backward" or "uncivilized" the people speaking it, has proved on investigation to be a complex and highly developed system of communication'[13]) which it is the task of linguistics to describe in its operation of the abstraction of *langue* from *langage*. Saussure comments that 'c'est du tout solidaire qu'il faut partir pour obtenir par analyse les éléments qu'il renferme',[14] to obtain, as it may be expressed, the structure of the system. It is thus that it was expressed by Trubetzkoy with respect to one of these systems (language being seen, in fact, as a set of interrelated systems) : 'la phonologie . . . part du système comme d'un tout organique, dont elle étudie la structure'.[15]

[13] John Lyons, *Introduction to Theoretical Linguistics*, p. 44. Cf. supra Chapter I, p. 18.
[14] *Cours de linguistique générale* (Paris, 1922) (second edition), p. 157.
[15] Cit. Benveniste, *Problèmes de linguistique générale*, p. 95. It may be recalled here that the Saussurian *langue/parole* model has been recast (which does not mean abandoned) by Chomsky in terms of *competence* ('the speaker-hearer's knowledge of his language') and *performance* ('the actual use of language in concrete situations') in the development of a linguistics within which the formal conditions of 'creative' individual acts of speech can be described. The limitations for Chomsky of the Saussurian model depend on its inability to 'come to grips with the recursive processes underlying sentence formation', it appearing to 'regard sentence formation as a matter of *parole* rather than *langue*' ('Current Issues in Linguistic Theory': in *The Structure of Language: Readings in the Philosophy of Language*, ed. J. A. Fodor and J. J. Katz, New Jersey, 1964, p. 59). In the actual stage of the development of semiotics the Saussurian model has lost none of its operational validity and in the context of the present discussion it is worth stressing the confusion of trying to 'romanticize' Chomsky's account into the rediscovery of the immediate presence of the full creative subject. Cf. Jean-Marie Benoist: 'The practitioners of structural analysis . . . are not bound to utilise one particular model from the area of linguistics—that of Saussure, Jakobson or Hjelmslev according to choice. On the contrary, they feel able to draw on new intellectual tools

Langue is defined by Saussure as a system of signs, a sign being the union of a *signifiant* and a *signifié* (that is, in the case of a linguistic sign, of a 'sound-image' and a 'concept'). Further, the sign has an arbitrary status : there is an arbitrary relation between sign and referent and between *signifiant* and *signifié*.[16] What is crucial, the area of the fabrication of sense, of sign-ification, is the system of relations and differences in which the individual signs are realized. Saussure is insisting on the systematic reality of *langue* : the two elements of the linguistic sign find their reality not in themselves via some direct analogical relation to 'reality', but in their relations in a system, that is, structurally : *'dans la langue il n'y a que des différences* . . . Qu'on prenne le signifié ou le signifiant, la langue ne comporte ni des idées ni des sons qui préexisteraient au système linguistique mais seulement des différences conceptuelles et des différences phoniques issues de ce système. Ce qu'il y a d'idée ou de matière phonique dans un signe importe moins que ce qu'il y a autour de lui dans les autres signes.'[17] Signification is a formal process : a structural analysis will operate not with contents but with forms, or rather—since what is crucial are structural relations and the old form/content opposition is radically rethought in the Saussurian model and its concept of the sign—with, precisely, structures : the structure of relations of the elements of a system within which they find their significance. Lévi-Strauss expressed this clearly in the course of an essay on the work of Vladimir Propp : 'La forme se définit par opposition à un contenu qui lui est extérieur; mais la structure n'a pas de contenu : elle est le contenu même, appréhendé dans une organisation logique conçue comme

---

when the material offered by the field which they are studying demands it. This confuses the rather naïve idea, sponsored by certain people, that Chomsky's generative grammar represents a kind of liberation from the monster structuralism which is coldly determined to choke human creativity in the coils of its systems and structures. To them, the idea of generation developed by Chomsky appeared to introduce the possibility of a return to the creativity of the free Ego. But this is clearly seen to be nonsense if we reflect that Chomsky is very far from abandoning the Saussurian distinction between *langue* and *parole*: indeed the linguistics of the act of speech which he builds up on the basis of this distinction lends itself particularly to formalisation and is totally at variance with Sartre's free, unpredictable pro-ject.' ('The End of Structuralisms': *Twentieth Century Studies*, May 1970, pp. 46–7).

16 The term 'immotivated' is now often preferred to 'arbitrary' in order to avoid the idea that the sign is arbitrary within the system, which would, of course, be in contradiction to the notion of system. Cf. the discussion by F. François in *Le Langage* (Encyclopédie de la Pléiade, Vol. XXV), ed. A. Martinet (Paris, 1968), pp. 20–5.

17 *Cours de linguistique générale*, p. 166.

propriété du réel'.[18] The Danish linguist Hjelmslev, whose glossematics may be considered as the extreme rigorous development of the teaching of Saussure's *Cours*, thus in 1944, in a now famous article, posited a structure as being *une entité autonome de dépendances internes'*, adding, 'l'analyse de cette entité permet de dégager constamment des parties qui se conditionnent réciproquement, et dont chacune dépend de certaines autres et ne serait concevable ni définissable sans ces autres parties. Elle ramène son objet à un réseau de dépendances, en considérant les faits linguistiques comme étant en raison l'un de l'autre.'[19]

It was in the context of this stress on the structural reality of the sign that Saussure proposed a general science of signs of which linguistics would be only a part (though an important part, *'le patron général'*). This was the science he named semiology, the object of which was to be the study of 'la vie des signes au sein de la vie sociale'.[20] The wager of semiology is a wager on the *sign*. 'C'est parce que la société, quelle qu'elle soit, s'emploie à structurer immédiatement le réel, que l'analyse structurale est nécessaire', comments Roland Barthes.[21] An object, as Husserl recognized, is not exhausted in its materiality (as for Saussure language is not exhausted in its phonic substance) but is held in an intelligibility, a system of relations of which—and here is the task of a practical semiology—is to be described. Faced with the text of a social practice, whether it be myth, cooking, kinship systems, fashion, or whatever, the semiologist or semiotician seeks to comprehend the process of signification. This search is an activity of description in the construction of models to render account of the system of relations that provides the code to the intelligibility of the practice, that realizes it as intelligible practice. Linguistics as a master-pattern may provide a basis for this activity in the possibility of the extension and modification of its models as elaborated in the description of the semiological system of language. Lévi-Strauss, understanding a culture as a body of semiotic practices, thus, in his inaugural lecture at the Collège de France, defined the scope of anthropology within the framework of this general science of signs, of semiology : 'Nous concevons donc l'anthropologie comme l'occupant de bonne foi de ce domaine de la sémiologie que la lin-

[18] 'L'analyse morphologique des contes russes', *International Journal of Slavic Linguistics and Poetics*, III, 1960, p. 122.
[19] *Acta Linguistica* IV, Fasc. 3, 1944, p. 3.
[20] *Cours de linguistique générale*, p. 33.
[21] 'Sociologie et socio-logique', *Informations sur les sciences sociales*, I., 4., December 1962, p. 115.

guistique n'a pas, déjà, revendiqué pour sien; et en attendant que, pour certains secteurs, au moins, de ce domaine, des sciences spéciales se constituent au sein de l'anthropologie.'[22] Here we may return to the concept of *Reaktivierung* in Husserl's thought. In the lecture given at the Vienna Kulturbund in May 1935, Husserl speaks of the crisis of European culture as a pathological sickness of which the dominant characteristic is a fall into passivity (*Passivität*).[23] The theme is a constant one in Husserl : man has lost contact with the sense of his activities, of his modes of knowledge and practice. In the natural attitude, the objective idealities, originally projections of man and evidently intelligible as such, are, as objective idealities, on the grounds of an *inter*subjectivity (the grounds of objectivity), transcendent to man and potentially and fatally receivable as without origin in Husserl's sense. It is the role assigned by Husserl to language and in particular to writing in the process of the foundation of the objective idealities (and thus, finally, of the crisis) that is crucial here. The problem is literally a problem of *reading*, a problem of the sign.[24] A system of signs is always for Husserl to be questioned at the level of its history, of its constitution, and it is in this connection that the concept of reactivation is centrally introduced. The system of signs that constitutes writing renders possible the permanence of the modes of human knowledge, but the foundation of this permanence which, in Husserl's phrase, is a *virtual* mode of communication,[25] is also, by this very virtuality, the possibility of the loss of the sense of this foundation. The movement from sign to meaning is passive, the system is constitut*ed*, and it is this passivity that gives rise to the problem, for, and here we touch on what is for Husserl a crucial element in the liberty of man, the movement should itself transcend the passive reception in a movement of reciprocal recreative conversion :

'that which is passively awakened must be, so to speak, converted in return [*zurückzuverwandeln*] in the corresponding activity (it is a conversion that is conscious of itself as a *Nachgestalt*) : this is the freedom [*Vermöglichkeit*, the faculty] of reactivation.'[26]

Language lies behind the erosion of this freedom for Husserl in so

[22] Claude Lévi-Strauss, *Leçon inaugurale* (Paris, 1960), p. 14.
[23] 'Die Krisis des europäischen Menschentums und die Philosophie', *G.W.* VI, pp. 314–48.
[24] 'Le moment de la crise est toujours celui du signe', Jacques Derrida: *La Voix et le Phénomène* (Paris 1967), p. 91.   [25] Cf. *G. W.* VI, p, 371.
[26] Ibid. (N.B. This quotation incorporates in ordinary parenthesis a comment given by Husserl as a footnote in the original text.)

far as it stands over against intersubjective practice. Husserl speaks, and the tone is indicative, of the *Verführung der Sprache* :

'In the life of the individual, from childhood to maturity, the originally intuitive life which creates in its activities, on the foundation of concrete experience, forms originally clearly evident as such, declines rapidly, and in proportion to the increasing diversion of language, into a mode of speaking and reading totally subservient to the play of associations.'[27]

The problem of origin will be of concern later in this chapter; for the moment it is important, in the context of these ideas of Husserl's, to characterize a natural attitude in respect of language itself, an attitude in which language is taken for granted and is, so to speak, *absent*. Language is *innocent* or *transparent*. 'Pour le sujet parlant, il y a entre la langue et la réalité adéquation complète : le signe recouvre et commande la réalité; mieux, il *est* cette réalité.'[28] Roland Barthes speaks in this connection of precisely a *naturalization* of language and sign : 'dans la langue le lien du signifiant et du signifié est contractuel dans son principe, mais ce contrat est collectif, inscrit dans une temporalité longue . . . et par conséquent en quelque sorte naturalisé.'[29] Language is grasped as an objective ideality in Husserl's sense : it is taken for granted, its reality as articulation of the real, as real articulation, as formal system (as much on the side

<hr/>

[27] Ibid., p. 372. This is to leave aside discussion of certain problems posed by these formulations by Husserl, with regard to which, however, one or two points that bear directly on issues raised in the present chapter may be briefly made. 1) The problem of the status of language in phenomenology is not resolved. The part played by language in the foundation of the crisis to which phenomenology is offered as a response has been seen. Derrida comments: 'on pourrait . . . interpréter le phénomène de *crise*—qui renvoie toujours pour Husserl à une maladie du langage—comme une dégradation du signe-expression en signe-indice, d'une visée "claire" en un symbole vide.' (*L'Origine de la géométrie*, p. 91.) The notion of clarity, the distrust of associations, of metaphor (reference should be made here to Derrida's account in his 'La mythologie blanche' of the position of metaphor in the philosophical text: *Poétique*, No. 5, pp. 1–52) develops in Husserl the notion of the necessity of *Eindeutigkeit*, of unequivocality in expression, recognized as impossible at the level of the language in the natural attitude in so far as that level is existential but posited as capable of foundation (a task for phenomenology) in terms of a science (e.g. geometry): all of which sends us back once again to the unresolved problem of the status of language in the phenomenological reduction. 2) The distinction posed by Husserl at the beginning of the *Logische Untersuchungen* of two types of sign (*Ausdruck/Anzeige*) and the attempt in the course of that work to distinguish a level of pure expressivity, the full immediate presence of the *signifié*, bring into question the *metaphysical* basis of phenomenology exactly to the extent to which it does run back into an original presence 'before' the sign. Reference should be made in this respect to Derrida's *La Voix et le Phénomène*.
[28] Emile Benveniste, op. cit., p. 52.
[29] *Eléments de sémiologie: Communications*, No. 4, p. 111.

of the *signifié* as on that of the *signifiant*), as in Marx's words 'practical consciousness', being lost in the acceptance of its perfection as the natural expression of 'Reality'. (Not for nothing, perhaps, do we speak of the '*mother* tongue', immediate and original gift of undifferentiated plenitude, outside the material process of inscription, of difference.) This loss is the very premiss of realist writing, as was seen at the very opening of this book; realist writing proffering the sign as *signifiant*, the *signifié* of which, in a moment of pure expressivity, is the thing itself, the sign being no more than the gangway to its presence.[30] Saussure's aim in the *Cours de linguistique générale* is the exact reverse of this suppression of the work of the sign. The sign in the *Cours* is not concealed but brought to the forefront of attention and 'emptied' of the full indiscriminate presence of 'Reality'. The sign is now defined as structural : it gains its significance 'negatively' via its relations to other signs, signifying diacritically by virtue of its difference that is apprehended in the system of which it is an element.

Evidently, this naturalization, this taking-for-grantedness, against which Saussure writes with regard to the linguistic sign, may encompass globally the full totality of the symbolic systems described by Lévi-Strauss, social integration being proportionate to the degree to which this totality, or totalization (to use a term that has the advantage of stressing its socio-historical reality as objectification in process) is not questioned but accepted as self-explicitly natural. At the level of absolute acceptance, meaning, paradoxically, would be everywhere and nowhere : everywhere in the perfect clarity of the immediately and always intelligible reality, nowhere in that this reality is lived as immediacy, as isomorphically simultaneous with Reality, in a manner which reduces the process of knowledge to one of recognition. It is in terms, then, of these symbolic systems that a social reality may be stabilized and sustained. A reality is legitimated by the projection and objectivization of bodies of knowledge (mythical, religious, philosophical, or whatever) which are described by Peter Berger and Thomas Luckmann in their book *The Social Construction of Reality* as, exactly, 'symbolic universes' :

'As man externalizes himself, he constructs the world *into* which he externalizes himself. In the process of externalization he projects his

[30] This image has, in fact, now been used by Derrida: 'Lieu de passage, passerelle entre deux moments de la présence pleine, le signe ne fonctionne dès lors que comme le renvoi *provisoire* d'une présence à une autre. La passerelle peut être *relevée*.' 'Le puits et la pyramide': in *Hegel et la pensée moderne* (Paris, 1970), p. 28.

189

own meanings into reality. Symbolic universes which proclaim that *all* reality is humanly meaningful and call up the entire cosmos to signify the validity of human existence, constitute the furtherest reaches of this projection.'[31]

This is, of course, the area of ideology, at once in its classic marxist sense and in the more general sense of the representation of reality a society gives itself, the montage of forms the extent of which is the very horizon of a given social reality.[32] The naturalization of these forms is their presentation as 'full-blown and inevitable totalities'.[33] The operation of a reactivation may be ascribed to semiological or semiotic practice in its comprehension of this systematic and meaningful reality. Understandably Barthes has talked of semiology as a *semioclastics*.[34]

Semiology, then, or semiotics is the science of signs and signification taking the term 'signification' as meaning the process of articulation or production of sense : 'signification, le procès systématique qui unit un sens et une forme, un signifiant et un signifié'.[35] ('Signification' could thus be written for clarity 'sign-ification'.) The field of study of semiology is the production of meanings and its purpose might be grasped as a purpose of *reading* : 'la sémiologie ne connaît qu'une seule opération : la lecture ou le déchiffrement.'[36] Foundations or elements of semiology were developed by Barthes in his *Eléments de sémiologie* and in the short history of semiology much work has already been accomplished in studies of fashion, cooking, theatre, advertising, visual art, gestural systems, cinema, signals and so on, not to mention those studies accomplished in the field of anthropology, which, as has been seen, is placed by Lévi-Strauss within the domain of semiology, and those in the field of literature to which further reference will be made below. At this point, however, it is necessary to develop more fully the notion of

31 *The Social Construction of Reality* (London, 1967), pp. 121–2.
32 'Les *idéologies pratiques* sont des formations complexes de *montages* de notions-représentations-images d'une part, et de *montages* de comportements-conduites-attitudes-gestes d'autre part. L'ensemble fonctionne comme des normes pratiques qui gouvernent l'attitude et la prise de position concrète des hommes à l'égard des objets réels et des problèmes réels de leur existence sociale et individuelle, et de leur histoire.' Louis Althusser, E.N.S., 1967/1968, Cours I. Cf. his essay 'Marxisme et humanisme': *Pour Marx* (Paris, 1965), pp. 225–49.
33 Berger and Luckmann, op. cit., p. 115.
34 *Mythologies* ('Collection Points') (Paris, 1970), p. 8.
35 Roland Barthes, *Essais critiques*, p. 197.
36 Roland Barthes, *Mythologies* (Paris, 1957), p. 221 (all further references to this work are to this edition).

190

reactivation in connection with the work carried out by Barthes in his *Mythologies*.

It may be remembered that Marx stresses that a commodity in its form as an exchange value retains not the slightest trace of its original value for usage nor of the piece of work that produced it; exchange value circulates over a level of production which it conceals, and the point of concealment is money, general equivalent or sign of work invested. 'The process is thus simply that the product becomes a commodity, that is, a *pure element of exchange* . . . The product becomes a commodity; the commodity becomes an exchange value : the exchange value of commodities is their inherent monetary property; and this monetary property is severed from them in the form of money, and achieves a social existence apart from all commodities and their natural mode of existence. The relation of the product to itself as an exchange value becomes its relation to money existing alongside it, or of all products to the money that exists outside them all.'[37] Marx tells of the necessity for an act of *decipherment* : the history of the circulation, its constitution in production, abstracted by ideology, must be reactivated, read at the level of the transformation which it operates. *Mythologies* is similarly in these terms a reading, a decipherment, as 'sémiologie générale de notre monde bourgeois',[38] of the process of a certain kind of abstraction operated in a particular form of society by a discourse all the activity of which is a certain kind of concealment that is founded in the very possibility of the sign itself.

As was seen earlier, Husserl described a 'structural' relation of objects and man within the general intelligibility of a culture so that the object is not exhausted simply in its materiality. It is exactly this area so to speak 'in excess of' the materiality of an object, the sense which is everywhere around us ('Combien, dans une journée, de champs véritablement *insignifiants* parcourons-nous?'[39]) that is the focus of Barthes' discourse. The object of *Mythologies* is the mode of sense that englobes facets of contemporary French life from the latest Citroen D.S. to the *Guide Michelin*, from wrestling to red wine, from the rhetoric of the colonial wars to the latest soappowder : the mode that is that of the discourse of *myth*, the function of which is no less than the transmutation of history into nature.

Myth is to be understood in this context as a second system of

[37] *Marx's Grundrisse*, ed. and trans. David McLellan (London, 1971), pp. 39–41.
[38] *Mythologies*, p. 7.
[39] Ibid., p. 219.

191

meaning 'hooked onto' an initial base system that is itself adequately denotative. This status of myth can be grasped clearly enough in the light of some of the simple examples given by Barthes. A schoolboy opens his Latin grammar and reads 'quia ego nominor leo'. Evidently, the words have a straightforward meaning and, equally evidently, they have a quite other meaning that is *the* meaning that they address to the schoolboy—namely that of the particular grammatical rule which the phrase is intended to illustrate. One system has become the *signifiant* of a second system. This example is innocent enough, but a second from amongst those given by Barthes will be a good deal less so. The cover of *Paris Match* shows a coloured soldier in army uniform saluting the French flag in the middle of jungle. Once again an initial system which gives a fully adequate sense (a coloured soldier salutes a French flag in the middle of the jungle) is overlaid by a second sense which is, of course, the sense intended by the cover's designers—a mixture of nationalism, colonialism and militarism, conveying an idea of brotherhood under the Empire and so on—and which is dependent on the first as *signifiant*.

This movement between two systems is crucial to mythical discourse as analysed by Barthes in his descriptions of those various aspects of everyday life which make up the first part of *Mythologies* and which he approaches theoretically in a long essay in the second part entitled 'Le mythe aujourd'hui'. It is in the moment of this movement that the discourse of myth is to be questioned. Confronted by 'quia ego nominor leo' or a traffic signal at red, I am directly confronted by a semiological system that announces itself as such : the rules of the system are clear and the system is learnt by me as a system via these rules (the grammar is headed *Grammar*, the code of traffic signals is learnt from a book called the *Highway Code*). Myth, on the contrary, is in this respect anti-semiological : it attempts to hide itself as fabrication of sense in the foundation of a kind of 'innocence', the achievement of which is the very condition of its success and, indeed, its central purpose. Confronted by the picture of the soldier, I am caught in a to-and-fro between the two systems, a game of hide-and-seek in which the second (the mythical) effaces itself in the first which is read as its proof, thus operating a tautology (the first *is* the second), a moment of innocence in which all becomes fully *natural*. The ceaseless to-and-fro hinges on the fact that where in the example of 'quia ego nominor leo' the meaning of the first system is of no interest to the functional purpose of the second, the significance of which has nothing to do with a lion, in the example of the photograph of the soldier saluting the flag the *signifiant* of the second system is not arbitrary but fully motivated; the image must *express* brotherhood under the Empire. This expression then *proves* the mythical meaning which is thus, in the reading the myth desires, never grasped as mythical: the soldier saluting is brotherhood under the Empire, brotherhood under the Empire is the soldier saluting—the oscillation hides the mythical fabrication and the continual full presence of the first system onto which the second is hooked founds the mythical meaning as natural. It is thus that mythical discourse that Barthes disengages from a consideration of seemingly normal and innocent facets of everyday social life is seen as no less than a continual transmutation of history into nature, a transmutation that eliminates, like realist writing, all questions (how can you question brotherhood under the Empire when you can see this fine coloured soldier proudly saluting our flag in the jungle?) and, purposefully, itself, in the absolution of the 'Natural'.

May one define a healthy state of the sign?[40] From the position of the semioclastics of *Mythologies*, Barthes' answer would lie in terms of the literality of the sign, the sign that is there as sign and not as the point of a concealment of its work as sign, the sign, then, that is there to be read. What is to be questioned, and it is the focus of Barthes' questioning or reactivation in *Mythologies* and elsewhere, is the *motivation* of the sign: 'dans les systèmes motivés, l'analogie du signifiant et du signifié semble fonder le système en nature et le soustraire à la responsabilité des créations purement humaines: la motivation semble bien un facteur de 'réification', elle développe des alibis d'ordre idéologique.'[41] To lead what Barthes calls an 'activity of the *signifiant*', an activity begun in the questioning of the sign operated by semiology or semiotics, to *write*, is to refuse this innocent immediacy grounded in the naturalized and diffuse repetition of encratic languages, the languages of the general social intelligibility, of the *doxa*, to adapt here an Aristotelian term, which have been submitted to a systematic 'rubbing-out' in their presentation as Nature and to which the novel is a central key. This is to return to our central theme of the reactivation of *the practice of writing* and to that interaction between that practice and the development of semiotics mentioned at the beginning of the present chapter. The nature of this interaction may be better understood if something of

[40] Ibid., p. 219.
[41] *Système de la Mode* (Paris, 1967), p. 226.

that development and the theoretical reflection it involved is now followed through.

It was seen that Barthes can speak of a naturalization of the linguistic sign, of the system of language, and that Benveniste can likewise describe a motivation of language in which its reality is hidden in its assimilation to 'Reality', as no more than its transparent expression. What must be stressed here is that the possibility of this concealment is that of inaugurating a distance between *signifiant* and *signifié* which will sustain the reduction of the process of signification to an expressivity in which the *signifiant* is the instrumental expression of a full natural sense. The mythical discourse studied by Barthes in *Mythologies* is simply an extreme example of this kind of repression of the work of the sign in the foundation of a Nature. In this connection it is indicative that in his semiotic analyses of various cultural systems Barthes has, in fact, been obliged to reverse Saussure's expectation with regard to the status of language in the development of semiology. Instead of finding a place as merely one semiological system amongst others, language is everywhere as the point of the foundation of other semiological systems. 'Il n'est pas du tout certain qu'il existe dans la vie sociale de notre temps des systèmes de signes d'une certaine ampleur autres que le langage humain',[42] remarks Barthes, and 'dès que l'on passe à des ensembles doués d'une véritable profondeur sociologique, on rencontre de nouveau le langage.'[43] Semiology or semiotics is called upon then to deal not so much with the extra-linguistic as with the trans-linguistic, with systems whose signification depends on the relation of language. The problem faced by Barthes in his *Système de la Mode* in the attempt to disengage the system of fashion indicates most strikingly his reversal of Saussure's expectation, since he is there brought to a definition of the object of his analysis in terms of the *descriptions* of fashion :

'La fonction essentielle de ce travail est de suggérer que, dans une société comme la nôtre, où mythes et rites ont pris la forme d'une raison, c'est-à-dire en définitive d'une parole, le langage humain n'est pas seulement le modèle du sens, mais aussi son fondement. Ainsi dès que l'on observe la Mode, l'écriture apparaît constitutive (au point qu'il a paru inutile de préciser dans le titre de cet ouvrage qu'il s'agissait de la Mode

---

[42] 'Entretien avec Roland Barthes': *Aletheia*, No. 4, p. 213.
[43] 'Présentation': *Communications*, No. 4, pp. 1–2.

écrite) . . . hors la parole il n'y a point de Mode essentielle . . . la vraie raison veut . . . que l'on aille de la parole instituante vers le réel qu'elle institue.'[44]

Semiology will thus be constituted as a *translinguistics* :

'La sémiologie est . . . peut-être appelée à s'absorber dans une *translinguistique*, dont la matière sera tantôt le mythe, le récit, l'article de presse, bref tous les ensembles signifiants dont la substance première est le langage articulé, tantôt les objets de notre civilisation, pour autant qu'ils sont parlés (à travers la presse, le prospectus, l'interview, la conversation et peut-être même le langage intérieur, d'ordre fantasmatique).'[45]

This is evidently a difficult and crucial point of reflection. *What is the status of language?* If in his work on contemporary semiotic systems Barthes finds language crossing his path at every turn (and many workers in this field would see in the extension of linguistic models into other domains in the elaboration of semiology an inevitable reflection of the founding primacy of language[46]), Lévi-Strauss, whose perspective is that of the study of the so-called primitive societies, stresses the irreducibility of culture to language and poses the problems that concern him semiologically in Saussure's terms : 'the problem about the origin of language,' he comments, 'is not about language itself. It is about the use of signs. Signs can be words, but they can also be women . . . Signs can be goods and services . . .'[47] It has also, of course, to be recognized that the extension and application of linguistic models in semiology has not been effected without, as Saussure foresaw, a considerable reformulation and critique of these models. The whole problem remains to be worked through in the future development of semiology; most fruitfully by thinking the kind of dialectical relation formulated by Julia Kristeva in the following passage from her *Semeiotiké* : 'toute prati-

[44] *Système de la Mode*, p. 9.
[45] 'Présentation', p. 2. Cf. the discussion of this reversal of the Saussurian postulate by Derrida: *De la Grammatologie*, p. 75.
[46] Cf. e.g. Tzvetan Todorov: 'c'est le langage qui a créé l'homme . . . On ne sera plus étonné, une fois saisie sa première fonction, de retrouver le langage dans toutes les activités proprement humaines, ou mieux, dans toute activité sociale. Ce n'est pas seulement que ces activités s'accomplissent par le truchement de la parole, c'est que dans leur structure profonde nous devons trouver et nous trouvons l'empreinte de cette même structure qui est à la base du langage.' 'La linguistique, science de l'homme': *Critique* Nos. 231–2, August-September 1966, p. 751.
[47] George Steiner, 'A Conversation with Claude Lévi-Strauss', *Encounter*, April 1966, p. 37.

que peut être scientifiquement étudiée en tant que modèle secondaire par rapport à la langue naturelle, modelée sur cette langue et la modelant.'[48] What it is important to grasp in the present context is that in returning contemporary semiotic systems to the foundation of language, Barthes refinds exactly that system where the myth of immediate expressivity and the absence of the sign is most pronounced in our culture. As Sollers puts it : 'Tout se passe comme si on conférait la réalité à n'importe quoi plutôt qu'au langage.'[49]

The basis of the practice of semiology is the recognition of the structural reality of the sign : the meaning of a sign is not in some sense immediate and innate, but differential, the production of its relations to other signs in which is realized its signification. It is this emphasis that was truly radical in the *Cours de linguistique générale* and its consequences need to be examined. Barthes comments in his *Eléments de sémiologie* :

'On notera qu'il ne saurait y avoir une linguistique de la Parole . . . puisque toute parole, dès lors qu'elle est saisie comme procès de communication, est *déjà* de la langue.'[50]

It is the *already* that is important there, posing the problem of the foundation of meaning and, in its most radical gesture, placing that problem in a position where it may be seen in its ideological formation and as to be fundamentally questioned from the standpoint of semiotic reflection.

Let us reconsider here, in the light of the work of Jacques Derrida,[51] Saussure's *Cours de linguistique générale*. What is radical in Saussure's teaching is the rejection of the traditional separation of *signifiant* and *signifié* as body and soul, the insistence on their unity in a single production and the location of the reality of a sign as production and productive in a system of signs. The key passage may be recalled at this point : 'Qu'on prenne le signifié ou le signifiant, la langue ne comporte ni des idées ni des sons qui préexisteraient au système linguistique, mais seulement des différences conceptuelles et des différences phoniques issues de ce système. Ce qu'il y a d'idée ou de matière phonique dans un signe importe moins que ce qu'il y a autour de lui dans les autres signes.' This insistence is accompanied, however, by a series of formulations that seem to define

48 *Semeiotiké*, p. 27.
49 *Logiques*, p. 245.
50 *Eléments de sémiologie*, p. 94.
51 Cf. *De la Grammatologie*, pp. 42–108.

the meaning of the *Cours* at a different and finally contradictory level. It is not, that is, fully contemporary with itself. A clear instance of this is the uneasy position Saussure accords to psychology : the reality of a sign is its place in a system of signs that signify diacritically in the system, but a sign is also defined as an 'entité *psychique* à deux faces'.[52] Saussure returns semiology to psychology as superstructure to infrastructure : 'C'est au psychologue à déterminer la place exacte de la sémiologie.'[53] A further instance is the attitude to writing. Writing is defined as a system of signs and Saussure insists that 'ce n'est pas le langage parlé qui est *naturel* à l'homme, mais la faculté de constituer une langue, c'est-à-dire un système de signes distincts.'[54] In addition, Saussure repeats at crucial points in the *Cours* the proposition that what is essential in *langue* is not related to the *phonic* character of the sign.[55] Yet a whole section of the *Cours* is then devoted to a discussion of the *natural* bond between thought and voice and of the necessity for avoiding the deceptive support of writing : to get away from writing is to substitute 'le naturel à l'artificiel';[56] if writing can sometimes be of help it is only because (and the attitude of Husserl to writing may be remembered here) the superficial bond of writing is much easier to grasp than the natural and only true bond, the bond of sound;[57] writing, finally, *obscures* language.[58] Writing, then, qualified as dangerous, bizarre, travesty of the voice, artificial, must be cast aside for the natural purity of sound, '*la pensée-son*'. Derrida has demonstrated the familiarity of this attitude to writing; it is part of the very basis of Western thought, of Plato, Aristotle, Rousseau, Husserl, even Lévi-Strauss : writing as *drug, parasite, artificial supplement to nature, moment of forgetfulness, moment of violence.*[59] Writing is rejected (with the violence these images suggest) because it is a mode of absence : the linguistic sign runs back into, has, so to speak, an interiority, an essence grasped in the full presence of the voice, is founded (and the foundation is the area of psychology, the context of Saussure's recourse to psychologism) and not produced-producing in the play of relations of a system without depth. Saussure's psy-

---

[52] *Cours de linguistique générale*, p. 99 (my italics).
[53] Ibid., p. 33.   [54] Ibid., p. 26 (my italics).
[55] Ibid., e.g. pp. 21, 56, 164, 166.
[56] Ibid., p. 55.   [57] Ibid., p. 46.
[58] Ibid., p. 51.
[59] See especially: *De la Grammatologie*; *La Voix et le Phénomène*; 'Le puits et la pyramide'; 'La pharmacie de Platon', *Tel Quel* Nos. 32 and 33; 'ΟΥΣΙΑ et ΓΡΑΜΜΗ' in *L'Endurance de la pensée* (Paris, 1968).

chologism short-circuits the idea of *langue* as system and, thereby, the arbitrary nature of the linguistic sign.

Moreover, for Derrida it is the very concept of the sign that is the root of the problem, as a concept inextricably involved (as indeed its very basis) with a 'logocentrism' characteristic of Western philosophy of which the reaction to writing is a startingly revealing symptom. Does not the concept of the sign entail necessarily the distinction *signifiant/signifié* that in turn entails, even when conceived in terms of unity (the recto and verso of a sheet of paper is Saussure's image for this unity), the possibility of thinking 'un concept signifié en lui-même, dans sa présence simple à la pensée, dans son indépendance par rapport à la langue, c'est-à-dire par rapport à un système de signifiants'?[60] Is not the psychologism and the privileging of the voice as realm of the natural exactly the realization in the *Cours* of such a possibility? Is not the repression of the sign paradoxically dependent precisely on the duality *(signifiant/signifié)* it encloses as condition of its reduction? Is not the two-faced sign held in the grip of expressivity, representation, communication opposed to production, constitution, transformation? Does not, finally, the image of body/soul always reemerge?[61] To understand Derrida's difficult work is to think one central theme against these inclinations: the theme of *already*.

In the radical moment of the *Cours de linguistique générale*, the idea of *parole* without *langue* is unthinkable, and, as Saussure puts it, in *langue* there are only *differences*. Every *signifié* is, therefore, always already elsewhere, in the position of *signifiant*. 'Il n'est pas de signifié qui échappe . . . au jeu des renvois signifiants qui constitue le langage.'[62] It is this that Lévi-Strauss recognizes in his emphasis on the inadequacy of thinking in terms of an opposition between form and content (an opposition, of course, exactly complicit with

[60] Jacques Derrida, 'Sémiologie et grammatologie', *Information sur les sciences sociales*, VII-3 June 1968, p. 137.
[61] 'Le contenu de ce vouloir-dire, cette *Bedeutung*, Hegel lui donne le nom et la dignité d'une *âme* (*Seele*). Ame déposée dans un corps, bien sûr, dans le corps du signifiant, dans la chair sensible de l'intuition. Le signe, unité du corps signifiant et de l'idéalité signifiée, devient une sorte d'incarnation. L'opposition de l'âme et du corps et, analogiquement, celle de l'intelligible et du sensible, conditionnent donc la différence entre le signifié et le signifiant, entre l'intention signifiante (*bedeuten*), qui est une activité d'animation, et le corps inerte du signifiant. Cela restera vrai chez Saussure; chez Husserl aussi . . .' 'Le puits et la pyramide', p. 44. Even Chomsky refinds this 'fundamental distinction' in the definition of his deep/surface structure distinction within the perspective of a Cartesian linguistics (Cf. Noam Chomsky, *Cartesian Linguistics* New York, 1966, pp. 32–3).
[62] *De la Grammatologie*, p. 16.

the opposition body/soul, the two oppositions being mutual images the one for the other) : 'il n'y a pas d'un côté de l'abstrait, de l'autre du concret. Forme et contenu sont de même nature, justiciables de la même analyse. Le contenu tire sa réalité de sa structure . . .'[63] It is necessary to think not presence but difference. Posit an original presence, a source, as God, the Soul, Being, Essence, the Absolute Idea, the phenomenological residuum or whatever, and after is thought before :

'Il y a des choses, des eaux et des images, un renvoi infini des unes aux autres mais plus de source. Il n'y a plus d'origine simple. Car ce qui est reflété se dédouble *en soi-même* et non seulement comme addition à soi de son image. Le reflet, l'image, le double dédouble ce qu'il redouble. L'origine de la spéculation devient une différence. Ce qui peut se regarder n'est pas un et la loi de l'addition de l'origine à sa représentation, de la chose à son image, c'est qu'un plus un font au moins trois.'[64]

This difficult recognition is developed by Derrida through a set of key terms : *écriture, trace, différance.* The violent reaction to writing from Plato on is, as has been said, symptomatic of the logocentric tradition of Western culture based on the thinking of a full presence as simple origin, and it is this tradition that must be 'deconstructed' : what must be grasped as origin is writing itself, *écriture* :

'L'idée même d'institution—donc d'arbitraire du signe—est impensable avant la possibilité de l'écriture et hors de son horizon. C'est-à-dire tout simplement hors de l'horizon lui-même, hors du monde comme espace d'inscription, ouverture à l'émission et à la *distribution* spatiale des signes, au *jeu réglé* de leurs différences, fussent-elles "phoniques".'[65]

Ecriture is not being used here in a straightforward narrow sense (elsewhere Derrida will talk of *archi-écriture* to make this clear) nor is the idea of *écriture* as origin to be taken as thinking some original presence : it is a question, as has been stressed, of thinking difference. As is implied in the radical moment of the *Cours de linguistique générale*, *langue* is 'originally' *écriture*, that is, a spacing, a play of differences in terms of which alone does the sign signify. *Archi-écriture* is nowhere present, a moment of distribution :

'l'archi-écriture, mouvement de la différance, archisynthèse irréductible, ouvrant à la fois, dans une seule et même possibilité, la temporalisation,

[63] 'L'analyse morphologique des contes russes', p. 137.
[64] *De la Grammatologie*, p. 55.   [65] Ibid., pp. 65–6.

le rapport à l'autre et le langage, ne peut pas, en tant que condition de tout système linguistique lui-même, être située comme un objet dans son champ. (Ce qui ne veut pas dire qu'elle ait un lieu réel *ailleurs*, un *autre site* assignable.[66])'

If a reading from what is radical in the *Cours* is followed through, are not presence/absence, subject/object, nature/culture (that 'methodological opposition' defined by Lévi-Strauss[67]) taken in the opposition *signifié/signifiant*, oppositions *nachträglich* (to adapt a term from Freud), not foundation but function, to be thought from this *archi-écriture* and not before, as moment of production understood by Derrida in the terms *trace* and *différance*? Every differential element (or sign, to retain the word) bears the inscription or *trace* of its difference (it has been said above that every *signifié* is always already also in the position of *signifiant*), *trace* which is nowhere but in the difference that can be grasped as a *differAnce*, at once difference and deference : $d^i{}_e$(f)ference :

'La différance, c'est ce qui fait que le mouvement de la signification n'est possible que si chaque élément dit 'présent' apparaissant sur la scène de la présence, se rapporte à autre chose que lui-même, gardant en lui la marque de l'élément passé et se laissant déjà creuser par la marque de son rapport à l'élément futur, la trace ne se rapportant pas moins à ce qu'on appelle le futur qu'à ce qu'on appelle le passé, et constituant ce qu'on appelle le présent par ce rapport même à ce qui n'est pas lui.'[68]

The crucial questions are to be formulated not at the level of truth as origin or presence in itself, but at the level of production and transformation that is *différance*. If Derrida can speak of passing beyond *man* and *humanism* in a way that can be placed in relation to that 'anti-humanism' mentioned in the opening chapter of this book, it is in so far as these concepts are part of that logocentric tradition which refuses to think itself in its adherence to a point of rest that veils the distribution of its own discourse. Derrida subverts the traditional notion of the *subject*, placing (in a gesture the history of which includes Nietzsche, Freud, Lautréamont, Mallarmé, Joyce and, in the definition given it by this book, the nouveau roman) subject and object not in opposition but as elements of a single milieu, or, better, of a single mise-en-scène, thus exorcising the idealism that phenomenology, for instance, was unable to avoid.

---

[66] Ibid., p. 88.   [67] Cf. *La Pensée sauvage*, p. 327n.
[68] 'La différance', *Théorie d'ensemble*, p. 51.

It will be clear that the very position of semiology/semiotics itself is difficult in the light of the work of Derrida, the difficulty of its position being clearly recognized by Derrida himself. (One might also read Julia Kristeva's *Semeiotiké* as a long exploration of the implications of this difficulty.) If, for Derrida, semiology is complicit with the opposition *signifiant/signifié* (with the idea of the sign), an opposition which in some sort potentially always offers the possibility of thinking a *signifié* intelligible before its 'fall' into the realm of the sensible, it is no less evident that semiology is not in some way to be rejected, that, indeed, semiology, precisely in its actual stress on the sign as such, is crucial for thinking critically a tradition of the repression of the sign. Derrida's work is itself to be seen as a part of the short history of semiology in the very act of suggesting its transformation. His proposed *grammatology* is to take semiology as the object of its discourse, thus, so to speak, liberating its practice from its metaphysical complicities, and it might be linked to that metasemiology that Barthes postulated under the name of *arthrology* in, significantly, the context of a discussion of one of the most radical passages in the *Cours de linguistique générale* where Saussure defines *langue* as the domain of *articulations*. Barthes wrote :

'le sens est avant tout découpage. Il s'ensuit que la tâche future de la sémiologie est beaucoup moins d'établir des lexiques d'objets que de retrouver les articulations que les hommes font subir au réel; on dira utopiquement que sémiologie et taxinomie, bien qu'elles ne soient pas encore nées, sont peut-être appelées à s'absorber un jour dans une science nouvelle, l'arthrologie ou science des partages.'[69]

That Barthes can postulate arthrology in these terms in the very act of elaborating the basic elements of semiology is indicative. Not from any kind of inadequacy are Barthes' texts ever cautious of themselves, continually grasped at the level of their own history that is itself grasped in the context of that of semiology. *Système de la Mode*, for instance, was recognized at once in the very moment of its publication as *already* a certain history of semiology.[70] The gesture is indicative of the nature of the theoretical practice of semiology, a practice which is always also at the level of itself; analysis, through the production of models of the process of signification of a given signifying practice *and* reflection on itself as production in its analysis.

[69] *Eléments de sémiologie*, p. 114. (For discussion of these points with respect to Barthes' work, see 'Conversation with Roland Barthes', in *Signs of the Times*, pp. 41–51).
[70] *Système de la Mode*, p. 7.

As Kristeva puts it : 'Ayant commencé avec, comme but, une connaissance, [la recherche sémiotique] finit par trouver comme résultat de son trajet une *théorie* qui, étant elle-même un système signifiant, renvoie la recherche sémiotique à son point de départ : au modèle de la sémiotique elle-même, pour le critiquer ou le renverser.'[71] Semiology/semiotics, that is, is developed as a fundamentally autocritical discourse, as, finally, writing. This development in the work of Barthes becomes the recognition of a homogeneity of theory and writing in which semiology defines itself precisely as a *practice* of *writing*, an activity in and of the *signifiant* :

'L'écriture, au sens actuel qu'on peut donner à ce mot, est une théorie. Elle a une dimension théorique et toute théorie ne doit pas refuser l'écriture, elle ne doit pas se mobiliser uniquement à l'intérieur d'une pure écrivance, c'est-à-dire d'une vue purement instrumentale du langage dont elle use . . . La théorie, précisément si on la conçoit comme une autocritique permanente, dissout sans cesse le signifié qui est toujours prêt à se réifier derrière la science. Et c'est en cela qu'elle s'articule . . . sur l'écriture comme règne du signifiant.'[72]

It is in the context of this autocritical practice that what might be seen as the consciousness of the semiotic choice is to be understood : a choice at the level of the object isolated by semiotics, which, as the discussion of *différance* will have suggested, is evidently problematic and must be thought as such, and a choice also at the level of semiotics itself between, to put it very crudely, on the one hand the description and analysis of a particular signifying system

[71] *Semeiotiké*, pp. 30–1. (Cf. the procedure of some other sciences: 'Neurophysiology, physiology, and certain parts of psychology are far ahead of contemporary physics in that they manage to make the discussion of fundamentals an essential part of even the most specific piece of research. Concepts are never completely stabilized but are left open and elucidated now by the one, now by the other theory.' Paul Feyerabend, 'Consolations for the Specialist': in *Criticism and the Growth of Knowledge*, ed. I. Lakatos and A. Musgrave, Cambridge, 1970, pp. 198–9). Evidently, such a conception of semiotics is articulated within a Marxist perspective. Kristeva writes: 'Une telle conception de la sémiotique n'implique aucunement un relativisme ou un scepticisme agnostique. Elle rejoint, par contre, la pratique scientifique de Marx dans la mesure où elle récuse un système absolu (y compris le système scientifique), mais garde la démarche scientifique, c'est-à-dire le processus d'élaboration de modèles doublé par la théorie qui sous-tend ces modèles. Se faisant dans le va-et-vient constant entre les deux, mais aussi en retrait par rapport à eux—donc du point de vue d'une prise de position dans la pratique sociale en cours—une telle pensée met en évidence cette "coupure épistémologique" que Marx a introduite.' Ibid., p. 32. 'Pour nous . . . la vérité absolue étant un *processus* il n'y a que des vérités *objectives* et *concrètes*, définies à chaque fois dans le cadre précis de la théorie et *de son objet*, dans l'histoire des sociétés et des sciences.' Philippe Sollers, *Tel Quel* No. 43, p. 85.
[72] Roland Barthes, 'Entretien': *VH 101* No. 2, pp. 6–9.

and the manifestation in that analysis of its own intelligibility as theory, and on the other the attempt to grasp the ('pre-') work that Derrida comprehends in the notions of *différance, trace, écriture*. In the context of the latter understood as activity of *writing* (as Barthes in *L'Empire des signes* places himself 'en situation d'écriture'), it is necessary now, in order to bring together some of the main emphases of this book and to place the discussion of Sollers for whom the relation of writing and theory is crucial, to consider the central fact of that area of semiotic activity that we call 'literature' in relation to the perspectives opened by a textual semiotics.

Literature has always occupied a key position in Barthes' work as semiologist and a vital point of this dependence is precisely what may be grasped as the reactivation of language operated by literature. This reactivation is not to be understood in terms of some ability in 'writing well' or 'writing with style', but rather as a *presentation* of forms of language attended to as such. The activity of literature is a specific semiotic *practice* : as that of semiotics, the effort of literature is fundamentally an effort of *reading* ('cette lecture —un acte de création', says Proust). The area of this activity is that of signification : the process of the signification of ourselves and our reality. Barthes speaks of the reactivation effected by literature as of a suspension of sense, an attention to the *process* of signification : its purpose is not to communicate some objective *signifié*, exterior and preexistent to the system, but to create an equilibrium of functioning, a signification in movement.[73] It is in these terms that Barthes in his *Essais critiques* values the work of Proust, Kafka, Brecht and, significantly, the nouveau roman, and we may recall in this connection Julia Kristeva's definition of literary practice as an exploration and discovery of possibilities of language, as activity of the subject that frees him from certain linguistic networks. The situation of Barthes' conception of literature (as of Kristeva's)—that of the development of a 'problematic of writing' analysed in his first book *Le Degré zéro de l'écriture* which, at the radical point of its consciousness, gives that mutation in writing that has been understood here in the term *the practice of writing*—is that which serves as part of the impetus for Derrida's interrogation of the sign, and the practice of literature can be regarded as within the dramatization of that

[73] *Essais critiques*, p. 156.

economy of distribution grasped by Derrida in the term *différance*, as recognition of the work of the *signifiant*, of the materiality of its inscription. The text in its activity hesitates forms fixed in sense,[74] achieving in the infinite deference of *signifié* to *signifiant* a totality as 'polyhedron of scripture'.[75] The *practice* of writing defines itself as a reading exactly in this hesitation in a way that has been finely suggested by Julia Kristeva in a passage where she makes one unity of the notions of reading and practice of writing :

'Le verbe "lire" avait, pour les Anciens, une signification qui mérite d'être rappelée et mise en valeur en vue d'une compréhension de la pratique littéraire. "Lire" était aussi "ramasser", "cueillir", "épier", "reconnaître les traces", "prendre", "voler". "Lire" dénote, donc, une participation agressive, une active appropriation de l'autre. "Ecrire" serait le "lire" devenu production, industrie : l'écriture-lecture, l'écriture paragrammatique serait l'aspiration vers une agressivité et une participation totale.'[76]

In these terms, the importance of the area of literature in the development of semiotics and the causes of this importance will be evident. Firstly, as was pointed out by Valéry in a lecture significantly entitled 'L'enseignement de la Poétique au Collège de France', literature is and cannot be other than a sort of extension

[74] This use of the term *hesitate* finds its source in the work of Proust for whom the moment of awakening is the moment of the reactivation of the work of 'la pensée' (normally locked, dead, in the grip of the habitual) which, writes Proust, 'hésitait au seuil des temps et des formes' (*A la recherche du temps perdu* I, 6). It is this hesitation at and of the forms of habitude which is to be practised actively and methodically in the text (and which is the practice learnt by the narrator in the course of his apprenticeship) in its hesitation of forms balanced across the oppositions 'grand jour'/'obscurité', 'parole'/'silence', etc.; across, that is, to adopt a formulation from the work of Philippe Sollers, the nocturnal and diurnal movement of the readable and the unreadable, within and without us. Later in the present chapter we shall have to return to this hesitation and its imagery.
[75] James Joyce, *Finnegans Wake* (London, 1968) (third edition), p. 107. Joyce, it may be remembered, was used as something of a 'touchstone' in the first chapter of this book and it is more than time for Joyce's text to be read—at last—in its specific practice of writing, tracing in its perpetual play around the missing letter (giving the text as 'A Comedy of Letters', p. 425) an activity of hesitation ('HeCitEncy', p. 421), a ceaseless losing and refinding of those 'normative letters' (p. 32), of 'plurability' (p. 104), in which the subject is read in the process of his inscription; the text as 'letter selfpenned to one's other' (p. 489), as 'idioglossary' (p. 423). In a real sense, it is only 'with Derrida' that our reading of Joyce becomes contemporary with the text: must we not, for instance, learn to read in the '*Wake*' not simply the play of birth (awakening) and death (the funeral wake), but also the wake of *différance*, the trace cut in the infinite deference of sign to sign? cf. my 'Ambiviolences (Notes pour la lecture de Joyce)', *Tel Quel* No. 50, (Summer, 1972) and No. 51, (Autumn, 1972).
[76] *Semeiotiké*, p. 181.

and application of certain properties of language.[77] Literature is thus privileged in that, semiology/semiotics being conceived from thinking the semiotic activity of language and developed in the extension and application of models elaborated in the study of that system, it offers a signifying practice directly dependent on the object that lies at the very centre of semiotic thinking. Secondly, the texts produced in that mutation of writing operated in the consciousness of the problematic of writing described by Barthes in *Le Degré zéro de l'écriture* themselves practise, in that writing-reading characterized by Kristeva, a semiotic activity that could not but demand and focus the attention of semiotics in the specificity of their manifestation of a work that traditional modes of thinking (or not thinking) the sign have been unable to contain. Thirdly, immediately following from this, literature can pose accutely the problem of the construction of the subject. It was seen in the discussion of the work of Claude Simon how the return to Freud effected in the theory of Jacques Lacan subverts the traditional Cartesian subject in the thinking of the articulation of the subject in relation to the instance of the *signifiant*. The texts of the practice of writing can be read as a questioning of this articulation, as a fracturation of what Flaubert nicely called the *declamatory personality*.[78] Such a reading will suggest itself later from the discussion here of Philippe Sollers' *Drame* and, indeed, the movement in Sollers' work from *Une Curieuse Solitude* to that later text will be seen exactly as a calling in question of the available and unquestioned writing of oneself, of that declamatory personality. Recent years have thus seen, in the light of these causes, the development of a body of work directed towards the elaboration of a textual semiotics. One seminal point in this development, which must be briefly discussed here for the help it may provide in understanding further the mutation represented by Sollers' texts by returning us to a consideration of realist writing, has been Barthes' long analysis of Balzac's story *Sarrasine*, pursued over two years in the course of his seminar at the Ecole Pratique des Hautes Etudes and published in a certain form in his book *S/Z*. It may be helpful, too, to approach this in the context of a short account of the history of Barthes' writings which will at once extend the discussion of his work given earlier in this chapter in the presentation of a certain perspective on semiotic thinking and at the same time allow a fuller

---

[77] Paul Valéry, *Oeuvres complètes* I, p. 1440.
[78] 27 March 1852, *Correspondance* Deuxième série, p. 379.

account of the definition of that problematic of writing made in *Le Degré zéro de l'écriture*.

A certain diversity seems to characterize Barthes' work as it is considered in its entirety from the earliest to the latest texts. He himself has defined its history as one of a successive play of models, a continual reflexive process of elaboration and criticism. It would be possible, however, to demonstrate an underlying concern in this play and it might perhaps best be described in terms of the implicit question, felt in every line Barthes writes and already defined above as basic to semiotics, *'comment lire?'*. Evidently, this question of reading is central to any critical discourse (though this evidence wilts before much of what has today been institutionalized as criticism in Britain) : Barthes' project is a reflection on that question in terms of an attention to the structuration of literary discourse, to its formation or, more exactly, signification, and, interdependently, a comprehension, from the fact of that mutation of writing to which reference has been made, of the activity of writing both in the retracing of the points of its emergence, thus reorganizing literary history from the perspective of the break represented by the practice of writing, and in the development through the notions of *texte* and *écriture* of the theoretical-practical reality of that activity.

What is literature? Sartre's famous question demands a reply in certain historical terms : what is a history of literature to be if not the history of the very idea of literature?[79] Semiotically, it is a history of the forms of the signification of literature that is in question— the attempt to trace a history of literary language which is not that of *langue* nor that of styles, but simply that of the signs of literature.[80] The process of this signification is that of connotation in which, as was seen in the discussion of the mythical discourse described by Barthes in *Mythologies*, an initial system is taken by a second as its *signifiant*. In the case of literature this process is especially complex since the initial system is here language itself : 'il faut que la littérature *se glisse* dans un système qui ne lui appartient pas mais qui fonctionne malgré tout aux mêmes fins qu'elle, à savoir : communiquer.'[81] Literature is signified additionally, as it were, to the fully adequate signification of the initial system of language itself. Barthes' image for this is that of a tourniquet between the two systems : 'voyez mes mots, je suis langage, voyez mon sens, je suis

[79] Roland Barthes, *Sur Racine* (Paris, 1963), p. 156.
[80] *Le Degré zéro de l'écriture*, p. 8.
[81] *Essais critiques*, p. 263.

littérature.'[82] This is simple enough if one thinks, for example, of the word *flamme* in French classical tragedy turning between its meaning of passionate love and its signifying of the rhetoric of tragedy, but it becomes of considerable importance in Barthes' working out in *Le Degré zéro de l'écriture* of the concept of *écriture* (in the first sense in which Barthes develops this term).

Le Degré zéro de l'écriture, which was, in fact, Barthes' first book, is characterized in *Mythologies* as a *mythology* of literary language : as *Mythologies* is to be read as a general semiology of our bourgeois world, so *Le Degré zéro de l'écriture* is to be read essentially as a semiology of the language of literature studied historically in relation to the crisis in the course of the nineteenth century in which, precisely, the processes of the signification of literature became a part of the consciousness of the writer, the moment, that is, of the problematic of writing. *Ecriture*, as the concept is understood in *Le Degré zéro de l'écriture*, is exactly the mode of the signification of literature, the *signifiant* of the literary myth,[83] and it can best be grasped in terms of Barthes' distinction between *écriture, langue* and *style*. *Langue*, then, is a body of limits and prescriptions, it functions negatively for the writer as a horizon, what Barthes calls the initial limit of the possible :[84] it is a reflex response, not a choice. *Style*, as Barthes understands it, is similarly outside the scope of the writer's choice, but where *langue* is the horizon of his art, *style* is, as it were, the vertical dimension, rooted in the 'biology' of the writer : 'des images, un débit, un lexique naissent du corps et du passé de l'écrivain et deviennent peu à peu les automatismes mêmes de son art.'[85] (It is this 'biology' of the writer that Barthes seeks to describe with regard to Michelet in his remarkable little book *Michelet par lui-même*, defined as a pre-criticism, an attempt to rediscover the structure of an existence, an organised network of obsessions[86]). *Ecriture* is located between *langue* and *style* as the writer's choice as to the form of the disposition of his project, the choice, that is, of *a way of thinking literature*.[87] The writer's discourse says always what it says, but also that it is literature, and the locus of this second meaning is *écriture*. Where, from the standpoint of the writer, *langue* and *style* are asocial, the one in its totality, the other in its particularity,

[82] Ibid.   [83] *Mythologies*, p. 242.
[84] *Le Degré zéro de l'écriture*, p. 23.
[85] Ibid., p. 19.
[86] *Michelet par lui-même* (Paris, 1954), p. 5.
[87] *Le Degré zéro de l'écriture*, p. 26.

an *écriture* is the moment of form, hence of value, and so of social engagement. The choice of an *écriture* is the choice of a set of values, a way of seeing, that it sustains : 'Ainsi adopter une écriture—on pourrait dire encore mieux—assumer une écriture, c'est faire l'économie de toutes les prémisses du choix, c'est manifester comme acquises les raisons de ce choix.'[88]

Roman Jakobson has remarked that freedom in usage of language grows in proportion to the size of the linguistic unit. In the combination of distinctive traits into phonemes, the user's liberty is nil; in the combination of phonemes into words, his liberty is heavily circumscribed; in the formation of sentences from words, he is much less constrained though regulated, of course, by the transformational generative rules of the grammar of his language; in the combination of sentences into blocks of discourse, his liberty grows substantially indeed.[89] This final liberty, however, must be qualified in the recognition of accepted and acceptable forms of discourse in a language that might be called *genres* of language and that, in one crucial area, are being identified by Barthes in his concept of *écriture*. An *écriture* is a mode of organization, of utilization of language (a form) which is social, beyond the individual in a body of texts that may, indeed, very well proffer it as an absence of form, as mirror, immediate representation, or whatever. It must be thought in all its implications that an *écriture* is not a simple question of style in our normal understanding of that term, but of a mode of articulating the real : it is neither natural nor innocent, it brings with it not simply a style, but, in its form, a whole series of received meanings. The assumption by a writer of an *écriture* is thus, as Barthes stresses, the assumption of a certain way of seeing the world, an act of socio-historical solidarity.

It is in this context that *Le Degré zéro de l'écriture* is proposed as an introduction to what a history of writing might be, as an introduction, in fact, to the particular moment and situation of the growth of the writer's awareness of the fact of *écriture*, an awareness which forming a real moral crisis of literary language founds that problematic of writing. The development of this awareness is situated by Barthes round about the middle of the nineteenth century and depends on the breakdown of the cohesion of classical writing. Classical writing is characterized by its unity which offers it as transparent : 'L'art classique ne pouvait se sentir comme un langage, il

[88] Ibid., p. 42.
[89] *Essais de linguistique générale*, pp. 47–8.

etait langage, c'est-à-dire transparence, circulation sans dépôt, concours idéal d'un esprit universel et d'un signe décoratif sans épaisseur et sans responsabilité.'[90] Thus it was, essentially, an absence of writing, absent in the very universalist conception (or mythology) of man that it founded, which then turned to guarantee its transparency, to confirm it as no more than a reflecting mirror : 'Ecriture instrumentale, puisque la forme était supposé au service du fond . . . un décor heureux sur lequel s'enlevait l'acte de la pensée.'[91] This single writing, argues Barthes, is not dramatically changed by the French Revolution and Romanticism : Fénelon and Mérimée use the same writing in the same way. (One can begin to understand in this context how a history of *écriture* could radically alter our accepted ideas of literary history.) The writing retains its transparent instrumentality, even if in certain individual writers the instrument is brought more and more into focus.

There is no form without language; thus form is the first and last arbiter of literary responsibility.[92] The moment of the assumption of this responsibility is the moment of the consciousness of forms of language and their values, in short, of the consciousness of language. Classical writing, witness to the universal, cannot support or create this consciousness precisely because of its universal confidence. It is not until this writing is forced into a recognition of its limits, forced to recognize itself as *écriture*, that that consciousness can be realized. It is at this moment that literature is established as an object : the form of writing is recognized along with the concept of literature for which it acts as the *signifiant*, and from then on the writer faces the problematic of writing. 'Depuis cent ans, toute écriture est ainsi un exercice d'apprivoisement ou de répulsion en face de cette Forme-Objet que l'écrivain rencontre fatalement sur son chemin, qu'il lui faut regarder, affronter, assumer, et qu'il ne peut jamais détruire sans se détruire lui-même comme écrivain.'[93] Literature becomes an object that can be accepted and signified as such in the craftsmanship of fine writing or challenged in the tortuous process of the elaboration of a writing which hesitates the forms which threaten to petrify it at every turn. It is within this latter challenge that is enacted that mutation of writing, marked by such names as Lautréamont, Mallarmé and Joyce, which refuses the transparent language of representation to think language as *signifying*. What Barthes begins

[90] *Le Degré zéro de l'écriture*, p. 10.
[91] Ibid., pp. 81–2.
[92] Ibid., p. 119.   [93] Ibid., pp. 10–11.

o

to describe in *Le Degré zéro de l'écriture* is an 'epistemological break' which recasts the whole nature of literary practice in terms of an activity of language, making of it no longer a simple discursive line at the service of a fixed logic of 'the True' or 'the Real', but a polygraphism aiming at the establishment of a dialogue between writings and logics.

From this break is grasped the key opposition between *écriture* as the practice of writing, the reflexive activity of polygraphism, and *écrivance*, the simple assumption of writing as purely instrumental. The classical writing (*écriture*) described by Barthes in *Le Degré zéro de l'écriture* was thus an *écrivance* in its 'innocent' transparency and Barthes' use of the term *écriture* in his recent work is generally in this sense (a sense in which it rejoins that given it by Derrida), found in opposition to *écrivance*, of a practice of writing, a practice that the growth of consciousness of *écriture* as described in *Le Degré zéro de l'écriture* prepares. From this break too, which remains exactly contemporary (the major points of the practice of writing, as today its radical theorization in the work of the *Tel Quel* group, have been massively resisted and recuperated and this break is constantly remade anew by, for instance, the work of Sollers) is developed the prospect of a textual semiotics as the comprehension of the literary work as writing and the analysis of its processes of signification, including, evidently, the description of those forms of writing characterized through the concept of *écriture* as used in *Le Degré zéro de l'écriture*. To turn to S/Z is to turn to such a description in a form that has particular relevance for our purpose here.

How do we read a text? What happens as the words succeed one another across the page under our gaze? Under what conditions do we 'make sense' of a text? How might we begin to describe the play of the opposition readable/unreadable the scene of which, as Sollers might put it, is no less than the guarantee of our reality? So many questions that lie at the foundations of a textual semiotics and that are at the centre of Barthes' S/Z, which is precisely the writing of the reading of a text in the transcription of Balzac's story *Sarrasine*.

The object of a textual semiotics is not, then, an account of 'the meaning' of a text but of its signification : what it seeks is the description of the conditions of the possibilities of sense of a text, the description of its *structuration*. The emphasis on structuration is important.

In an initial moment—that, say, of the work leading up to the publication in 1966 of the special number of the review *Communications* devoted to the structural analysis of narrative[94]—two complementary tendencies could be noted in the thinking of a textual semiotics : the attempt (for which Vladimir Propp's *Morphology of the Russian Folk-Tale* was a major point of reference) to construct general descriptive models to account structurally for a mass of individual narratives, to define, that is, on the basis of the Saussurian model, a narrative *langue*, and, the second tendency, the assumption of the structural closure of a given text and the consequent attempt to render account of its coherence (and it is here that old notions of organicism crept in again) in the description of the structure *it proposes*. Pursued rigorously, there is friction between the two tendencies : if a *langue* may be defined to describe the realization of a mass of individual texts, how can a particular text be seen as closed in the proposition of its own structure? There, on the ground of the recasting of this problem, is the site of *S/Z* : 'il faut à la fois dégager le texte de son extérieur et de sa totalité.'[95]

The foundation of this recasting is the concept of intertextuality, elaborated by Julia Kristeva (originally in the context of Barthes' seminar) in critique of the notion of structural closure. A text is not some absolute origin or source, but an intertextual space, traversed by modes of writing which write it as it writes them; there is a dialogue of texts within the space of the text. An approach to this recognition can be read in *Le Degré zéro de l'écriture* in the very concept of *écriture* as Barthes there defines it in terms of 'an ever more dense cryptography', the structure of a tissue of texts, the form(alization) of a discourse.[96] Kristeva speaks in similar fashion of a 'croisement de surfaces textuelles'.[97] There is, in the moment of reading, the single text, but this single text is the scene of a series of texts. A given text is literally a dense cryptography, a fabric knit from a multitude of strands, that can be read not simply horizontally, but also, as it were, simultaneously vertically in terms of the relations of its structuration. It is this that is grasped in the notion of intertextuality, the interaction of texts that takes place in a single text. Thus the project of *S/Z* can be understood literally and without contradiction as simultaneously the disengagement of the text from its exterior and from its totality.

[94] 'L'analyse structurale du récit', *Communications*, No. 8.
[95] *S/Z*, p. 12.
[96] *Le Degré zéro de l'écriture*, p. 28.   [97] *Semeiotiké*, p. 144.

It is necessary to stress again at this point that mutation in writing which itself poses these problems of readability and which the development of a textual semiotics helps us to read in its activity in the texts of the practice of writing. These texts that are 'unreadable' and 'aberrations' (here we trace the mark of our desire not to read our own limits) refuse that which makes the readability of the classic text, the *Signifié* : they work in the *signifiant*, offering a multiplicity without centre which calls for a continual retextualization, a reading-writing such as we have tried to approach in discussing the work of Robbe-Grillet and Claude Simon, calls us to traverse their writing with a fresh inscription.[98] These texts are to be contrasted as *écriture* with those texts that simply repeat, in an *écrivance*, the text proposed as real in a society, that move within the natural attitude of an accepted readability which allows the fixing of the text outside of any process of production in Truth or the Real or whatever. Here is the distinction on which *S/Z* opens, that between the *texte scriptible*, that is given as an experience of reading, and the *texte lisible*, given as an absence of language, outside itself, and it is the latter that is Barthes' focus in *S/Z* : its object, that is, is the classic text and its readability which is characterized, as has been suggested, by its *limited* plurality. The task of *S/Z* is to appreciate this limited plurality, to transcribe what Barthes refers to as the stereographic space of a mode of writing. Briefly (and fully recognizing the reduction of Barthes' text that this will involve) some points of this transcription must now be outlined.

The transcription proceeds 'step by step' in the division of Balzac's text into over five hundred *lexies* or units of reading. The area of the division is that of connotation. 'La connotation est la voie d'accès à la polysémie du texte classique';[99] its systems 'hooking onto' the initial system (*langue*) taken as basis for the production of their *signifiants*. 'Sémiologiquement, toute connotation est le départ d'un code.'[100] Barthes' transcription will, therefore, articulate a series of codes in the play of which the reading of Balzac's text is held. The term 'code', however, is not to be understood as the necessity for the exhaustive reconstruction of a particular system : 'Ce qu'on appelle *Code* ici, n'est donc pas une liste, un paradigme qu'il faille à tout prix reconstituer. Le code est une perspective de citations, un mirage de structures; on ne connaît de lui que des départs et des

98 Roland Barthes, 'Musica Practica', p. 17.
99 *S/Z*, p. 14.
100 Ibid., p. 15.

retours.'[101] What is described in *S/Z* as code is essentially the prospect of a code, a horizon the tracing of which reveals the text as inter-textual space: 'Latéralement à chaque énoncé, on dirait en effet que des voix *off* se font entendre : ce sont les codes : en se tressant, eux dont l'origine "se perd" dans la masse perspective du *déjà-écrit*, ils désoriginent l'énonciation : le concours des voix (des codes) devient l'écriture, espace stéréographique où se croisent les codes, les voix.'[102] This is the space of the situation of the text in the general intelligibility of its historico-social context, of its relation to the forms and conventions of articulation (the already-written) proposed by its society which it may, monologistically, simply assume and repeat or, dialogistically, begin to read in that reflexive activity here referred to as hesitation. It is this interwoven tress of codes, moreover, that assures that limited plurality the classic text does possess and that Barthes' analysis sets itself to appreciate even in defining its limita-tion; hence what Barthes regards as the impertinence of attempting to place the codes in a hierarchy, such an attempt offering precisely to read monologistically, to end the plurality of the text in returning everything to a privileged, fixed (there is the privilege) level, so absenting (refusing to read) the work of the text.

Barthes distinguishes five codes at work in the signification of the Balzac text: the *proairetic code* (Barthes adapts from Aristotle the term *proairesis* which refers to the process of deliberative choice between courses of action; thus the proairetic code is the code of the narrative choices of the text, the code of actions and behaviour, articulated in sequences of functions the relation of which in the process of reading is assured by the code); the *semic code* (the code of the *semes*, or units of meaning, that the reading deciphers in the definition of, say, a character or a theme); the *cultural code* (the code of the knowledge assumed by the text); the *hermeneutic code* (the code of the articulation and resolution of the mysteries posed in the text); the *symbolic code* (the code of the symbolic forms taken in charge by the text of *Sarrasine*, the major articulation of which is the antithesis—hot/cold, inner/outer, life/death, etc. and of which the unity is the human body). The interwoven tress of these five codes assures, as well as the limited plurality, the readability of the classic text, which Barthes likens in this respect to a score in classical (tonal) music, in the very limitation of its plurality at the levels of two of the codes which impose on the text an irreversible order, an

101 Ibid., p. 27.
102 Ibid., p. 28.

213

unfolding progression—the proairetic code with its sequences of actions and the hermeneutic code with its march towards the discovery of the truth. It is here that the classic text is fixed outside itself in the image of a 'Real' towards which its writing is an opening out : what Barthes' analysis indicates is that this image is itself sustained in a body of writing on which the classic text, tressing itself from the various codes that go to make up that body, founds its direct, 'natural' truth to reality.

But why *Sarrasine*? For the perfection of its 'tressing' (Barthes' text would here have to be copied out in its entirety for a proper appreciation of this) and also, so to speak, for the intelligibility of its play, already noted by Georges Bataille in his *Le Bleu du ciel* and finely reemphasized by Philippe Sollers in a review of Barthes' book.[103] What Bataille had recognized in *Sarrasine* was its reality as a 'limit-text', one of those texts which in the work of a great writer seem to prefigure modernity, to open out onto that mutation of writing. *Sarrasine* opens, in fact, onto the 'trouble' of plurality, the lack of a full final *Signifié*, and that in striking fashion, for its theme is that of castration. The young sculptor *S*arrasine blindly pursues his desire for Zambinella who is, in fact, a castrato, and he is thus finally faced with the recognition of a lack, an absence, in which mirror-like (as *S/Z*) he reads his own castration. The narration of the story of Sarrasine and Zambinella, which is offered in a contract in exchange for possession of the woman to whom it is recounted (as—and this was seen in the discussion of *Dans le labyrinthe*—realist writing is a contract for 'the Real'), itself ends in a castration : herself touched by the castration of the story, the woman refuses her body to the narrator. This troubled circulation (at its centre there is an emptiness or, in other words, it finds no centre) is found in the circulation of money which is now without origin, without *Signifié* ('les écus ne trahissent rien', says Balzac's text). Everywhere, then, there is a trouble of *representation*, the classic text thus troubling—and this is its reality as 'limit-text'— that which it takes as its foundation : the possibility of exchange, of authentification against an original plenitude. The tressing of the codes places the text in a scene without beginning, the movement of the *signifiant* : '*Sarrasine* représente le trouble même de la représentation, la circulation déréglée (pandémique) des signes, des sexes, des fortunes.'[104]

103 '*S/Z*', *La Quinzaine Littéraire*, 1/15 March 1970, pp. 22–3.
104 *S/Z*, p. 222.

The analysis of *Sarrasine* in these terms is precious for our present purpose. The absence of the plenitude of an ultimate *Signifié* leaves a network of *signifiants* that circulate without point of rest, in a ceaseless process of making and remaking meaning, a circulation that Balzac in the moment of writing the premisses of the readability of the classic text cannot but feel as trouble : *Sarrasine* represents the very trouble of representation. At the centre of Sollers' work— a work which is situated consciously and powerfully in the perspective of the work of Barthes and Derrida that has been described here— is exactly the recognition of that process, of the work of the *signifiant*, of the process of production of our known and knowable reality. It is a process that for him is to be grasped '*tel quel*' in a practice of writing-reading.

II

'. . . le seul moyen d'agir et non d'être agi, est justement celui que j'ai choisi, l'écriture.'

FRANCIS PONGE

'La question qui se pose aujourd'hui à la littérature tout entière, dans la mesure où elle veut être révolutionnaire, c'est-à-dire en état de renouvellement permanent, est d'ailleurs l'unification du lieu où elle s'exerce (en dehors des qualifications secondaires comme "poésie", "roman", "essai"). Cette unification doit, bien entendu, rencontrer les plus grandes résistances, étant donné qu'elle s'attaque à ce que l'on pourrait appeler le statut éternellement platonique de l'expression. Mais si nous voulons prendre conscience du sommeil entretenu par les dualismes, les antinomies, si, reprenant "le fil indestructible de la poésie impersonnelle", nous voulons, avec Lautréamont, qu'elle ait pour but la "vérité pratique", alors nous sommes contraints d'en venir à cette pratique spécifique de la langue qui affirme simultanément les contra-dictions et se cherche en elles.'

PHILIPPE SOLLERS

In the course of this book the attempt has been made to introduce the nouveau roman by situating it in the context of the practice of writing. It has been seen, particularly in the discussion of the work of Alain Robbe-Grillet and Claude Simon, how the novel becomes in this context the space of a reading of the 'novelistic', a 'grammar of fiction' that involves an exploration at once of the novel form and, in this, of those forms in which we grasp ourselves, of those forms of language, or fictions, in which we find our definitions and of which a basic source is that form, or variety of forms, that our culture has been able to canonize as 'the Novel'. The attempt that has been made here to understand this work on processes of signification carried through in the *text* as, in Sollers' phrase, specific practice of language, has led naturally to the description of that work in the first part of this chapter alongside the general development of semiotic thinking. What has been grasped, then, as being at the core of this textual practice is the drama of the recognition of the production of meanings: the trouble felt in Balzac's *Sarrasine* which placed that work in the wings of modernity now occupies the centre of the stage:

> 'Le drame dont le ressort est cette passion peu étudiée en elle-même qu'est la rage de l'expression : voilà quels pourraient être la spécialité de l'art littéraire, le lieu de ses sujets.'

This passage is cited by Philippe Sollers from the work of Francis Ponge in the course of a review of Ponge's brilliant *Pour un Malherbe* (*Logiques*, p. 199). Significantly, Sollers published a novel in 1965 under the very title *Drame*, the title indicating clearly enough the situation of his work within the context of the practice of writing. Sollers' work may thus be regarded as following on from that of the nouveau roman, but it must also be seen, together with the general body of work accomplished in the review *Tel Quel* of which Sollers is an editor, as offering in some sort, in its high degree of theoretical-practical comprehension, a radical advance on and critique of the nouveau roman in so far as that enterprise (its very assimilation as the 'noveau roman' being, indeed, symptomatic in this respect) slipped back into postures and attitudes foreign to that radical redefinition of literary practice which gave it its impetus and vitality: we have already examined the role played by Robbe-Grillet's theoretical writings in this connection and noted Sollers' critical *Tel Quel* review of *Pour un Nouveau Roman*. The nouveau roman, that is, the definition and institutionalization of which have been effected with particular regard to the opportunities provided by the case of Robbe-Grillet, has been too easily available to what Sollers calls those 'tentatives incessantes de récupération et de déviation qui ont pour but de masquer *la réalité d'un travail*' (*Entretiens de Francis Ponge avec Philippe Sollers*, p. 12, my italics). It is in stressing some of the key elements of the kind of theoretical

216

comprehension being developed by Sollers that we may usefully begin
to approach the reality of his work in *Drame*, and in so doing turn
back again to the nouveau roman with the central emphasis its work
has been given here against the meanings with which it has been
recuperatively overlaid, that of the *practice* of *writing*.

1. This comprehension is developed from the 'epistemological
break' (the term has been derived from work in the philosophy of
science done by Gaston Bachelard) that is marked by the texts of
Lautréamont, Mallarmé, Roussel, Joyce, Artaud and so on—
remember Barthes' analysis in *Le Degré zéro de l'écriture* of the
development of a problematic of writing in the latter half of the
nineteenth century from which is developed the decisive break
indicated by these texts of the practice of writing, by the work of Marx
and Freud, and by the work, briefly discussed above, of the elaboration of semiotic thinking. Evidently, the development of this comprehension involves a continual work of theoretical reflection and this
has been carried through in the collective activity of the review
Tel Quel with which Sollers, as has been indicated, is closely connected, having, in fact, been a member of the editorial board since
its inception. In this context, Sollers has accomplished major studies
of Mallarmé, Lautréamont, Roussel, Artaud and Bataille, all of
which, together with others, are collected in his *Logiques*, a book
conceived as the study of a certain number of key texts in history,
the 's' of the title, the plural 'logics', stressing the varying attempts
made by these writers to pierce the space of classical logic in a work
of writing. In this sense, *Logiques* itself can be read as a text, as a
polygraphism aiming at the establishment of, precisely, a dialogue
between writings and logics. The assimilation of these logics in this
way provides Sollers and the *Tel Quel* group with a perspective for
their aim of the constitution of a general theory of writing : 'une
théorie de l'écriture . . . son champ s'ouvre sur tout l'espace des
significations dans l'histoire . . . son objet est complexe, c'est la
théorie générale des significations. Elle peut avoir une branche
linguistique, une branche sémiotique, une branche psychanalytique,
une branche qui serait la littérature, etc. . .'[105] Such a theory, of
course, will need to be thought through in connection with a science
of modes of production and social transformation, a crucial point
of its attempt being precisely the definition of the modes of juncture
of the two in a way that will restate dynamically the superstructure/

[105] Philippe Sollers, (interview) *VH 101* No. 2, p. 107.

infrastructure model. The work achieved in *Tel Quel* from the starting point of the understanding of the practice of literature has been, in the writings of Sollers, Julia Kristeva, Marcelin Pleynet and others, the beginnings of the development of such a theory of writing through the elaboration of the concepts of *texte, écriture, intertextualité*, etc.

The review *Tel Quel* has been in existence for over ten years and an adequate account of its history would demand a close and detailed study of particular texts of a kind that cannot be undertaken here. The brief discussion of that history that follows is limited, therefore, to a simple indication of one or two key stages and factors in the development of the review.

Tel Quel was founded in 1960 with an opening 'Déclaration', that Sollers now regards as an example of 'aesthetic ambiguity', stressing the specificity of literature and the necessity for a process of reflection on that specificity :

'Ce qu'il faut dire aujourd'hui, c'est que l'écriture n'est plus concevable sans une claire prévision de ses pouvoirs, un sang-froid à la mesure du chaos où elle s'éveille, une détermination qui mettra la poésie à la plus haute place de l'esprit. Tout le reste ne sera pas littérature.'
Tel Quel No. 1, Spring 1960, p. 3

The response offered by the review in its early development to the declaration of this responsibility was one qualified, both within and without the review, as a *formalism*. One result of this was the interest shown in the work of the Russian Formalists of the 1920s which led to the publication in 1965 in the 'Collection *Tel Quel*' (a series of full-length books generally linked with the work of the review) of *Théorie de la littérature*, a body of Formalist texts edited by Tzvetan Todorov and prefaced by Roman Jakobson, himself, of course, an original member of the Russian movement. The ambiguity of which Sollers now speaks can effectively be located in the review in these early years in a certain lack of precision and in certain lapses of standard seemingly connected with clashes of viewpoint on the editorial board. (One moment at which contradictions and difficulties are, as it were, clarified for the review comes in the questions which Roland Barthes poses to *Tel Quel* at the end of an interview published in the seventh number in the Autumn of 1961.)[106] The implications of the radically new kind of theoretical

106 This interview is reprinted in Barthes' *Essais critiques*, pp. 155–66.

consciousness increasingly developed in the review through a range of activities—literary (major texts by Sollers, Jean Thibaudeau, Claude Ollier, Jean Ricardou, Pleynet in these first years), critical (the beginnings of a sharp criticism of Robbe-Grillet by Sollers, as also by Gérard Genette[107]) and, so to speak, informative (publication of texts by Pound, T. S. Eliot, Musil, Hölderlin, Heidegger, Borges, etc., as well as unpublished texts by Ponge, Artaud, Bataille) —were grasped and defined in the colloquium organized by the review at Cerisy in September 1963 in which Michel Foucault played a crucial 'formulating' role, as can be read in the proceedings later published (*Tel Quel* No. 17, Spring 1964). In an interview given to the paper *France Nouvelle* in 1967, Sollers acknowledged the importance of this colloquium for the review and characterized the subsequent orientation of its work as follows :

'A partir de ce colloque . . . l'accent ne fut plus mis seulement sur les recherches formelles de fiction mais sur l'élaboration d'un terrain critique qui permettait de ne plus distinguer entre les niveaux des textes, qu'ils soient dits critiques, poétiques ou romanesques. En même temps se précisait la recherche de la manière dont la série littéraire s'insérait dans la politique même; et nous en arrivons aujourd'hui à l'élaboration simultanée d'une *théorie de l'écriture* et d'une *théorie de l'action littéraire*, laquelle se trouve entièrement transformée par rapport au début.'[108]

As Sollers there makes clear, it is from the Cerisy colloquium that is begun, through an encounter with work in linguistics and semiotics (*Tel Quel* has published work by, *inter alia*, Jakobson, Saussure and contemporary Russian semioticians), the elaboration of that theory of writing of which mention has already been made and in which a decisive stage is reached by the review in 1967 with the impetus provided by the writings of Jacques Derrida[109] and the subsequent textual theory progressively being constructed in the researches of Julia Kristeva.[110] The publication by the *Tel Quel* group in 1968 of a collective *Théorie d'ensemble* represents, in this

[107] Genette's essay 'Vertige fixé' first appeared (in a preliminary version) in *Tel Quel*: 'Sur Robbe-Grillet', No. 8, Winter 1962, pp. 34–44.

[108] '*Tel Quel* aujourd'hui', *France Nouvelle* No. 1128, 31 May 1967, p. 21.

[109] For an account of this impetus, reference may be made to the introduction written by Sollers for the Latin American version of Derrida's *De la Grammatologie*: 'Un pas sur la lune', *Tel Quel* No. 39, Autumn 1969, pp. 3–12.

[110] Vid. *Semeiotiké*. For a detailed introduction to the context of Kristeva's work reference may be made to her essay 'La mutation sémiotique' *Annales*, November-December 1970, pp. 1497–1522.

light, both an account of work accomplished and a decisive ground from which the theory of writing must be worked out and defined. It was seen in the first section of this chapter that semiotics in its thinking of the sign, in its activity of reading, can be defined as a *semioclastics* and, in its thinking of the production of meanings, in its recognition of the *materiality* of the *signifiant* repressed by Western culture in a hypostatizing transcendalization of the *signifié* (a recognition in the foundation of which the consideration of the semiotic practices of *other* cultures—Indian, Chinese, Japanese— plays a fundamental role), the theory of writing at the centre of the project of the *Tel Quel* group encompasses the practice of writing as semioclastic in a theory of literary action. The year 1968, indeed, marked for the review not simply the publication of the *Théorie d'ensemble*, but also, in the events of May, the clear definition of a political position in the social conflict, of a political participation without ambiguity,[111] *in essential mutual relation with* the theoretical work of the review that is seen as a contribution within Marxism-Leninism, 'seule théorie révolutionnaire de notre temps'. If the political nature of this theoretical practice and the terms of the encounter with Marx (in which the work of Louis Althusser has played a seminal part) receive little explicit emphasis in the following discussion of Sollers' work, the major emphasis of which is on the development of the novel in relation to the elaboration of the concept of *texte* and, hence, on that work which Sollers has continued to publish under the general heading of '*roman*', then it has to be stressed from the outset against that lack of emphasis (which is in itself and however unintentionally already a mode of recuperation) that the situation of the work *in* a political struggle is *central* to the activity of Sollers and *Tel Quel*. The aim of *Tel Quel* has been defined by Sollers as the articulation of a politics connected logically with a non-representative dynamic of writing; an aim that involves a constant analysis of the misunderstandings provoked by this position and the explanation of their social and economic derivation and the elaboration of the relations between such a reflexive non-representative writing in its activity and historical and dialectical materialism.[112] It is neither accident nor irrelevance that Sollers is currently working on a book to be called *Sur le matérialisme*.

---

111 'Nous y participons politiquement sans ambiguités', 'La révolution ici maintenant', *Tel Quel* No. 34, Summer 1968, p. 3. Cf. Sollers' 'Printemps rouge' in J. Thibaudeau, *Mai 1968 en France* (Paris, 1970), pp. 7–24.
112 Vid. *Théorie d'ensemble*, p. 10.

What does need to be outlined in a little more detail for present purposes in this brief sketch of the history of *Tel Quel* is the relation of the review and of Sollers in particular to the nouveau roman. In the first chapter of this book, the nouveau roman was described —in so far as its development was concerned—as a phenomenon of the 1950s. *Tel Quel*, founded in 1960, can be regarded as finding its beginning exactly in the ascendant moment of the nouveau roman, just at the time of the publication of the major works that finally established the seriousness of the new novelists: Robbe-Grillet's *Dans le labyrinthe* of 1959, Nathalie Sarraute's *Le Planétarium* of the same year, Simon's *La Route des Flandres* and Butor's *Degrés* of 1960, all of which novels had, of course, been preceded by (quantitatively and qualitatively) considerable bodies of work. To place *Tel Quel* 'in the wake of' the nouveau roman is no more than to assent to the explicit acknowledgements of the group: Sollers in 1962 was able to characterize the nouveau roman as 'l'expérience qui m'a appris à être sérieux'.[113] It was this lesson of seriousness, provided by its attention to the specificity of writing, that made the nouveau roman the determining factor in the possibility of the foundation of the review. As Sollers put it in 1967: 'En 1960 la seule force qui se présente du point de vue formel en même temps que du point de vue d'une reconversion idéologique possible des manières de traiter de la littérature, c'est le nouveau roman.'[114] The nouveau roman, that is, in its consciousness as fiction and its exploration of fictions, acknowledged a reflection on the specificity of literature that we have been able to define in these pages in terms of a practice of writing, offering in that acknowledgement a point of challenge to the general recuperation and institutionalization of literature as confirmation operated by society. In the very first number of *Tel Quel* Sollers indicates admiration for *Dans le labyrinthe* and *Le Planétarium* amongst recently published books and subsequent numbers continued to manifest the importance of the nouveau roman for the review's enterprise by the publication of texts (by Simon, Pinget, Butor), interviews (with Robbe-Grillet, Nathalie Sarraute, Butor), and critical studies (by Genette, Ricardou, Sollers himself). In view of the confusion that was indicated above in the discussion of the theoretical writings of Robbe-Grillet, however, it is not surprising to find admiration increasingly qualified by a central critique, the terms of which are firmly set out

113 (Interview) *Le Figaro Littéraire*, 27 September 1962, p. 3.
114 '*Tel Quel* aujourd'hui', p. 21.

in Sollers' review of *Pour un Nouveau Roman* in 1964 and which is made precisely in the name of a practice of writing. Sollers concludes his review:

'Où trouver un roman nouveau? Peut-être se montrera-t-il, en dépit de toutes les résistances, dans une pratique vraiment intégrale du langage et de la pensée. C'est-à-dire dans la seule dimension enfin avouée (et démystifiée), dans le relatif absolu de l'écrire : à tous les niveaux.' *Tel Quel*, No. 18, Summer 1964, p. 94

Hence the characterization by 1968 of the 'positivist ideology' of the nouveau roman, described, in terms that recall those of our discussion of Robbe-Grillet's initial theories, as oscillating between a survival from psychologism, the stream of mental life, and a decoratively structural 'descriptionism' (*Théorie d'ensemble*, p. 392). Evidently, the present book has moved against this simple dismissal of the nouveau roman by attempting to read its work in the context of its situation within the practice of writing : that attempt has been possible, in no small part, thanks to the perspective provided by the work of the *Tel Quel* group that has allowed the disengagement of the texts of a Robbe-Grillet or a Simon or a Nathalie Sarraute from the 'noise' of the theoretical pronouncements of Robbe-Grillet with which they have been massively covered; inversely, as has been seen, for all the recuperative possibilities of the phenomenon of the nouveau roman, its importance for the instigation of the work of the *Tel Quel* group may be reasonably underlined here.

2. Crucial in the process of comprehension developed by Sollers is a radical experience of language in the face of a general ignorance or blindness : 'Tout se passe comme si on conférait la *réalité à n'importe quoi plutôt qu'au langage*, et le langage ne serait donc pas une réalité, situation, il faut l'avouer, des plus étranges, si l'on considère qu'il est justement ce qui nous fait autant que nous le faisons.' (*Logiques*, p. 245). Language—and to be understood here is that system of differences which Saussure defines as 'the natural' for man, the productive reality of *signifiant* or *letter* or *number* (Sollers calls one of his 'novels' *Nombres*, insisting on the number as concept of relation and difference[115]), the spacing in which the real is produced—is grasped as *milieu, space intermediary* (a collection of essays by Sollers is given the title *L'Intermédiaire*), *area, scene,* in, on and through which are realized the structures of experience. Man

---

[115] Cf. the idea of number developed by Ponge: *Pour un Malherbe* (Paris, 1965) p. 137.

is taken up in that *réson* defined by Ponge : system or network of signifiants in the inter-resonances of which he finds his reason.[116] The choice is clear : either the recognition of the reality of language, its experience, and the loss of one's fixed reality (that given reason) finding oneself *other, outside*, or the unquestioning assumption of one's given reality in the refusal of the (social and productive) language as anything other than non-experience of instrument of representation. The choice is put by Sollers in these terms in one of the essays in *Logiques* (p. 234) :

'—ou bien nous acceptons en tant qu'individus sociaux (et au-delà de la simple nécessité matérielle) la garantie de la réalité que nous donne cette société en échange d'un abandon implicite de toute revendication fondamentale (de toute atteinte aux principes de cette société)—et dans ce cas le langage devient pour nous un phénomène secondaire, c'est "l'art"
'—ou bien nous décidons de nous vivre nous-mêmes et quoi qu'il nous en coûte comme *fiction*, et c'est alors que se produit un renversement décisif, scandaleux sans doute, mais dont la nature singulière constitue l'expérience littéraire.'

The illusion, the fiction, remains first and foremost that of oneself and it is in the experience of language in a work of writing that Sollers will live himself as fiction, read himself in the reactivation of the reality of language as milieu of production, in the drama of the text—'expérience textuelle qui résout la dualité réalité/fiction' (*Logiques*, p. 22).

3. Thus is constituted the literary experience—in the grasping of the experience of language in a practice of writing, which is not to be assimilated to the linguistic activity of speech : 'on écrit pour se taire de plus en plus, pour atteindre ce silence écrit de la mémoire qui, paradoxalement, nous rend le monde dans son mouvement chiffré, ce monde dont chacun de nous est le chiffre dissimulé et irréductible' (*Logiques*, p. 238).[117] This practice of writing is, therefore, in no

---

116 Cf. Sollers, 'Francis Ponge ou la raison à plus haut prix', *Francis Ponge* ('Collection Poètes d'aujourd'hui') (Paris, 1963), pp. 56–7; Jacques Lacan, *Ecrits*, p. 322.
117 Cf. the decisive formulation by Julia Kristeva at the beginning of her *Semeiotiké*: '*Faire de la langue un travail*— ποιεῖν —oeuvrer dans la *matérialité* de ce qui pour la société, est un moyen de contact et de compréhension, n'est-ce pas se faire, d'emblée, étranger à la langue? L'acte dit littéraire, à force de ne pas admettre de distance *idéale* par rapport à *ce* qui signifie, introduit l'étrangeté radicale par rapport à ce que la langue est censée être: un porteur de sens. Etrangement proche, intimement étrangère à la matière de nos discours et de nos rêves, la "littérature" nous paraît aujourd'hui être l'acte même qui saisit comment la langue travaille et indique ce qu'elle a le pouvoir, demain, de transformer.' (p. 7).

sense an attempt at *representation,* but rather a presentation as reading of the movement, the play, of signification. This presentation which offers a production of sense for reading, and not the product of a representation ('Ce livre est tout sauf un objet', comments Sollers introducing *Compact* by Maurice Roche, a contributor to *Tel Quel*)[118] makes of writing/reading, writer/reader simultaneous functions of the textual process. The radical experience of language is the recognition of man's position in the practice of signification, in the specificity of writing-reading : 'nous sommes sans cesse en train de lire et d'écrire, dans nos rêves, notre perception, nos actes, nos fantasmes, notre pensée—mais nous l'ignorons dans la mesure où nous *croyons savoir lire et écrire.*' (*Logiques,* p. 247). It is this ignorance, lived in the modes of separation (between language and thought, language and real, writing and reading, *signifié* and *signifiant*), that Sollers' work (theory-practice) takes as its point for reactivation : 'sommes-nous si sûrs que l'on ne nous a pas appris à ne plus savoir lire et écrire *notre vie* du jour où l'on nous a dit que nous savions lire et écrire?' (*Logiques,* p. 247). The text as materialist practice of language ('pratique spécifique de la langue') in its redistribution and reading of texts, its attention to the functioning of language and the production of sense, recasts the accepted logic of separations in its activity as real process/process of the real, putting writer in position as reader, reader as writer in an interrelation. 'C'est parce que l'auteur est en état de "lecture" qu'il écrit' (*Logiques,* p. 206), the author, that is, reads himself, his construction, in the activity of writing; and the reader in his reading is to become 'sa propre écriture—c'est-à-dire briser la parole qui en lui est parlée par les préjugés afin de juger lui-même sur pièces, d'accéder à sa propre *génération*' (*Logiques,* p. 243). Writer and reader are confounded in the process of the text : they become actors in its process —'le scripteur et le lecteur de ce texte sont astreints à en devenir les acteurs', comments Sollers with regard to his own *Nombres* (*Théorie d'ensemble,* p. 321). (This has already been touched on in the course of the discussion of Simon and, through him, obliquely, of Proust.)

4. Whence the experience of writing, its practice, as an experience of *limits*—'La littérature . . . se bat aux frontières où l'individu se fait autre qu'il n'est permis' ('Alternative', *Tel Quel* No. 24, Winter 1966, p. 95)—that may be understood here in the opposition readable/unreadable; limits presented by Sollers in his work on those

[118] 'La douleur du nom', Maurice Roche, *Compact* (Paris, 1966), p. 11.

writers declared unreadable by his society in *Logiques*, his confrontation of Logic and logics. Is readable that which repeats the generalized text of the social real institutionalized as Natural; that discourse that copies the discourse assumed as representative of Reality by the society (it is the *vraisemblable* of the society). To practise writing is fundamentally to call into question that *realism* (key of the readable, its founding fiction), to effect :

'la dénonciation du prétendu *réalisme* (de quelque nom qu'il se travestisse, qu'il soit naturaliste ou mental), ce préjugé qui consiste à croire qu'une écriture doit *exprimer* quelque chose qui ne serait pas donnée dans cette écriture, quelque chose sur quoi l'unanimité pourrait être réalisée immédiatement. Mais il faut bien voir que cet accord ne peut porter que sur des conventions préalables, la notion de *réalité* étant elle-même une convention et un conformisme, une sorte de contrat tacite passé entre l'individu et son groupe social : est déclaré réel, dans des circonstances historiques données, ce que le plus grand nombre à travers le nombre au pouvoir, et pour des raisons économiques précises, est obligé de tenir pour réel. Ce réel, d'autre part, n'est pas manifesté ailleurs que dans un langage, et le langage d'une société, ses mythes, est ce qu'elle décide être sa réalité.'
Logiques, p. 236

To accomplish a practice of writing, achieve a *text* that demands to be *read* as activity, production, is to transgress automatically the limits of the readable which are always *outside* in a discourse (lost as such in a natural) that it repeats or copies to be consumed. The symptomatic appropriateness of so many of the criticisms of the nouveau roman in the name of Human Nature as *unreadable* has already been remarked. It is then no surprise that *Tel Quel* has become a kind of glib synonym for 'unreadable' in the French literary world and that a certain criticism feels it necessary to declare Sollers' work 'cold' and 'inhuman', talking of 'une sorte de Jean-Baptiste du Désert qui prépare la venue d'une littérature désincarnée, sans chaleur, lunaire.'[119]

Perhaps the criticism made by Alain Robbe-Grillet should be noted here in order to conclude the brief history of the relations of *Tel Quel* and nouveau roman presented above. In the course of an interview in 1965 Robbe-Grillet commented : 'Je ne suis pas du tout d'accord avec certains romanciers plus jeunes que moi qui prétendent être les descendants du nouveau roman et que je ne nommerai pas, et

---

[119] Georges Borgeaud, *L'Année dans le monde 1965* (Paris, 1966), p. 278.

qui pensent que l'idéal est qu'il n'y ait rien d'autre dans le livre que le romancier en face de son papier, en train d'écrire un roman qui ne serait que le roman du roman qu'il ne réussit pas à écrire.'[120] This was answered by Sollers in his essay 'Le roman et l'expérience des limites' published in *Tel Quel* in the Spring of 1966 : 'Il ne s'agit pas . . . d'écrire "le roman du roman", d'écrire que l'on est incapable d'écrire un roman—mais de toucher de façon renouvelée ce point, semblable en chacun—ce centre nerveux—ce "nombril des rêves" dont parlait Freud—ce "centre de suspens vibratoire", disait Mallarmé—qui est à la source de toute fiction et par conséquent de notre vie se communiquant à nous' (*Logiques*, p. 243).

5. Sollers' practice of writing in these terms is the production of a series of texts. A text by Sollers is published, distributed and sold through the channels instituted by the society it wishes to transform like any other novel, and is, in fact, inscribed 'roman'. (That inscription is made as a key to the area of contestation that Sollers defines, as has been seen at various points in the present essay, as the *romanesque* : 'Et s'il s'appelle "roman", c'est peut-être justement pour porter la contestation là où elle devrait avoir lieu' *Logiques*, p. 229). The text is there available for recuperation, to be inserted into the Library, placed in a history (fundamental mode of a society's self-presence), covered by a discourse aimed at the fixing of the activity of the text in an accepted (and acceptable) mode. *Drame* and *Nombres*, however, are not there to be spoken, but to be rewritten, cited, copied out, read, transformed in the production of another text, as *Nombres* will extend *Drame*, as Derrida will extend *Nombres* in his brilliant text 'La dissémination'.[121] (It will be understood why this present essay attempts no more than a pre-text, attempts to remain 'this side' of a reading, in signalling even in this attempt the possibilities of recuperation it may open.) Product/ production, novel/text, object/activity, literature/writing-reading, finished work/continuous fragment ('Le texte n'est donc pas l'objet plein et frontal exprimant un sujet substantiel ultime mais le fragment, l'oblique d'un jeu numérique et différentiel . . . le *reste* d'une opération à construire ou à relancer' : 'Survol/Rapports (Blocs)/ Conflit', *Tel Quel* No. 36, Winter 1969, p. 8); thus may be expressed the difficult point of resistance of Sollers' practice of writing.

[120] 'Robbe-Grillet avait rendez-vous avec Hong-Kong', *Le Figaro Littéraire*, 7–13 Oct. 1965, p. 3.
[121] Jacques Derrida, 'La dissémination', *Critique* No. 261, February 1969, pp. 99–139; No. 262, March 1969, pp. 215–49.

6. Central then is the notion of *text*. By *text* (a text such as *Drame*) is understood a series of relations, produced in language in a practice of writing, as plurality, without centre or point of arrest. The text has as its function, *against* the linearity of the traditional novel founded in the separation language/world (real), the reduction of the distance between *signifié* and *signifiant* in refusing the distance of *representation* (the dissimulation of production) for the *materialization* of the signs in its literarity (as productive) in a paragrammatic writing, a network of relations 'qui nous aidera à formaliser le fonctionnement symbolique du langage comme marque dynamique, comme "gramme" mouvant (donc comme *paragramme*) qui *fait* plutôt qu'il *n'exprime* un *sens*.'[122] Thus the definition by Sollers of textual writing in the 'Programme' placed at the head of an issue of *Tel Quel* in 1967 : 'réseau littéral à plusieurs dimensions, chaînes de générations et de transformations réciproques, sommes vides de consumation du langage par son articulation.' (*Logiques*, p. 13). The text *se li*^{e}$_t$ (reads itself and is tissued) as an intertextual space : presents itself as reading of the texts by which it is crossed. It is thus dialogistic : 'un espace nouveau (inter-textuel) où les livres se liraient, s'éclaireraient, s'écriraient les uns les autres, laissant place à un texte enfin réel qui serait l'explication permanente du monde . . .' (*Logiques*, p. 110). Thus also it opens into the text of the real : Sollers specifies : 'par *texte*, j'entends non seulement l'objet saisissable par l'impression de ce qu'on appelle un livre (un roman), mais la totalité concrète à la fois comme produit déchiffrable et comme travail d'élaboration transformateur. En ce sens, la lecture et l'écriture du texte font à chaque reprise partie intégrante du texte qui, d'ailleurs, se calcule en conséquence. Il s'agit donc d'un texte ouvert donnant sur un texte généralisé' (*Théorie d'ensemble*, p. 319). The text, then, is to be understood as a production in every sense of the term (practice, activity, fabrication, mise-en-scène, drama, theatre) :

'Le livre n'est rien d'autre que le passage du monde au théâtre, l'apparition théâtrale du monde comme texte . . . IL NOUS FAUT DONC RÉALISER LA POSSIBILITÉ DU TEXTE COMME THÉÂTRE EN MÊME TEMPS QUE CELLE DU THÉÂTRE ET DE LA VIE COMME TEXTE.'
Logiques, pp. 112–5

---

[122] J. Kristeva, *Semeiotiké*, p. 184. This notion of paragrammatism is elaborated from the example provided by Saussure in his work on anagram in poetry, which, even if erroneous in the particular point of the analysis, brings to the fore a notion of the constitution of the literary text beyond that of the simple category of 'communication', 'expression,' etc.

In this context it is time to move—with all the reservations set out in the preceding section above—to a consideration of one of Sollers' major texts, his *Drame*.[123]

III

'Je vous propose moins un discours qu'une méthode, moins une méthode qu'un jeu. Ce qui doit jouer : la région qu'en ce moment j'éprouve et traverse pour vous joindre.'

PHILIPPE SOLLERS

The *I-Ching*, the Chinese manual of divination which became a repository of concepts for the explanation of natural phenomena, orders the universe, in a ceaseless process of transformation, in the sixty-four hexagrams derived from the mark of difference, the continuous or the broken line. The writing of *Drame* is ordered in sixty-four sequences, or fragments, or 'chants' (Sollers' terms), or 'houses' (traditional term for the divisions of the *I-Ching* and with the resonance for us in English—and the significance of this resonance will become apparent in a moment—of its use in the seventeenth century as the term for the squares of the chess-board), which alternate between 'il' and 'je', non-person and person, *histoire* and *discours*. As well as the organization of the *I-Ching*, that of the chess-board is referred to as model for the sixty-four squares of *Drame*,

---

[123] This is to leave aside here Sollers' earlier works, only one of which, *Le Parc* (Paris, 1961), awarded the Prix Médicis by a jury that included Alain Robbe-Grillet and Nathalie Sarraute, is still listed inside the cover of *Drame*, and in connection with which reference should be made to the two excellent studies by Jean Ricardou ('Premières lectures du *Parc*', *Médiations*, Winter 1961–1962, pp. 175–85) and Jean Thibaudeau ('Un écrivain averti en vaut deux', *Critique* No. 177, February 1962, pp. 134–43). The two works which have 'slipped' from the list are *Le Défi* (Paris, 1957) and *Une Curieuse Solitude* (Paris, 1958). Both won acclaim (from, among others, François Mauriac!) and both are cast in the mould of traditional 'psychological' fiction, though with a certain edgy bitterness of tone that jars oddly in the latter with a feeling of naïvety. *Une Curieuse Solitude*, the narrator of which is named Philippe and who in the course of the novel turns to a project of writing, a 'research' on memory through writing (Proust is heavily present at certain points), reads a little like a protrait of the artist as a young man. It has recently been reissued as a paperback (Collection Livre de poche, Paris, 1970) with a prefatory note by Sollers referring to it as a *faux livre* written in an *écriture décadente*, though insisting at the same time that it was written ironically. That irony is not *obvious* in the text, and the difficulties of reading it presents in this sense are perhaps a point of comparison with Joyce's *Portrait*, itself now read ironically, now literally by critics.

'échiquier mobile' (p. 20)—squares that might be called, then, with full appropriateness, 'houses'. It was chess that provided Saussure with a crucial image for the structural reality of language as system of relations, formal play of differences.[124] Chess was also a central image for Raymond Roussel (himself a noted chess player) who found in the chess-board with its sixty-four squares the representation of the projection of time into space.[125] This conception is recalled by Sollers in his cover-note for *Drame*, which adds : 'De même, les fragments s'enchaînant ici par l'écriture, voudraient dévoiler une projection immédiate de la pensée dans le langage qui cependant la comprend.'

This 'comprehension' is to be understood in the play of language. 'D'abord (premier état, lignes, gravure—le jeu commence) . . .' (p. 11); thus the drama, this *Drame*, begins. But the notion of beginning is precarious : as in chess, the particular beginning is the entry into the system of relations that are its precedent and the participants are players. The third section of *Drame* opens with the question 'Prisonnier du jeu?' (p. 21). There is no 'beginning' but in the terms of the process of 'comprehension' defined by Sollers. The 'I', for instance, in which the subject finds his expression, can be defined only as the effect of a language which can never know any beginning.[126] The 'I' does not inaugurate, it is inaugurated in the subject's insertion in language; defined—given and limited— in the assumption of the 'I', the subject, in his awakening, is always what *Nombres* refers to as an 'effet décalé'. The recognition is that of Nietzsche; 'I' is never a truth, but the mark of a limit.[127] *Drame* is the advance of a writing held at the point of this recognition : 'Il écrit : 'Dans le jeu, sur cet échiquier invisible (et sans attendre, sans chercher plus loin pour l'instant), je décris celui que j'ignore. J'avance . . .' (p. 73).

This advance is a work on that 'celui que j'ignore' which, shatter-

124 For the chess image in Saussure, see *Cours de linguistique générale*, pp. 43, 125–7, 153.

125 See Raymond Roussel, *Comment j'ai écrit certains de mes livres* (Paris, 1963), p. 154. (It is precisely in terms of the game of chess that Saussure is also able to understand the 'fait diachronique'; see *Cours*, pp. 126–7).

126 As Saussure writes of the system of *langue*: 'En fait, aucune société ne connaît et n'a jamais connu la langue autrement que comme un produit hérité des générations précédentes et à prendre tel quel.' *Cours*, p. 105. This same passage was used as motto for an issue of *Tel Quel* (No. 13, Spring 1963). *Drame* writes of 'quelque chose qui aurait toujours précédé ce qu'il est obligé de voir, de penser,' (p. 64).

127 F. Nietzsche, *Der Wille zur Macht*; *Gesammelte Werke* Vol. XIX, (Munich, 1926). p. 13.

ing the plenitude of the 'I', refinds the subject in his production. The space of the text, in which the subject is turned inside out like a glove ('nous pouvions là être retournés comme des gants', *Nombres*, p. 44), is that of the development of a negativity; 'celui d'une langue négative, d'un "réseau ondoyant et négatif"qui se donne, du côté lisible, un effet de production double, celui de la trace et de son déchiffrement, de son retracement,—procès sans commencement ni fin qui traverse à la fois le savoir et sa parole, le corps et le sexe, le réel et sa métaphore, la narration et ses limites "conscientes", bref le tout d'une culture à un moment quelconque donné' (*Logiques*, p. 255). That negativity is thus the deconstruction of the subject and his discourse, of the world and its sense, of the theatre of representation ('du théâtre où nous allons et venons encore, récitant sans y penser le texte ancien . . .', *Nombres*, p. 37). The text is constructed not as a communication, accomplished in the repetition of the 'déjà dit' but as, in the process of the development of that negativity, the 'crossing' of communication : 'Le monde que je vis, c'est celui que je parle, que je suis capable de dire . . . Ces limites sont grammaticales dans la mesure où je tiens à rester dans la communication—mais je sais que je n'atteindrai vraiment la communication que si, par un mouvement brisant et sans retour, je suis aussi celui qui nie ces limites, qui atteint par cette affirmation la pulsion du sens.' (*Logiques*, p. 148). What must be set in play is the area crossed by the writing and this process can know neither beginning nor end; it is a refusal, for instance, of that point of fixity derived from the institution of the relation 'author'/'reader' (sender/ receiver) in which the book is the point of exchange of a message, of a sense or truth. It was seen in the preceding section of this chapter how Sollers disengages the notion of *text* from that accepted schema and the play of pronouns in *Drame* in which writer and reader are inscribed is a crucial point of its refusal. *Drame* is founded in an exploration (reactivation) of that region that is crossed in its writing :

'Entre les séries incalculables qui se bousculent et s'annulent, vocabulaire en fusion (ne suis-je pas aussi le négatif de tout ce que je suis?), voici celle qui enfin me limite : cette forme, ce corps. Ce que je dis en dépend, n'oublie pas cela . . . Cependant je dois garder le contact au plus près. Je n'avancerai que par rapport à cette carte, le voyage n'est possible que par elle et sur le terrain obligatoire où je suis placé. Et d'ailleurs, cette équation en vaut une autre, c'est elle qui, chaque matin (et je vois par la fenêtre les acacias de la place sous le soleil et le vent;

j'accepte de me contempler du dehors), me remet en face des données,
sur cet échiquier mobile . . .'
Drame, pp. 20–1

There then is the basic focus of *Drame* (that is, of this drama
of writing), that of limits. The focus is grasped from a problem on
which the text is articulated : 'Comment revenir? Comment être là?
Comment accepter l'aventure?' (p. 16). A series of questions
(repeated at later points in the text) pose the project of the writing
and its problem. 'Comment être là?'; the 'je' replies at once in the
second sequence of the text, 'je suis là, déposé par hasard dans un
brouillard lumineux . . .' (p. 19). It will be necessary to return later
to that image of the 'brouillard lumineux', the antynomical resonance
of which takes up a major articulation of the text. For the moment
what is to be retained is that fact of a problem of situation, of 'being
there', and the project of a return ('Comment revenir?'), invoking
at once the task of the acceptance of an adventure ('Comment
accepter l'aventure?'). The adventure is followed in the text as the
pursuit of *'la véritable histoire'* which is announced on the first page
of the text and announced, furthermore, in its difficulty : 'Surprise :
toujours il a pensé qu'au moment voulu la véritable histoire se
laisserait dire. Loin, sous une apparence abandonnée, il la sentait pas
à pas immuable. Même maintenant, il se persuade de pouvoir la
définir simplement . . . Manqué.' (pp. 11–12). The pursuit and
the difficulty are marked again at the close of the second block of
eight sequences : 'De nouveau la véritable histoire? Non. Et pourtant
c'est elle que j'essaie de dire, elle qui probablement dit tout, depuis
toujours, silencieusement . . .' (p. 46). This *véritable histoire* and the
problem of its demonstration form the drama of the text as it returns
again and again to those questions :

'Comment être là? Comment accepter l'aventure? Arrêté, il n'insiste
pas, il attend. Sentant fuir et se dissoudre la véritable histoire, le drame
implicite qu'il était sur le point d'esquisser, qui déjà s'édifiait et se
chantait imperceptiblement en lui par grandes zones transparentes, en
marchant le long des quais, le soir, sous le ciel rouge et noir, dans le
désordre et le bruit et la poussière chaude, l'odeur d'essence brûlée
occupant les rues. Cependant—Il écrit :'
pp. 61–2

Il écrit. It would be appropriate to call that *histoire* (the word
has to be understood as history and story, as fiction) which the text
seeks in its writing a *biography*, if that term is taken with the

force Sollers gives it in *Logiques* in the course of an essay on the logic of fiction : 'bio-graphie, *écriture vivante* et multiple' (*Logiques*, p. 31), a writing that will be the negation of the classic biography in the dispersion of its subject, a name inaugurating and unifying a simple line of discourse, into a plurality of positions and functions. *Drame* comments at one point on the writing of the *histoire* in a manner not without echo of the project in Proust of a textual reality, the project of the 'seul livre vrai' : 'Rien ne ressemble moins à un roman que notre histoire, et pourtant c'est bien le seul roman dont j'aurais envie de te parler (celui que personne ne pourrait écrire, celui qui s'écrit en nous devant nous). Le seul qui serait gagné sur ce que nous pourrions, cédant au mensonge, appeler, comme dans les romans, notre vie.' (p. 27). *Drame*, as *écriture vivante*, is woven through from dream, memory, images of *ville, port, bateaux, lumières, étoiles, jardin, chambre*, forming a network ('cette ville (ce livre)' p. 138) realizing the presence of the body (and the presence of the woman, but there we return to the play of pronouns : under the 'elle' woman and *histoire* are one) in a writing the fine activity of which is not to be arrested, as the passage previously cited stresses, into a novel. 'Un rêve se constitue de lui-même et je suis à la limite voilée du paysage qu'il traverse, ligne de fuite, (les mots dans l'encre) d'où il vient, où il se dissipe . . . Sans fin . . . Dans ce mouvement régulier, balancé, où la terre glisse et se dérobe sans fin sous le ciel . . . Signes, personnages debout, distraits sous le ciel . . .' (p. 125).

It is here in this bio-*graphy* that the *histoire* is to be discovered; its centre is exactly that of the problem of limits. 'Problème : être en attente et vide au bord de ce monde encombré de signes, où je suis expulsé de moi-même . . .' (p. 81). The *histoire*, the true, *véritable histoire*, is the problem of limits, images of which run through the text as a fundamental 'motif' (*bord, lisière, marge, mur, de l'autre côté, limite*, etc.) and of which the writing is the dramatization approaching in the text, in 'le théâtre en action' (p. 64), the 'trace cherchée : passage transposé, lisière où le dénouement a lieu' (p. 24). The image is that of difference, foundation, without depth, against which the subject is described. Another central image of this drama of being there inside/outside in the limits of self/non-self (and 'n'importe quoi peut devenir limite, point critique . . .' p. 36) is that of the accident invoked in the course of *Drame* : 'A ce moment, chacun se trouve à l'intérieur et au-dehors du vertige, du tourbillon qui vient de transparaître brièvement. Encore un instant d'immobilité, d'interrogation, puis c'est la course, le regroupement, l'unification autour du corps désarticulé : quelqu'un soutient la tête ensanglanté, le blessé est en entier rendu au choeur des témoins placé maintenant au centre de leur certitude "moi je vis".' (p. 37). Another is that of the paintings in a gallery that it is necessary to view not simply in their spacing, their arrangement but also, as it were, from 'behind' or, as in the following passage, to see the surface in which they distinguish themselves : 'il faut dégager le chemin qui ne cache plus rien, accéder à l'envers des tableaux, être capable de passer derrière eux et, sans transition, de l'un à l'autre . . . Ecrivant enfin le mur unique où ils sont accrochés, la surface invisible qui les multiplie . . .' (p. 58). Another is that of a picture of a battle (the tracing of the *histoire* is itself a 'combat', p. 50)

'où le même personnage devient à chaque instant deux armées cuirassées entrant par la gauche, sortant par la droite, mais revenant en somme après avoir fait le tour des collines plates, des plaines surélevées, terre brune, argileuse . . . Les lances des cavaliers—double unique— crevant le centre, formant le compas et traçant le cercle souterrain qui les remet encore et toujours face à face dans une agression figée . . . Dans la violence d'être pour soi-même insaisissable et durci au- dehors . . .'
p. 57

Drame defines a method for this passage 'outside', to the condi- tions of subject-ivity; that of writing, that bio-graphy grasping a plurality, a multiple series of relations in which the subject is com- prehended, grasping, that is, a text. Of this method *Drame* proposes a succession of images based on the opposition night/day, wake/ sleep and including the third term of their intermediation. (Remem- ber the image of the *brouillard lumineux* mentioned above.) Central to *Drame* is the series *sommeil—éveil—veille* of which the first and third elements (the opposition *sommeil/veille*) will be reversed in the text. The state of wakefulness (*veille*) is that of fixity, of certainty, of the stability of language. One passage refers to 'la translation instan- tanée qui le ramène à la veille, à l'ensemble matériel et fixe qu'il a pris l'habitude d'appeler "le port".' (p. 22).[128] This fixity is that of a captivity ('Prisonnier du jeu?'), thus of a sleep, a 'sommeil mécanique soigneusement entretenu et réglé' (p. 83). Elsewhere this wakefulness that is a sleep is referred to simply as 'le sommeil éveillé' and opposed

---

[128] τοῖς ἐγρηγορόσιν ἕνα καὶ κοινὸν κόσμον εἶναι ('to those who are awake there is one common world'). Heraclitus (attributed by Plutarch, *De Superstitione* 3, 166c.: G. S. Kirk, *Heraclitus: The Cosmic Fragments*, Cambridge, 1954, p. 63).

to the real sleep which is a possibility of wakefulness; 'le sommeil éveillé qui revient fabriquer une fausse histoire et un faux récit dont le vrai sommeil est justement la mise en question régulière . . .' (p. 93). Thus the reversal of the elements in the series : wakefulness= sleep; putting itself in the security of a *fausse histoire* : sleep= wakefulness; the possibility of the questioning of the stability of wakefulness. The ground of this latter possibility is the fact of the work of the dream (Freud's Traum*arbeit*) which plays a key rôle in *Drame*. It is from the account of the text of a dream that the drama begins (cf. pp. 12–14). Remember that the dream for Freud is the royal road to the limitless (without negation) realm of the unconscious and that, as Michel Foucault stressed in the course of a brilliant essay on Binswanger's *Traum und Existenz*, the dream is the radical experience by the subject of his world, in which experience he is perpetually displaced from his identity in the dream-work :

'le malade qui rêve est bien le personnage angoissé, mais c'est aussi la mer, mais c'est aussi l'homme inquiétant qui déploie son filet mortel, mais c'est aussi, et surtout, ce monde d'abord en vacarme, puis frappé d'immobilité et de mort, qui revient finalement au mouvement allègre de la vie. Le sujet du rêve ou la première personne onirique, c'est le rêve lui-même, c'est le rêve tout entier. Dans le rêve tout dit "je", même les objets et les bêtes, même l'espace vide, même les choses lointaines et étranges, qui en peuplent la fantasmagorie.'[129]

The dream, the wakefulness of sleep, is *another* scene. The problem is to be there on the edge turned out of oneself in the world of signs, to be there 'between', 'in the moment of limits'. Hence the intermediary stage in the series *veille—sommeil*. Between the sleep of wakefulness and the wakefulness of sleep is the shadowy realm of awakening ('lieu de pénombre', p. 141), of *éveil* (or *demi-sommeil*, p. 11, or *avant-sommeil*, p. 40) : 'le bref et interminable passage de la nuit au réveil' (p. 94). This is exactly the state of hesitation; marginal, on the edge, a moment of limits, a moment of questioning, of mise-en-scène, of drama, of, in fact, that *véritable histoire*; a moment to be read in its images here, for instance, in the following passage from the nineteenth fragment of the text :

'En fermant les yeux, il cherche à laisser s'épancher "la source", "là d'où ça vient". Vibration, alors, de plus en plus forte : le corps entier, mais un corps pensé plutôt que perçu, semble à présent osciller sur

[129] Michel Foucault, 'Introduction': L. Binswanger, *Le Rêve et l'Existence* (Paris, 1954), p. 85.

place, c'est comme si—mais la comparaison le fait aussitôt déraper—il voyait au loin la courbe, la courbure . . . Fuite : tout ce qu'il ne veut pas penser faisant exprès de se penser . . . Le lieu se réduit, une sorte de main se referme sur tout paysage, ramasse, replie, largue les amarres de tout paysage . . . Déploiement invisible, frontière organique, chaude, dans le soir . . . Il s'appuie sur cette tapisserie menaçante . . . Etoffe comme enroulée hors de l'espace, mais dont l'espace est seul à pouvoir parler, suite d'images inutiles affrontées désormais à la possibilité d'un langage muet, immédiat . . . C'est bien "le monde entier" qui est palpé dans cette ombre chaude, fragile, dans cette insaisissable demeure d'ombre et de nuit . . . (et la nuit, dehors, s'infiltre avec la brume dans la ville de plus en plus silencieuse, tandis que les lumières persistent, que, les moyens d'information se déploient et persistent à l'intérieur, brefs communiqués, musiques, journaux en préparation, décalage, retard qu'une veille incessante s'emploie à combler, commentaires et rappels du langage direct assuré en plein jour . . .) Et la nuit prend possession de lui, pour finir, tirant le rideau derrière lequel il peut feindre d'échapper au problème, bien que tout, à partir de là, soit transposé dans une élaboration parallèle, travail dont il tirera au réveil seulement quelques fragments masqués hors du courant . . . quelques indications scéniques insignifiantes pour la somme de texte qu'il est sûr d'avoir lu, entendu, souplement vécu . . . toujours cette marge, cette coupure, mince immensité latente . . .'
Il écrit :
pp. 52–3

The awakening is achieved in the practice of writing. The series *sommeil—éveil—veille* is that of an exploration of language.[130] In

130 The names of Proust and Joyce have occurred again and again (and necessarily) in the present essay. They will be mentioned here once more, for the last time, in remarking the analogues provided in their work to this series articulated in the text of *Drame* and in Sollers' writings in general. The following table gives a schematic account of the correspondences.

sommeil	éveil	veille
obscurité		grand jour
silence		causerie
livre ('ce livre essentiel')		conversation/monde
	découverte	
	traduction	
	écriture/lecture	
	texte	
wake	wake*	wake
(sleep, death)	(trace)	(wakefulness)
night	writing	day
	(book, text)	

Continued at the foot of the next page.

* See page 236.

that passage from *Logiques* cited in the course of the discussion earlier in this book of the work of Nathalie Sarraute the reality of these images is clearly defined in the terms of that exploration: 'Nous vivons dans le faux jour d'une langue morte aux significations bornées : nous manquons le jour dans la mesure où nous manquons la nuit que nous sommes. Mais nous ne sommes pas autre chose que ce mouvement nocturne et diurne du lisible et de l'illisible en nous, hors de nous—et cela nous ne voulons pas le savoir' (*Logiques*, p. 240). This knowledge is that which *Drame* seeks to discover in its writing, to unfold. Such an unfolding, which is the adventure of *Drame*, is a question of 'origins' but this question is not posed in terms of a movement towards the discovery of some point of rest, some final moment of full presence : the question is that of the writing of limits, of the scene of the effect of presence. The term 'unfolding' is dangerous in so far as its use, perhaps inevitably, implies a whole metaphysics linked to the idea of re-finding, in some depth, *a lost sense* (whether it be called essence, real self, phenomenological residuum or whatever); it is to appeal to some original site, in short, to a beginning. *Drame*, however, is written precisely as an absence of beginning, as recognition of that absence. To accede to the 'other side' is to accede not to some essence, but to a movement of production and transformation, to disarticulate oneself (literally; it is on a language that one works) in reading that movement, as in the following difficult passage (not without an echo of that equally difficult passage in the *Cours de linguistique générale* in which Saussure, striving to express the reality of language as a formal play of differences, turns to the image of the encounter of two undifferentiated masses, of sky and sea in the trace of waves) :[131]

'Mais à ce point, il est dans son envers incompréhensible, dans la réorganisation de sa propre pensée dont il est à la fois l'auteur, la

signifiant	sign	signifié
	(signifiant + signifié)	
nuit	pénombre	jour
sommeil	éveil	veille
	écriture-lecture	
	texte	

* As one speaks of the *wake* of a ship; the disturbance, division, difference, traced on a smooth surface: the writing in *Finnegans Wake* forged between night and day.

[131] Cf. *Cours de linguistique générale*, pp. 155–6. (One is reminded too here of Valéry's description of *Homo Scriptor*: 'Je regarde la mer en furie, et le Dictionnaire caché, tapi dans *l'être de lettres*, veut à chaque plus beau coup *joué* par les lames ou les nues et *gagné* par les yeux, lâcher un vol de mots dans la région sensible où passe dans la lumière spirituelle ce qui se fait articuler et écrire . . .' *Oeuvres* II, pp. 805–6.)

victime, le produit semblable et nouveau. Cela occupe un cercle et une sphère sans limites où les bombardements d'idées (enveloppant mots et images) ont lieu et n'ont jamais lieu. Tassements, fuites, désintégrations, réapparitions . . .'
p. 104

The text often refers to a silence, or void, against/on/through which the production is mounted, as here at the opening of the twenty-seventh section : 'il retrouve la marge de vide qui permet de tenir immédiatement sous les yeux, sous la main . . . le théâtre en action . . . C'est un vide entourant chaque histoire, projetant sur sa propre scène chaque histoire—' (p. 64). It is a silence situated in the very presence of the sign, of the world as theatre : 'C'est en lui, par lui mais toujours apparemment sans lui que l'ensemble a lieu . . .' (p. 65). There is no presence but in that theatre in action, that circulation, in which it is founded on the ground of a movement that marks it as difference, and there as absence; no *signifié* that is not already in place as *signifiant*. Hence the obligation to place oneself 'en scène', 'sur le bord' (p. 29); between moi/non-moi, 'je'/'il', day/ night, wake/sleep. What counts is that *drama* ('Comment être là?'), that *production*, that *activity*, not some result or product : 'il est obligé à un certain geste pour saisir le "tout"—*mais seul le geste compte* puisqu'il sait d'avance que la main restera vide (le sable fuyant, l'eau n'étant jamais enfermée). Pourtant, ceci ou cela peut être touché *au passage* . . .' (p. 127, my italics).

The scene of this activity, of this awakening, is language. As *Nombres* puts it at one point; 'Je m'étais réveillé en train de parler, éclair glissé dans un tourbillon noirci de paroles . . .' (p. 25). Awake in language, placed there, what has to be accomplished is, as it were, the hesitation of that 'there' in thinking its production. The drama is the accession to the world of signs : 'signes mobiles, solides, où il trace et recoupe un ensemble de canaux lumineux . . . Il est choisi, mais il peut choisir. Il vit de plus en plus dans un dévoilement hési- tant : c'est "l'insertion" (où il prend individuellement la place d'une veine, d'une ligne—mais aussi du mouvement global où cette image apparaît).' (*Drame*, pp. 112–3). *Insertion between.* Hence the prac- tice of writing, precisely as the scene of this insertion (between the silence—'il y a   . (Un point dans du blanc, c'est cela)' (p. 111) —and the blackened vortex of speech) in the elaboration in the *text* ('réseau paragrammatique'[132]) of a logic of fiction (*la véritable his-*

---

[132] Cf. the brief discussion of *Drame* in Julia Kristeva's essay 'Pour une sémiologie des paragrammes': *Semeiotiké*, pp. 198–9.

toire) following the production of meaning, awakening, for example, to the logic, the fiction, of words ('c'est du sens des mots qu'il s'agit, non des choses dans les mots' p. 113), as in the attention to the word *fougère* in the thirty-sixth section of the book (p. 88). The text then, finally, is *margin* or *frontier* : 'Il me semble que je suis à la frontière des mots, juste avant qu'ils deviennent visibles et audibles, près d'un livre . . .'(p. 87).

It is in this context that the writing of *Drame*, which is itself the *'véritable histoire'*, is to be understood. 'Récit de la pensée dans les mots et réciproquement. Ablatif absolu. Cela ne se passe pas dans le temps mais sur la page où l'on dispose des temps' (p. 98). This presence of the text ('sur la page') is found in the coincidence of *discours* and *histoire*; what is narrated is this narration. *Drame* is performative, the accomplishment of an action. The alternation between 'il' and 'je' in the concatenation of the sequences is the dramatization of this coincidence in its continual resumption of the writing of 'je' as insertion into the narration of the 'il'. In the dialogue of 'il' and 'je' the writing is maintained at a kind of degree zero of narrativity, remaining 'between', in the very opening of narration. The criss-cross of the squares of the chess-board ('système de réflexion et d'encadrement' p. 89), a paragrammatic network returning each square to the others in its pattern of relations, to its reading of them and theirs of it,[133] serves to present the text entirely in its activity, in a *lexis* comprehending author-reader in its process. It serves too to remove the text from the notion of a 'beginning' ('Aucun début n'offre les garanties nécessaires de neutralité' p. 11) and from that of an 'ending'. The sixty-fourth section reads, in fact, as follows :

'On doit pouvoir considérer que le livre échoue ici—(brûle) (s'efface) (dans la pensée qui n'a pas de dernière pensée—"plus nombreuse que l'herbe"—"l'agile, la rapide entre toutes, qui prend appui sur le coeur")—.'
p. 159

The text does not end (it will be taken up in *Nombres* as *Drame* has taken up in quotation *Le Parc*[134]), it *burns* in the reflection of its own production, consumed entirely in its activity as *text*.

---

[133] In this plurality the text may be assimilated to the tabular model described by Michel Serres in the opening pages of his *Hermès ou la communication* (Paris, 1968, pp. 11–20).

[134] Sollers comments: 'le *Parc* et *Drame* deviennent en effet des anneaux, des groupes réactivés ou réinvestis dans leur matérialité même dans un texte nouveau', *Théorie d'ensemble*, p. 74.

238

The motif of *burning* links *Drame* and *Nombres*, a dense and difficult text published in 1968,[135] the opening phrase of which takes up this same motif that will recur throughout the book; 'le papier brûlait' (p. 11). It is a motif that recurs too in *Logiques* in the prospect it defines of 'une littérature non-expressive, une littérature en train de brûler dans le moment même où elle s'accomplit' (*Logiques*, p. 200): 'Le roman doit donc brûler et consumer toutes traces de roman ou se résigner à n'être qu'un roman' (ibid., p. 244).[136] For Balzac the image of burning was to be applied to the world of social ambition and of passion ('une passion brûlante') in contrast to the calm clarity of observation, of that knowledge of which the novelist will furnish the text : '*Vouloir* nous brûle et *Pouvoir* nous détruit, mais *Savoir* laisse notre faible organisation dans un perpétuel état de calme.'[137] For Sollers it is the text that burns in the reading of its own production, in that *écriture-lecture* that it operates in its activity held in the plural organization of the text. The square of sixty-four houses in *Drame*, the matrix of the square in *Nombres* (written in a hundred sections derived from a series of squares) offer, in opposition to the *linearity* of the traditional novel (the Balzacian text of knowledge will *end* in the accomplishment, via demonstration, of a truth), a multiplication, a constant plurality, a series of relations and returns. 'Fonctionnement difficile à saisir dans ses glissements, ses coupures, ses rapprochements, son absence de centre et de but, son tissu ramifié de lois.' (*Nombres*, p. 31).

'Laws' which are to be discovered in the formal play of the text, which, in the demonstration of the activity of its writing, aims at the mise-en-scène of the drama of its production. It is here that the concept of intertextuality, introduced above, is of fundamental importance. The concept is related directly to the motif of burning with its reference to the activity of the text as *écriture/lecture*, *construction/destruction*, as the following comment by Sollers with

---

135 For discussion of *Nombres* reference should be made to the two accounts of the text given by Sollers himself, 'Ecriture et révolution' and 'Niveaux sémantiques d'un texte moderne', both reprinted in *Théorie d'ensemble*, pp. 67–79, 318–25, and also to that given by Julia Kristeva in her 'L'engendrement de la formule', *Semeiotiké*, pp. 278–371.
136 The image is prefigured in Sollers' commentary on *Le Défi* published in 1957 where it is used, however, with a different emphasis in which can be glimpsed something of the radical development that distances the later from the earlier work: 'Pas de désir dans *Le Défi*. Le style ne brûle pas ou, s'il brûle, c'est sans réchauffer, comme une abstraction.' (*Le Défi*, p. 32). The crucial reference for the motif of 'brûlure' is to the work of Lautréamont.
137 *La Comédie Humaine* IX, p. 40.

regard to the 'quotations' that traverse *Drame* and *Nombres* makes clear :

'Les fragments lisibles entre guillemets ne sont pas des citations mais des prélèvements opérés sur des tissus textuels différents pour montrer que le texte global est précisément le lieu de structuration de leurs différences. Le concept d'intertextualité (Kristeva) est ici essentiel : tout texte se situe à la jonction de plusieurs textes dont il est à la fois la relecture, l'accentuation, la condensation, le déplacement et la profondeur. D'une certaine manière, un texte vaut ce que vaut son action intégratrice et destructrice d'autres textes.'
Théorie d'ensemble, p. 75

Effectively, Sollers operates a distinction or opposition of text / ideology : the text is the space of the production (in the theatrical sense) of the discursive modes of the general cultural text.[138] Sollers speaks in this connection of a 'scenography', in the same way that *Finnegans Wake* is described as a 'scribenery'; the scene of an inter-action of texts which are not 'sources' but the point of its activity of writing-reading, of its questioning.[139] The 'author' as writing subject is equally taken in this scenography, prospected, as it were ('production se servant de moi comme base', *Nombres*, p. 59), is broken, fragmented, in the plurality of discourses, (' "moi" cependant de plus en plus égaré dans le texte', ibid., p. 62). The text offers a topology of the subject : founded in the other (the order of dis-course), the subject becomes (written-read) other to himself (author-actor) :

'Il se réveille un matin dans ce qu'il a écrit. A la lettre : sans transi-tion en ouvrant les yeux, le récit continue, se répète—il traverse avant de revenir ici les mêmes formes tournoyantes comme suspendu en elles, respirant en elles un air réfléchi . . . Il sort en effet du texte, naturelle-ment, il vient d'en toucher l'existence autonome, directe.'
Drame, pp. 157–8

The practice of writing as it can be understood in Sollers' texts, and it is from the perspective of this understanding that this book

---

[138] It is in this manner that the 'Sieg des Realismus' referred to by Engels (see above, p. 35) is to be understood and from which a theory of the *realism* of the novel may properly be elaborated, as the present writer hopes to demonstrate in another work now in progress.

[139] It was seen in the discussion of Barthes' work on *Sarrasine* how a textual semiotics could establish the scenography of the classic text in describing the various codes sustaining its realization. For Sollers' account of a 'scenography' in relation to a prac-tice of writing, see his 'Dante et la traversée de l'écriture', *Logiques*, pp. 44–77.

has been concerned to describe the significance of the *nouveau roman*, is a ceaseless practice of fracturation. *Nombres* is not a sequel to *Drame* but its resumption, in the sense in which *Drame* itself is a series of resumptions in the dialogue of 'il' and 'je' and in which *Nombres* again is a series of permutations of imperfect and present sequences moving from square to square. It is in this movement of the square, three sides imperfect with the fourth giving the present always already caught up in a text which is there as the condition of its presence, that the writing breaks the linearity of representation. Where the classic novel establishes the depth of representation, Sollers' text (*Drame* or *Nombres*) finds 'ni salle ni scène mais bien au contraire, une seule nappe capable de donner à la fois la sensation de profondeur, de représentation et de réflexion : la page est, pour l'instant l'indice de cette nappe . . .' (*Nombres*, pp. 22–3). The image is that again of Saussure finding in the tracing of the furrows of the waves, dividing sea and sky, the expression of the reality of language; that again of Joyce, the wake inscribing the play of death and life, night and day, sleep and wakefulness; that again of Proust ever appealing to the sea as image of primordial undifferentiated purity but only to know, in the obliquity of his writing pursued in the wake of a reality of forms, a ceaseless play of differences in which that purity is always lost, a myth of origin. Sollers' writing, its activity of 'brisure', is a response to those images : not the pursuit of a presence, but the questioning of presence; the development of a negativity in resting 'between', ceaselessly running through the mesh of the tissue (of sense, of the body, of all the text of 'Reality'), grasping it 'inside out' in its composition. The gage of the writing is the breaking of the sign, of the assurance of sense and 'Reality'. The writing is exactly an 'écriture de la brisure' and the term 'brisure' should be allowed all the multiple resonances it finds in Sollers' text. The fracturation of the sign is the attempt to hold the writing in the hollow of *différance,* 'dans la partie creuse et concave de l'édifice' (*Nombres*, p. 34; Proust speaks precisely of a writing between sleep and wakefulness producing a 'concavité nouvelle'); to read the sign in its fracturation, its perpetual opening onto other signs in a play of differences, to read it in its 'brisure', its jointure, its articulation. Thus too, the writing itself held in the jointure of its articulation, always to be broken and resumed, 'se ruinant et tombant dans sa propre action', fragmented by the texts with which, as scenography, it is furrowed. The negativity developed in this experience of limits, for it as this that the writing proceeds, is powerfully marked in *Nombres* in the string of citations (Bruno, Spinoza, Marx, Lenin, Artaud, Bataille, Nietzsche, Mao) and in the opposition of West and East articulated materially in the Chinese characters inscribed in the text, which at once produce the shock of ignorance and resume its fundamental figures (*fang*—square, *tiao* —penis, *chou*—number, *hsiae*—blood, *houo*—fire, *yi*—transformation, *k'o-wen*—text). That experience of limits cannot but be, and we return to a point raised at the beginning of this chapter, political in its specificity; and that specificity, the gage of negativity, is that, precisely, of an 'écriture de la brisure'. As Sollers puts it : 'L'écriture est la continuation de la politique par d'autres moyens. Ces moyens, il faut le souligner, sont spécifiques . . .', those, let us say, of a *practice of writing*.

Select Bibliography

The following bibliography is necessarily limited in extent. No attempt is made to provide a comprehensive list of works devoted to the nouveau roman and/or to particular novelists, nor to provide a complete list of all those works to which reference has been made in the course of the present essay, full details of which are given on the occasion of their mention there. The bibliography is divided into three sections:

1 A checklist of the major works of the four novelists who have received particular discussion in Chapters 2–5.

2 A brief selection of books and special numbers of periodicals which deal generally with the nouveau roman and to which reference may be made for further bibliographical information.

3 A short list of works that offer, as it were, a prospect of the situation of the work of the nouveau roman and of the writing of the present essay.

Unless otherwise stated, the place of publication throughout is Paris.

I

ALAIN ROBBE-GRILLET :   *Les Gommes,* Editions de Minuit, 1953 (trans : *The Erasers,* Calder & Boyars, London 1966; Grove Press, New York 1964)

Le Voyeur, Editions de Minuit, 1955 (trans : *The Voyeur,* John Calder, London 1959; Grove Press, New York 1958)

La Jalousie, Editions de Minuit, 1957; Macmillan, New York 1963 (trans : *Jealousy,* John Calder, London 1960; in *Two Novels by Robbe-Grillet,* Grove Press, New York 1965)

Dans le labyrinthe, Editions de Minuit,

1959 (trans : *In the Labyrinth,* Calder & Boyars, London 1967; in *Two Novels by Robbe-Grillet,* Grove Press, New York 1965)

L'Année dernière à Marienbad, Editions de Minuit, 1961 (trans : *Last Year at Marienbad,* John Calder, London 1962)

Instantanés, Editions de Minuit, 1962 (trans : *Snapshots,* in *Snapshots and Towards a New Novel,* Calder & Boyars, London 1965; *Snapshots,* Grove Press, New York 1968)

L'Immortelle, Editions de Minuit, 1963

Pour un Nouveau Roman, Editions de Minuit, 1963 (trans : *Towards a New Novel,* in *Snapshots and Towards a New Novel,* Calder & Boyars, London 1965; *For a New Novel,* Grove Press, New York 1966)

La Maison de rendez-vous, Editions de Minuit, 1965 (trans : *The House of Assignation,* Calder & Boyars, London 1970; *La Maison de rendez-vous,* Grove Press, New York 1966)

Projet pour une révolution à New York, Editions de Minuit, 1970

NATHALIE SARRAUTE :

Tropismes, Denoël, 1939 (Reprinted Editions de Minuit, 1957 with one text omitted and six new ones added; trans : *Tropisms,* in *Tropisms and The Age of Suspicion,* John Calder, London 1963; *Tropisms,* G. Braziller, New York 1967)

Portrait d'un inconnu, Robert Marin, 1948, Gallimard, 1956 (trans : *Portrait of a Man Unknown,* John Calder, London 1959; G. Braziller, New York 1958)

Martereau, Gallimard, 1953 (trans : *Martereau,* John Calder, London 1964; G. Braziller, New York 1959)

L'Ere du soupçon, Gallimard, 1956 (trans : *The Age of Suspicion,* in

Tropisms and The Age of Suspicion, John Calder, London 1963; *The Age of Suspicion,* G. Braziller, New York 1963)

Le Planétarium, Gallimard, 1959 (trans: *The Planetarium,* John Calder, London 1961)

Les Fruits d'or, Gallimard, 1963 (trans: *The Golden Fruits,* John Calder, London 1965; G. Braziller, New York 1964)

Le Silence/Le Mensonge, Gallimard, 1967

Entre la vie et la mort, Gallimard, 1968 (trans: *Between Life and Death,* Calder & Boyars, London 1970; G. Braziller, New York 1969)

Isma, Gallimard, 1970; *Vous les entendez?,* Gallimard, 1971

CLAUDE SIMON :

Le Tricheur, Editions du Sagittaire, 1946

La Corde raide, Editions de Minuit, 1947

Gulliver, Calmann-Lévy, 1952

Le Sacre du printemps, Calmann-Lévy, 1954

Le Vent, Editions de Minuit, 1957 (trans: *The Wind,* G. Braziller, New York 1959)

L'Herbe, Editions de Minuit, 1958 (trans: *The Grass,* Jonathan Cape, London 1961; G. Braziller, New York 1960)

La Route des Flandres, Editions de Minuit, 1960 (trans: *The Flanders Road,* Jonathan Cape, London 1962; G. Braziller, New York 1961)

Le Palace, Editions de Minuit, 1962 (trans: *The Palace,* Jonathan Cape, London 1964; G. Braziller, New York 1963)

Histoire, Editions de Minuit, 1967 (trans: *Histoire,* Jonathan Cape,

London 1969; G. Braziller, New York 1968)

La Bataille de Pharsale, Editions de Minuit, 1969 (trans: *The Battle of Pharsalus*, Jonathan Cape, London 1971; G. Braziller, New York 1971)

Orion aveugle, Skira, Geneva 1970

Les Corps conducteurs, Editions de Minuit, 1971

PHILIPPE SOLLERS :

Le Défi, Editions du Seuil, 1957

Une Curieuse Solitude, Editions du Seuil, 1958 (trans: *A Strange Solitude*, Eyre & Spottiswoode, London 1961; Grove Press, New York 1961)

Le Parc, Editions du Seuil, 1961 (trans: *The Park*, Calder & Boyars, London 1968; Red Dust, New York 1969)

L'Intermédiaire, Editions du Seuil, 1963

Francis Ponge, Seghers, 1963

Drame, Editions du Seuil, 1965

Logiques, Editions du Seuil, 1968

Nombres, Editions du Seuil, 1968

Entretiens de Francis Ponge avec Philippe Sollers, Seuil/Gallimard, 1970

Lois, Editions du Seuil, 1972

II

ASTIER, PIERRE A. G. :

Encyclopédie du nouveau roman, ou, La Crise du roman français et le nouveau réalisme, Debresse, 1969

BLOCH-MICHEL, JEAN :

Le Présent de l'indicatif, Gallimard, 1963

Cahiers Internationaux du Symbolisme Nos 9–10 (1965–1966), 'Formalisme et signification (A propos des oeuvres littéraires et cinématographiques du Nouveau Roman)'

Esprit Nos. 7–8 (July–August 1958), 'Le Nouveau Roman'

GASTAUT-CHARPY, DANIELLE : *Le Nouveau Roman* (Publications des Annales de la Faculté des Lettres et

246

| | des Sciences Humaines d'Aix-en-Provence, Série 'Travaux et Mémoires', No. 37), Aix-en-Provence 1966 |
| JANVIER, L. : | *Une Parole exigeante*, Editions de Minuit, 1964 |

Revue des Lettres Modernes Nos. 94–99 (1964) 'Un Nouveau Roman? Recherches et traditions'

| STURROCK, JOHN : | *The French New Novel*, Oxford University Press, London and New York 1969 |

Yale French Studies No. 24 (Summer 1959) 'Midnight Novelists'

III

BARTHES, ROLAND :	*Le Degré zéro de l'écriture*, Editions du Seuil, 1953 (trans : *Writing Degree Zero*, Jonathan Cape, London 1967; Hill & Wang, New York 1968; in *Writing Degree Zero and Elements of Semiology*, Beacon Press, Boston 1970) *Mythologies*, Editions du Seuil, 1957 (trans. *Mythologies*, Jonathan Cape, London 1972) *Essais critiques*, Editions du Seuil, 1964 *Eléments de sémiologie*, in *Communications* No. 4, Editions du Seuil, 1964 (trans : *Elements of Semiology*, Jonathan Cape, London 1967; Hill & Wang, New York 1968; in *Writing Degree Zero and Elements of Semiology*, Beacon Press, Boston 1970) *S/Z*, Editions du Seuil, 1970 *L'Empire des signes*, Skira, Geneva 1970
BLANCHOT, MAURICE :	*L'Espace littéraire*, Gallimard, 1955 *Le Livre à venir*, Gallimard, 1959 *L'Entretien infini*, Gallimard, 1969
DELEUZE, GILLES :	*Différence et répétition*, Presses Universitaires de France, 1968 *Logique du sens*, Editions de Minuit, 1969

DERRIDA, JACQUES :   *L'Ecriture et la Différence*, Editions du Seuil, 1967
De la Grammatologie, Editions de Minuit, 1967

FOUCAULT, MICHEL :   *Raymond Roussel*, Gallimard, 1963
Les Mots et les Choses, Gallimard, 1966 (trans : *The Order of Things*, Tavistock, London 1971)
L'Archéologie du savoir, Gallimard, 1969

GENETTE, GÉRARD :   *Figures*, Editions du Seuil, 1966
Figures II, Editions du Seuil, 1969

GREIMAS, A. J. :   *Du Sens*, Editions du Seuil, 1970

KRISTEVA, JULIA :   *Semeiotiké: Recherches pour une sémanalyse*, Editions du Seuil, 1969
Le Texte du roman, Mouton, The Hague 1970

LACAN, JACQUES :   *Ecrits*, Editions du Seuil, 1966

LECLAIRE, SERGE :   *Psychanalyser*, Editions du Seuil, 1968

MALLARMÉ, S. :   *Oeuvres complètes*, Gallimard (Bibliothèque de la Pléiade), 1956

MERLEAU-PONTY, MAURICE :   *Signes*, Gallimard, 1960 (trans : *Signs*, North-western U.P., Evanston, Illinois 1964)
Résumés de cours, Gallimard, 1968
La Prose du monde, Gallimard, 1969

PONGE, FRANCIS :   *Pour un Malherbe*, Gallimard, 1965

RICARDOU, JEAN :   *Problèmes du nouveau roman*, Editions du Seuil, 1967

SERRES, MICHEL :   *Hermès ou la communication*, Editions de Minuit, 1968

Tel Quel   *Théorie d'ensemble*, Editions du Seuil, 1968

VALÉRY, PAUL :   *Oeuvres*, Gallimard (Bibliothèque de la Pléiade, 2 vols) 1957

Index